OPPOSING
VIEWPOINTS®
SERIES

# Mass Incarceration

# Other Books of Related Interest

## Opposing Viewpoints Series

Police Brutality
Race in America

## At Issue Series

Guns and Crime
Minorities and the Law
Poverty in America

## Current Controversies Series

Capital Punishment
Drug Legalization
Prisons
Racial Profiling

> "Congress shall make no law … abridging the freedom of speech, or of the press."
>
> *First Amendment to the US Constitution*

The basic foundation of our democracy is the First Amendment guarantee of freedom of expression. The Opposing Viewpoints series is dedicated to the concept of this basic freedom and the idea that it is more important to practice it than to enshrine it.

OPPOSING
VIEWPOINTS®
SERIES

# Mass Incarceration

Rebecca Aldridge, Book Editor

GREENHAVEN
PUBLISHING

Published in 2018 by Greenhaven Publishing, LLC
353 3rd Avenue, Suite 255, New York, NY 10010

Cover image: Joseph Sohm/Shutterstock.com

**Library of Congress Cataloging-in-Publication Data**

Names: Aldridge, Rebecca, editor.
Title: Mass incarceration / edited by Rebecca Aldridge.
Description: New York : Greenhaven Publishing, 2018. | Series: Opposing viewpoints
 | Includes bibliographical references and index. | Audience: Grades 9-12.
Identifiers: LCCN ISBN 9781534500457 (library bound) | ISBN 9781534500433
 (pbk.)
Subjects: LCSH: Imprisonment--United States--History. | Criminal justice,
 Administration of--United States--History. | Alternatives to imprisonment--United
 States. | Civil rights--United States. | Criminals--Rehabilitation--United States.
Classification: LCC HV9466.M377 2018 | DDC 365.973--dc23

Manufactured in the United States of America

Website: http://greenhavenpublishing.com

# Contents

## Chapter 5: How Do We Handle Crime?

# The Importance of Opposing Viewpoints

Perhaps every generation experiences a period in time in which the populace seems especially polarized, starkly divided on the important issues of the day and gravitating toward the far ends of the political spectrum and away from a consensus-facilitating middle ground. The world that today's students are growing up in and that they will soon enter into as active and engaged citizens is deeply fragmented in just this way. Issues relating to terrorism, immigration, women's rights, minority rights, race relations, health care, taxation, wealth and poverty, the environment, policing, military intervention, the proper role of government—in some ways, perennial issues that are freshly and uniquely urgent and vital with each new generation—are currently roiling the world.

If we are to foster a knowledgeable, responsible, active, and engaged citizenry among today's youth, we must provide them with the intellectual, interpretive, and critical-thinking tools and experience necessary to make sense of the world around them and of the all-important debates and arguments that inform it. After all, the outcome of these debates will in large measure determine the future course, prospects, and outcomes of the world and its peoples, particularly its youth. If they are to become successful members of society and productive and informed citizens, students need to learn how to evaluate the strengths and weaknesses of someone else's arguments, how to sift fact from opinion and fallacy, and how to test the relative merits and validity of their own opinions against the known facts and the best possible available information. The landmark series Opposing Viewpoints has been providing students with just such critical-thinking skills and exposure to the debates surrounding society's most urgent contemporary issues for many years, and it continues to serve this essential role with undiminished commitment, care, and rigor.

The key to the series's success in achieving its goal of sharpening students' critical-thinking and analytic skills resides in its title—

Opposing Viewpoints. In every intriguing, compelling, and engaging volume of this series, readers are presented with the widest possible spectrum of distinct viewpoints, expert opinions, and informed argumentation and commentary, supplied by some of today's leading academics, thinkers, analysts, politicians, policy makers, economists, activists, change agents, and advocates. Every opinion and argument anthologized here is presented objectively and accorded respect. There is no editorializing in any introductory text or in the arrangement and order of the pieces. No piece is included as a "straw man," an easy ideological target for cheap point-scoring. As wide and inclusive a range of viewpoints as possible is offered, with no privileging of one particular political ideology or cultural perspective over another. It is left to each individual reader to evaluate the relative merits of each argument— as he or she sees it, and with the use of ever-growing critical-thinking skills—and grapple with his or her own assumptions, beliefs, and perspectives to determine how convincing or successful any given argument is and how the reader's own stance on the issue may be modified or altered in response to it.

This process is facilitated and supported by volume, chapter, and selection introductions that provide readers with the essential context they need to begin engaging with the spotlighted issues, with the debates surrounding them, and with their own perhaps shifting or nascent opinions on them. In addition, guided reading and discussion questions encourage readers to determine the authors' point of view and purpose, interrogate and analyze the various arguments and their rhetoric and structure, evaluate the arguments' strengths and weaknesses, test their claims against available facts and evidence, judge the validity of the reasoning, and bring into clearer, sharper focus the reader's own beliefs and conclusions and how they may differ from or align with those in the collection or those of their classmates.

Research has shown that reading comprehension skills improve dramatically when students are provided with compelling, intriguing, and relevant "discussable" texts. The subject matter of these collections could not be more compelling, intriguing, or urgently relevant to today's students and the world they are poised to inherit. The anthologized articles and the reading and discussion questions that are included with them also provide the basis for stimulating, lively, and passionate classroom debates. Students who are compelled to anticipate objections to their own argument and identify the flaws in those of an opponent read more carefully, think more critically, and steep themselves in relevant context, facts, and information more thoroughly. In short, using discussable text of the kind provided by every single volume in the Opposing Viewpoints series encourages close reading, facilitates reading comprehension, fosters research, strengthens critical thinking, and greatly enlivens and energizes classroom discussion and participation. The entire learning process is deepened, extended, and strengthened.

For all of these reasons, Opposing Viewpoints continues to be exactly the right resource at exactly the right time—when we most need to provide readers with the critical-thinking tools and skills that will not only serve them well in school but also in their careers and their daily lives as decision-making family members, community members, and citizens. This series encourages respectful engagement with and analysis of opposing viewpoints and fosters a resulting increase in the strength and rigor of one's own opinions and stances. As such, it helps make readers "future ready," and that readiness will pay rich dividends for the readers themselves, for the citizenry, for our society, and for the world at large.

# Introduction

> "*The nature of the criminal justice system has changed. It is no longer primarily concerned with the prevention and punishment of crime, but rather with the management and control of the dispossessed.*"
>
> —*Michelle Alexander,*
> *The New Jim Crow: Mass*
> *Incarceration in the*
> *Age of Colorblindness*
> *(New Press, 2010)*

Over the past 40 years, the incarceration rate in the United States—the number of prisoners per capita—has more than quadrupled. In fact, we incarcerate more of our citizens than any other nation in the world. Approximately 2.2 million people in the United States are living behind bars; that equates to approximately 716 people for every 100,000 citizens. And the money spent has increased, too. In the past two decades, states have increased the dollars spent on prisons at a rate six times that of the money spent on higher education.

Some have called this shocking increase "the New Jim Crow," a new form of enslavement for African Americans. Partly to blame for this unsurpassed incarceration is the war on drugs declared several decades ago and a "law and order" movement that started in late 1960s just after the civil rights era. The argument is a difficult one to ignore. Sixty percent of those incarcerated are people of color and 40 percent are black men. In fact, there are currently more black prisoners today than black slaves in 1850.

The argument has been made that the entire justice system—from the first encounter with a police officer to sentencing—is unfair and biased. The result has a definite impact on who we are as a nation. Whether a result of mandatory well-intentioned minimum sentences or zero tolerance policies, incarceration affects not only the individual but also his or her family and, consequently, society as a whole. Once on the outside, a former inmate may find it difficult to find employment, may be denied food and housing assistance, and may have lost their right to vote. Together these factors can trap ex-offenders and their loved ones in a life cycle of poverty and struggle.

Other factors to consider when it comes to mass imprisonment are mental health and addiction issues. People in prison are two to three times more likely to report having mental health issues than the population at large; drug and alcohol abuse is more common as well. Some suggest that if we altered our system and treated drugs as a public health issue rather than a criminal justice one, the prison population rate would drop and those who need help would be more effectively treated.

These factors lead to questions surrounding the choice of rehabilitation or punishment and which kind of society we want to be. They also lead to discussion on the effectiveness of alternative approaches to imprisonment, such as probation, community service, electronic monitoring, and treatment programs. And if we make such changes, another question arises: Will they come at a risk to society's safety?

For those people trapped in a prison's revolving doors, that place becomes their primary provider of health care, counseling, and job training. In light of that, another aspect of the mass incarceration debate has become prison privatization, which involves for-profit companies that operate a significant number of state and federal prisons. Both inmates and people on the outside wonder if a prison population's needs are best met through companies that may care more about profit than human welfare.

Today, most people on all sides of the issue recognize that mass incarceration is a problem that desperately needs a solution, but there is little consensus on its contributors and causes. This leads to a great deal of debate on what steps should be taken to solve the problem, and how best to handle crime and punishment in general.

*Opposing Viewpoints: Mass Incarceration* examines this epidemic of overpopulated prisons in chapters that ask the following questions: Is mass incarceration an effective system for curbing crime? What are the societal effects of incarceration? Are there problems with our prison system? How do we perceive crime? How do we handle crime?

OPPOSING
VIEWPOINTS®
SERIES

# CHAPTER 1

# Is Mass Incarceration an Effective System for Curbing Crime?

# Chapter Preface

The prison system in the United States exists for two main reasons—to keep its citizens safe; and to punish, and possibly rehabilitate, the individuals who break societal laws. However, over the past several decades the rate at which this nation places offenders behind bars has increased at a skyrocketing rate, in part due to aggressive laws passed decades ago. Simply put, today's prisons are overcrowded. Few dispute the overpopulation, but debate exists when it comes to related issues such as how did we arrive at this point, who or what is at fault, and what is the best way to approach and solve this incarceration crisis.

Some people see the benefits of mass incarceration as minimal. They point to its costs—both social and cultural—that affect the poor, minorities, and people with mental illnesses more than any other societal groups. They also tie imprisonment and long sentences to high recidivism rates.

To solve this prison problem, the cause must be understood, and experts vary in their explanations for America's severe prison overcrowding. Some point to racial disparities and suggest that racism within the criminal justice system is to blame. Another commonly cited cause is the war on drugs.

And just as there are numerous ideas regarding the reasons behind prison overcrowding, the suggested solutions are equally as varied. Some experts suggest we focus on incarceration alternatives, such as treatment programs, or changing sentencing laws. Some people believe the answer is more police on the street. A great deal of attention has also been focused on drug offenses and their relationship to the incarceration rate; some say changing these laws and sentences would have a positive effect, while others claim this would address only a small sliver of the problem.

Across the country, correctional institutions are struggling with this overpopulation, and without question steps will need to be taken to solve the problem. The following chapter examines the effectiveness of mass incarceration. The authors of the viewpoints present opinions on the roots of the problem and solutions to a problem that many consider a national disgrace.

> "*Mass incarceration is not only unnecessary to keep down crime but also ineffective at it. Increasing incarceration offers rapidly diminishing returns. Extensive research shows incarceration can increase future crime in some cases, as prison often acts as a 'crime school.'*"

# Mass Incarceration Is Unnecessary and Ineffective

*Inimai M. Chettiar*

*In the following viewpoint, Inimai M. Chettiar argues that mass incarceration is not only unnecessary, but ineffective, causing more harm than good. She provides detail on how we came to this point in our society and offers three solutions for what she believes would be a more equitable and reasonable system. Chettiar is the director of the Justice Program at the Brennan Center for Justice and was previously employed by the American Civil Liberties Union. Her work has been featured in The New York Times, Washington Post, Wall Street Journal, The Economist, MSNBC, National Public Radio, and Bloomberg.*

"A National Agenda to Reduce Mass Incarceration", by Inimai M. Chettiar, Brennan Center for Justice, April 27, 2015. Reprinted by Permission.

As you read, consider the following questions:

1. Why does Chettiar say that an increase in incarceration offers rapidly diminishing returns?
2. According to the author, what are some of the more suitable punishments for low-level offenses?
3. What are some of the financial incentives that Chettiar says help fuel mass incarceration?

Mass incarceration threatens American democracy. Hiding in plain sight, it drives economic inequality, racial injustice, and poverty. It will ultimately make it harder to compete in the global economy. The United States has 5 percent of the world's population, yet it has 25 percent of the world's prisoners. More black men serve time in our correctional system today than were held in slavery in 1850. If the prison population were a state, it would be the 36th largest—bigger than Delaware, Vermont, and Wyoming combined. Our current penal policies do not work. Mass incarceration is not only unnecessary to keep down crime but also ineffective at it. Increasing incarceration offers rapidly diminishing returns. Extensive research shows incarceration can increase future crime in some cases, as prison often acts as a "crime school."

Mass incarceration has startling harmful effects. The criminal justice system costs taxpayers $260 billion a year. Spending grew almost 400 percent over the past 30 years. With so many withdrawn from society, and returning stigmatized as "convicts," the criminal justice system drains overall economic growth. Best estimates suggest it contributed to as much as 20 percent of the U.S. poverty rate. Nearly two-thirds of the 600,000 people who exit prisons each year face long-term unemployment. The social and human costs are even higher.

How did we get here? In response to the crime wave of the 1980s, politicians vied to be the most punitive—from the 1977 New York City mayoral election, which improbably turned on the issue of the death penalty (over which a mayor has no power), to

# The Growing Problem of the Prison System

For most of the 20th century, U.S. prison rates were fairly low and stable by comparison with contemporary levels. From 1930 to 1970, for example, the average annual rate of imprisonment was around 110 per 100,000.

But beginning in the 1970s, a number of political and economic factors gave rise to the prison boom, which was to bring the nation to the age of mass incarceration, which in turn would have far reaching and sometimes devastating impacts on those affected. Incarceration became the default setting rather than the backstop of the criminal justice system. This would most heavily impact low-income, low skilled young men without high school diplomas or post-secondary education—and this was disproportionately true for young African Americans.

Contributing factors to the prison boom included fears of crime and unrest, political hysteria regarding drugs, a backlash against the gains of the civil rights movement, widening economic inequality and a decline in the demand for low-skilled labor.

The policy response around the nation included new criminal penalties, more severe sentencing and parole systems, less reliance on probation and other alternatives to incarceration, and a mushrooming prison building industry.

While drug use occurs throughout society, low-income urban communities are more heavily policed, in part because more daily life occurs in public spaces and illegal activities are more difficult to hide.

According to the American Civil Liberties Union, "The racial disparities resulting from this system have been staggering. Black individuals are imprisoned at nearly six times the rate of their white counterparts—and Latinos are locked up at nearly double the white rate. Most of this racial disparity is a result of the War on Drugs. While these groups engage in drug use, possession, and sales at rates comparable to their representation in the general population, the system disparately impacts people of color. For example, black individuals comprise 13% of the U.S. population and 14% of drug users, yet they are 37% of the people arrested for drug offenses and 56% of those incarcerated for drug crimes."

> When young people are incarcerated, the effects last a lifetime, impacting job quality, earnings, assets, home ownership, marriage and family life, public benefits and, in some states, voting rights. When this occurs disproportionally in low income and minority communities, the effects reach far beyond those immediately involved.
>
> **"The Growing Problems of the Prison System," Rick Wilson, West Virginia Economic Justice Project, American Friends Service Committee, 11/27/12.**

the 1994 referendum that passed "three-strikes-and-you're-out" in California.

But times have changed. Reducing mass incarceration is now one of the few issues on which the left and right are coming to agree. Notably, Republicans are leading the charge, while Democrats largely play catch up. Lawmakers approach the issue from different perspectives. Their concerns vary from spiraling prison costs to intrusion of big government, from religious redemption to civil rights concerns.

We now know that we can reduce crime and reduce incarceration. States like Texas, New York, Georgia, and California have changed their laws to do just that. For the first time in 40 years, crime and incarceration fell nationwide. The state reforms provide modest fines and short-term relief. Local grassroots and state advocacy groups were vital to these wins, working tirelessly to build momentum. Although these reforms are heartening, they are not the wholesale systemic changes needed to strike a blow to mass incarceration.

To end mass incarceration, the American people and their top leaders must also embrace the cause. We need a national conversation, led by national voices, off national solutions. The ideas must be big and aim high.

But, since criminal justice is largely a province of states and cities, how can there be "national" solutions? Each state struggles with the same challenges: too many arrests, prosecutions, pretrial detentions, prison sentences, and probation and parole revocations.

Trends of overcriminalization, overincarceration, and selective enforcement play out across the country, with some variation. It is a false choice to debate whether we need powerful, state-focused efforts or a vibrant, national conversation. A change in national attitude will create the space for bolder state reforms.

This essay offers three national solutions, executed through a mix of federal, state, and local reforms. Though a President or other national leader may not have legal authority to enact all of them, they can and should be champions for these changes.

## Eliminate incarceration by law for most low-level offenses, except in extraordinary circumstances.

Incarceration is the punishment of first resort for too many offenses. Half of state prisoners are behind bars for nonviolent crimes; half of federal prisoners are locked up for drug crimes. Roughly one in three new prison admissions are for violations of parole or probation conditions. And 6 out of 10 local jail inmates await trial, though research suggests that as many as 80 percent could be released with little or no threat to public safety. All told, as many as 1.07 million people may be behind bars without a public safety rationale.

Many states increased the discretion of judges so they can decide—or a prosecutor or parole officer can recommend— whether to send a defendant to prison or to an alternative punishment. However, prison is still a legally permissible option for low-level crimes.

But we should ask: Why do our laws allow prison—the harshest punishment available short of execution—for many of these crimes in the first place? Of course, those who commit crimes should be punished (and some low-level offenders may need prison), but generally such severe punishment simply is not warranted. Ample research demonstrates that alternatives to incarceration in such cases often reduce recidivism and are cheaper than prison time.

We can safely reduce the ranks of the incarcerated in several ways:

- Change criminal laws to remove prison as an option for most low-level, nonviolent, or non-serious crimes— except in extraordinary circumstances. More suitable punishments include: probation, community service, electronic monitoring, or psychiatric or medical treatment. This holds especially true for an array of drug crimes. Many argue for drug legalization. Many argue against it. The same neighborhoods where drugs wreaked havoc in the 1980s are now devastated by mass incarceration. It remains unclear whether drug legalization would be helpful or harmful to communities of color. However, one fact is clear: It is neither efficient nor cheap to throw a person into prison for years for possessing a joint or a bag of cocaine.

- Make treatment, not prison, the standard response for people with mental health or addiction issues. Half of prisoners suff from mental health or drug addiction issues. There are more Americans with mental illness in prisons than in hospitals. Prison does not treat health issues; it makes them worse. Treatment will help people get back on their feet and become productive members of society. (Of course, they should also be supervised; and incarceration may be needed for some due to the nature of the crime or threat posed.)

- End incarceration as a sanction for technical violations of terms of parole and probation. Texas found a way to safely curb these revocations. In 2007, the state introduced a system of progressively stronger punishments for violations. It invested $241 million in alternatives, including treatment. By 2015, the state cut revocations to prison by 40 percent. It also saved $2 billion, closed three prisons, and dropped its crime rate to the lowest since 1968.

- Detain defendants who await trial based on dangerousness, not wealth. Last year, New Jersey overhauled its bail process: the state will now release defendants charged with low-level crimes under conditions that protect public safety, while detaining those who pose risks of violence. These defendants are required to remain in the custody of a guardian, maintain a job or school enrollment, report to a law enforcement officer, undergo drug or mental health treatment, or submit to electronic monitoring. Other states use social science tools to assess danger and flight risks to make detention decisions.

## Reduce mandatory sentences set by law.

Sentencing laws must change. Mandatory minimum, "three strikes you're out," and "truth-in-sentencing" regimes set overly-punitive sentences for defendants. Not only are people now incarcerated at higher rates than ever before, they are incarcerated for longer. According to the Pew Center, the average prison stay increased 36 percent since 1990.

Lawmakers enacted these regimes partly out of a concern for uniformity and equal treatment. If states simply eliminate these laws and return discretion entirely to judges, they could create the very problems of inequity some of these laws were intended to fix.

Instead, we should reduce the mandatory minimum sentences set by law, and reduce the maximum sentences ranges set by codes. Sentence lengths are often wildly disproportionate to the crimes committed. And research shows that longer sentences, beyond a certain point, do not decrease recidivism.

## Create financial incentives to steer toward curbing crime and reducing mass incarceration.

A web of perverse financial incentives drives mass incarceration. For example, police departments often report their "success" by tallying the number of arrests and drug seizures. Prosecutors are often hailed when they increase the number of convictions and prison sentences. These counts are reported as part of the budget process. And prisons—public and private—get more funds when their populations swell.

Instead, a new way forward, termed "Success-Oriented Funding," prescribes that government should fund what works.

Government should closely tie the hundreds of billions of dollars spent on criminal justice to the twin goals of reducing crime and incarceration. Harnessing the power of incentives, this approach can be implemented at the federal, state, and local levels.

The federal government has been one of the largest instigators of perverse incentives. For example, the 1994 Crime Bill included $9 billion to encourage states to drastically limit parole eligibility. Unsurprisingly, 20 states promptly enacted such laws, yielding a dramatic rise in incarceration. Today, the federal government continues to subsidize state and local criminal justice costs to the tune of $3.8 billion annually. One basic, yet effective, step: The federal government should provide funds to states that cut both crime and imprisonment. California, Texas, and other states succeeded by changing financial incentives. They awarded additional funds to local probation departments that reduced the number of people revoked to prison. In its first year alone, California reduced revocations to prison by 23 percent, saving the state nearly $90 million. In one year, Texas reduced the number of people revoked to prison by 12 percent. In both states, crime continued to drop.

A federal program to reward states that reduce crime and incarceration would spur vital change. States should also implement similar financial incentives for budgets to police, prosecutors, jails, prisons, and parole and probation offices. Success-Oriented Funding steers decision making toward broad goals, while allowing local officials the flexibility to decide how to achieve these outcomes.

What political strategy can achieve the change needed? A strategy that firmly puts mass incarceration at the forefront of a national political conversation. One in which the President, U.S. Senators, governors, mayors, police chiefs, civil rights leaders, and business heads call for change. One that puts forward big solutions that can also secure political support. As Abraham Lincoln said of the debate over slavery: "Public sentiment is everything. With public sentiment, nothing can fail. Without it, nothing can succeed."

Mass incarceration—the fundamental civil rights issue of our time—will only end when there is a collective American will do so. The challenge at hand is to find bold, practical ways to cut the prison population while keeping the public safe. Three ideas to start: eliminate incarceration for low-level offenses, except in exceptional circumstances; reduce mandatory sentences set by law; and create financial incentives to steer toward reducing crime and incarceration.

More broadly, this book provides an array of additional solutions from our nation's leading bipartisan public figures and criminal justice experts to reduce mass incarceration. It aims to ignite a conversation that national leaders will join, support, and encourage. Now is the moment to push forward to revitalize our justice system and our democracy.

> *"More police reduce crime, while longer sentences don't, because of how criminals perceive risk. Most people commit crime thinking they won't get caught. Seeing more police changes this and increases the perceived cost of committing crime."*

# What We Need Is More Police on the Street

*Allison Schrager*

*In the following viewpoint, Allison Schrager points to the failure of mass incarceration to act as a deterrent to crime. Using material from economics professor Michael Mueller-Smith, she demonstrates that imprisonment and long sentences lead to recidivism rather than reform. Instead, Schrager argues that putting more police on the street would increase the perception by would-be criminals that more is at stake for committing a crime and that the threat of arrest would act as a true deterrent. Schrager is an economist and writer, and a columnist for the website Quartz. She has written for the Economist, Businessweek, Wired, National Review, and Reuters.*

"In America, Mass Incarceration Has Caused More Crime Than It's Prevented," by Allison Schrager, Quartz, July 22, 2015. Reprinted by Permission.

As you read, consider the following questions:

1.  How much has the U.S. incarceration rate changed since the 1970s?
2.  According to the author, what role does prison play in turning people into career criminals?
3.  What does Schrager believe potential criminals need to perceive in order to deter them?

L ast week, president Obama vowed to end mass incarceration, the imprisonment of 2.2 million Americans. He's commuted the sentences of 46 drug offenders—but ending the practice will require a major policy change at the state and federal level. The sooner this is done, the better. Evidence from the last 40 years suggests the mass imprisonment policy was a tragic failure. Putting more people in prison not only ruined lives, it may have created more new crime than it prevented.

There are five times as many people in prison today—nearly 5% of the population will be imprisoned at some point—as there were in the 1970s. The increase in crime during the 1960s and '70s motivated Americans to get tough on crime, which took several forms. The most striking of these was putting lots of people in prison. Imprisonment is supposed to reduce crime in two ways: it takes criminals off the street so they can't commit new crimes (incapacitation) and it discourages would-be criminals from committing crime (deterrence).

But neither of these outcomes came to pass.

A new paper from University of Michigan economics professor Michael Mueller-Smith measures how much incapacitation reduced crime. He looked at court records from Harris County, Texas from 1980 to 2009. Mueller-Smith observed that in Harris County people charged with similar crimes received totally different sentences depending on the judge to whom they were randomly assigned. Mueller-Smith then tracked what happened to these prisoners. He estimated that each year in prison increases the odds that a prisoner would reoffend by 5.6% a quarter. Even people who went to prison for lesser crimes wound up committing more serious offenses subsequently, the more time they spent in prison. His conclusion: Any benefit from taking criminals out of the general population is more than off-set by the increase in crime from turning small offenders into career criminals.

High recidivism rates are not unique to Texas: Within 5 years of release more than 75% of prisoners are arrested again.

Why does prison turn people into career criminals?

Prison obliterates your earnings potential. Being a convicted felon disqualifies you from certain jobs, housing, or voting. Mueller-Smith estimates that each year in prison reduces the odds of post-release employment by 24% and increases the odds you'll live on public assistance. Time in prison also lowers the odds you'll get or stay married. Being in prison and out of the labor force degrades legitimate skills and exposes you to criminal skills and a criminal network. This makes crime a more attractive alternative upon release, even if you run a high risk of returning to prison.

You could argue prison is still worth it if long sentences discouraged people from committing crime in the first place. Mueller-Smith estimates a one-year prison sentence would only be worth it (in terms of prison cost and forgone economic potential) if it deterred at least 0.4 fewer rapes, 2.2 assaults, 2.5 robberies, 62 larcenies or prevented 4.8 people from becoming a habitual drug user. And the deterrent effect is not this powerful—not even close. There exists little evidence that the possibility of a long prison sentence is much of a crime deterrent at all.

If long prison sentences was truly a deterrent, juveniles would stop committing crimes when they turn 18 and face the possibility of more jail time. But they don't. There are several reasons why: First, criminals, who are often young men, tend to be impulsive and to discount the future. The possibility of a longer prison sentence is too far away to pose as a deterrent. Second, even after they turn 18, there's still a fair amount of uncertainty around the length of their sentence. The Harris County data show jail time often depends on the judge that's assigned, the prosecutor, available evidence, and how busy the court is, which determines the odds that someone convicted ends up with a plea bargain. Longer sentences aren't much of a deterrent because, even in our era of mass incarceration, the possibility of actually going to prison is too uncertain and too far in the future to meaningfully impact behavior.

The one exception seems to be when there's a high degree of certainty around the punishment. The 3-strikes rule in California levies draconian sentences on 3-time offenders—with near certainty, even if the crimes are fairly minor. There is some evidence that if someone has two strikes, they are less likely to commit a third offense.

So if mass incarceration has not deterred crime, what could work?

Would-be criminals respond to incentives like everyone else. If they sense the cost and risk associated with crime has increased in a meaningful way, they are more likely to obey the law. That's why an effective deterrent is increasing the perceived probability of being arrested. Studies show if arrests increase 10%, crime falls by 3% to 5%. The simplest way to increase the perceived probability is to put more police on the street. Florida State's Jonathan Klick and George Mason economist Alex Tabarrok estimate that raising terror alert levels increased police presence by 50%. It is not clear if that meant less terrorism, but more police decreased auto-theft by 43% and burglary by 15%.

More police reduce crime, while longer sentences don't, because of how criminals perceive risk. Most people commit crime thinking they won't get caught. Seeing more police changes this and increases the perceived cost of committing crime.

A notorious example of this is the dramatic crime drop that occurred in New York City in the 1990s. There are many reasons crime fell, including a stronger economy that offered better, legal alternatives to crime. But a major factor was that the New York police force grew by 35%. There is little evidence that arresting people for misdemeanors prevented them from committing more serious crimes later, which was the philosophy at the time. But crime did fall because arrests increased for all kinds of crime.

The rest of America also experienced a big drop in crime during mass incarceration. But this was for myriad reasons: Crime fell because of a booming economy, changing trends in drug and alcohol use, an aging population, and other more effective police methods. It's possible that crime would have been even lower if we hadn't put so many people in prison, and turned a generation of young men into hardened criminals.

> "*The U.S.–Mexico drug challenge remains stark and disturbing. Mexican-based traffickers smuggle an estimated 500 to 700 metric tons of cocaine into the U.S. every year.*"

# There Are No Easy Solutions for the Nation's Drug Habit

*Ray Walser*

*In the following viewpoint, Dr. Ray Walser claims that the U.S. strategy for dealing with Mexican drug cartels is flawed and uncertain. He praises the Obama Administration for continuing with policies first set by George W. Bush but states the former has placed too much blame on U.S. gun laws and American drug use. Walser outlines a plan that he believes would help put a stop to the wave of drug violence. Walser is executive director at Americas Forum and served as a senior policy analyst on Latin America at the Heritage Foundation.*

"U.S. Strategy Against Mexican Drug Cartels: Flawed and Uncertain," by Ray Walser, The Heritage Foundation, April 26, 2010. Reprinted by Permission.

As you read, consider the following questions:

1. What encompasses the "blame America" strategy that Walser is against?
2. What did foreign minister Jorge Castañeda have to say about the attitude toward drugs in the United States?
3. How does Walser feel about laws regarding recreational drug use?

In 2010, the United States and Mexico face yet another critical year in their mutual confrontation with Mexico's deadly criminal cartels. In 2009, the death toll caused by drug-related mayhem in Mexico was over 9,000, making it the worst year since President Felipe Calderón took office.

Barbarous murders, military-like firefights, rampant corruption, a traumatized citizenry, and high-stakes political gamesmanship frame Mexico's ongoing challenges. Despite some successes, the high levels of violence in Mexico, the slow pace of law enforcement reform, persistent and deep-rooted corruption, and a potential loss of public confidence in the Mexican government's ability and will to sustain the drug fight are warning signs that the Obama Administration should not ignore.

The Obama Administration has continued a cooperative assistance program established by President George W. Bush and known as the Mérida Initiative. The Administration has also committed to "dual containment," securing the U.S.–Mexico border and heartland against Mexican drug-trafficking organizations (DTOs) or cartels operating in the U.S. while attempting to reduce substantially the illegal movement of guns and bulk transfers of cash from the U.S. into Mexico that feed the cartel's lust for profits and power. These efforts are important but insufficient.

Domestically, the White House has sent mixed signals on the "war on drugs." Senior officials, as well as the President himself, declared efforts aimed at reducing supply through eradication, interdiction, and police action a "historic failure" and promised a new mix of more rational and effective strategies. Commenting on performance by previous Administrations, Secretary of State Hillary Clinton in March 2009 declared despairingly that "We have been pursuing these strategies for 30 years. Neither interdiction [of drugs] nor reducing demand have been successful."[1]

Yet the Administration has done little to act on these pronouncements. The Obama White House has remained generally aloof to complex issues relating to drug consumption in the United States.

The current policy mix is inadequate, and this must change. The threat that drug-induced violence and potential instability in Mexico pose to core U.S. security interests are substantial. The Administration and Congress must play a bolder, more aggressive leadership role. The elements of such an approach would feature:

- A comprehensive, well-articulated anti-narcotics strategy for the Americas;
- An adequately funded multi-year program that includes sustained support for Mexico, Colombia, and other regional allies;
- Enhanced law enforcement and military-to-military cooperation, especially with Mexico; and
- An informed national strategy for public diplomacy and reduced demand that addresses the links between the murderous criminality of traffickers and the individual drug consumer.

## Flashing Red Warning Lights

The U.S.–Mexico drug challenge remains stark and disturbing. Mexican-based traffickers smuggle an estimated 500 to 700 metric tons of cocaine into the U.S. every year. Mexican DTOs or cartels have dominated cocaine-smuggling into the U.S. increasingly since the 1990s.

Mexico is the top foreign source of marijuana, cultivating and harvesting an estimated 15,800 metric tons in 2007.[2] Cannabis is a highly profitable mainstay for the Mexican cartels, reportedly accounting for 50 to 60 percent of their profits. Mexican drug-smuggling organizations are also expanding marijuana production inside the U.S. to increase profits and minimize detection.

Mexico is a major provider of heroin and methamphetamines to the U.S. Estimates of the revenue generated from illicit sales of drugs range from $13 billion to $38 billion. Only Mexico's oil and auto industries generate greater revenue streams.

Since 2007, the Mexican government has struck hard at the Mexican cartels. Just in recent months, government officials have killed or arrested three major drug chieftains: Teodor Garcia Semental, a key crime figure in hundreds of Tijuana murders (arrested January 12, 2010); Carlos Beltran Leyva (arrested January 2, 2010); and Arturo Beltran Leyva, the Boss of Bosses (killed in a gunfight with Mexican special forces on December 16, 2009).[3]

In the past two years, the Mexican government claims to have seized 70 metric tons of cocaine, recovered $260 million in cash, captured 31,000 weapons, and made more than 58,000 arrests. Mexico has extradited 284 indicted traffickers for prosecution and trial in the U.S.[4] But the number of dead from drug violence has continued to climb steadily over the past five years: 1,537 killed in 2005; 2,221 killed in 2006; 2,673 killed in 2007; 5,630 killed in 2008; and 9,635 killed in 2009.[5]

Because they control entry into the U.S., the Mexican states of Baja California, Chihuahua, Guerrero, Michoacan, and Sinaloa account for nearly 75 percent of Mexico's drug murders. Ciudad Juarez, across the Rio Grande from El Paso, has developed a reputation as the deadliest city on the planet. In the past five years, more than 1,000 police and military officers have lost their lives in the fight. Targets of cartel gunmen have included former generals, active-duty military officers, and heads of federal and local police agencies, as well as individuals in witness protection programs, print and media journalists, and even recovering addicts seeking help in drug treatment and rehabilitation centers.

Moreover, Mexico's drug violence has spawned a variety of hybrid, hyper-violent criminal organizations such as the cartel-like Zetas that are able to employ military-like professionalism coupled with terrorist-like methods of indiscriminate murders—tactics ominously new to North America. Mexico's Zetas are studied closely and with considerable intensity by U.S. law enforcement and security strategists.[6] Security analysts describe Mexico's transition from gangsterism to dangerous hybrid forms of "paramilitary terrorism" with "guerrilla tactics."[7] The capabilities of the Zetas, for example, include sophisticated intelligence-gathering, often with insider information, coordinated military actions, and deployment of concentrated levels of lethal firepower, as well as an ability to exploit new vulnerabilities such as extortion and the wholesale theft of oil from pipelines. In essence, Mexico's narco-cartels have constructed what one expert labeled "a parallel government" in which power is shared between elected officials and drug barons.[8]

A fierce debate rages over whether Mexico is in fact winning or losing its war on the cartels. Optimists say violence is still rising because increasingly leaderless cartels are fighting for a diminishing slice of the criminal-earnings pie. Former Salvadoran guerrilla Joaquin Villalobos, for example, believes the state is gaining the upper hand. "It takes time to reduce violence, but drug trafficking is going through a process of self-destruction that deepens when the state confronts it," he states.[9] Skeptics believe a Darwinian process of survival is underway and that key Mexican cartels such as the Sinaloa have not been seriously weakened.

The present assessments of Mexico's progress in the war on the drug cartels need to be tempered with uncertainty about the inadequacy of police and judicial reform, the persistent problem of corruption, and the danger of a loss of political will to continue the drug fight.

[…]

## Cooperation, Containment, and Blame America

U.S. drug strategy for Mexico rests on three fundamental pillars. The first pillar seeks to broaden cross-border, bilateral cooperation with the Mexican government for actions against a shared transnational threat and common enemy. The second involves domestic actions taken by U.S. law enforcement and other agencies to contain or negate the real or potential harm done by drug trafficking and other forms of criminality originating in Mexico and committed on U.S. soil. This includes actions aimed at preventing any major spillover of violence from Mexico into the U.S.

The third element in the United States' Mexico drug strategy, more prominently emphasized by the Obama Administration, is an official acceptance of "co-responsibility" for Mexico's narcotics and cartel crisis. At its core, this pillar is yet another example of the "blame America" strategy embraced by the Obama White House.

The willingness to accept co-responsibility focuses attention on American drug consumption habits (the demand side) and the need for effective demand reduction as well as targeted actions aimed at reducing access of Mexican cartels to U.S. guns, bulk currency, and other accessories that make their criminal businesses both profitable and deadly. It potentially includes changes in U.S. domestic law and law enforcement, particularly laws governing firearms, and tightens restrictions on international financial and monetary transactions.

**Cooperation.** When President George W. Bush met with President Calderón in Mérida, Mexico, in March 2007, the two leaders sketched out a new vision of greater cooperation, a change many considered to be a paradigm-like shift away from grudging association toward genuine cooperation and potential partnership.[22] When finally sent to Congress in October 2008, the Mérida Initiative constituted the largest and most comprehensive package of assistance for the Western Hemisphere since Plan Colombia was begun in 1999.[23] The three-year program proposed an expenditure of $1.4 billion and was "premised on a partnership between our countries and recognition that the multifaceted problems associated with these criminal organizations remain a shared responsibility whose solution requires a coordinated response."[24]

The primary objective of the Mérida Initiative is to strengthen the capabilities of Mexican institutions to fight complex criminal and trafficking organizations. It involves the dispatch of aircraft and vehicles, technology transfers, and training to enhance Mexican law enforcement skills and professional efficiency.

Over half of the Mérida Initiative budget is assigned to the acquisition of 20 airplanes and helicopters.[25] Other big-ticket items include 26 armored vehicles and 30 ion scanners to detect drugs and explosives, five X-ray vans, and forensic equipment. Assistance targets include equipping and training police, supporting judicial reform efforts, developing prosecutorial capacity, and cooperating with a host of Mexican agencies. The Mérida Initiative also addresses needs outside of law enforcement and the judiciary to include helping drug treatment centers, promoting gang prevention strategies, and supporting drug awareness education.

The Obama Administration reports that it is sharing more sensitive drug intelligence with Mexican officials on a regular basis. This is critical if the U.S. and Mexican governments are to stay ahead of the cartels. U.S. assistance was instrumental in helping to set up Platforma Mexico, a nationwide network for intelligence analysis that substantially increases the capacity of Mexican law enforcement to collect, analyze, and disseminate drug intelligence. The U.S. is also working to expand Mexico's Sensitive Investigative Unit, which allows the U.S. Drug Enforcement Administration (DEA) to recruit, select, and train foreign police officers to work cooperatively with the DEA in major case development and the exchange of intelligence.[26] In many respects, this intelligence-sharing ability may be among the most important and most effective of the tools needed to bring the Mexican cartels to heel.

[...]

Overall, the levels of cooperation and trust appear to be improving, but preserving these gains will be critical for the long-term sustainability of joint cooperation.[29] A major issue with the Mérida Initiative has been the painfully slow delivery of promised assistance. A December 2009 report by the Government Accountability Office (GAO) found that at the end of FY 2009 (September 30, 2009), a disappointing 3 percent of appropriated assistance had been delivered to the Mexican government.[30]

The Obama Administration argues that long lead times are required in order to allow the letting of contracts for aircraft and other expensive, high-tech acquisitions, inevitably slowing the delivery process. The Administration managed to deliver five Bell helicopters to Mexico on December 15, 2009.[31] The disbursement of Mérida funds has also been the subject of disputes between Congress and the Administration over human rights.

**Containment.** Since the beginning of the 20th century, the U.S. has sought to contain or block smuggling as diverse as illegal migration, human trafficking, and the illicit movement of goods (such as liquor during Prohibition) in order to keep the problems associated with such activity on the Mexican side of the border. From the establishment of the U.S. Border Patrol in 1924 to the enactment of the Secure Fence Act of 2006 and experimentation with virtual barriers such as SBInet, the U.S. has relied on a combination of uniformed guardians, physical barriers, and an array of detectors and sensors to protect the border and the country from threats arising outside of the borders of the U.S.

The Obama Administration believes it can contain the drug crisis in Mexico to a significant degree. It continues to modify border security policy through modest revisions of the Bush-era Southwest Border Security Initiative, repackaged and reissued by Secretary of Homeland Security Janet Napolitano in March 2009.[32]

In April, the Administration named Alan Bersin, former U.S. Attorney in San Diego and a former San Diego County school superintendent, as Assistant Secretary for International Affairs and Special Representative for Border Affairs, loosely termed the new "border tsar." DHS also directed more than $400 million in government stimulus funds from the American Recovery and

Reinvestment Act to support law enforcement activities on the southwest border.

In June 2009, the Office of National Drug Control Policy (ONDCP), in conjunction with DHS and the Department of Justice, issued its National Southwest Border Counternarcotics Strategy.[33] The strategy aims at "substantially reducing the flow of illicit drugs, drug proceeds, and associated instruments of violence across the Southwest Border."[34] The strategy committed the Obama Administration to enhancing intelligence capabilities; improving controls at ports of entry and in the ground, air, and maritime domains of the border; disrupting the smuggling of guns and bulk currency; disrupting and dismantling drug trafficking organizations; enhancing counterdrug technologies for drug detection and interdiction; and enhancing U.S.– Mexico cooperation in counterdrug operations.

In August 2009, Secretary Napolitano highlighted the achievements of the Administration during its first six months:

> In the past six months, we have added hundreds of agents and deployed additional technology to the border. We've doubled the number of agents that ICE [U.S. Immigration and Customs Enforcement] has assigned to the border enforcement security teams.... We have tripled the number of DHS intelligence analysts working on the Southwest border. We have doubled the number of DHS agents collaborating on looking for and apprehending violent criminal aliens [and have] ramped up southbound inspections to search for illegal weapons and cash, adding mobile X-ray machines, license plate readers, more Border patrol agents, and K-9 detection teams to that effort. For the first time we have begun inspecting all southbound rail shipments into Mexico.[35]

The Obama Administration has largely upheld the Bush Administration's commitment to enhanced border security,[36] but certain projects, such as the creation of a segment of virtual fencing known as SBInet, continue to be ensnared in technical reviews of effectiveness.[37] The distribution of $720 million in economic stimulus money for completing upgrades in border security infrastructure has also become the subject of considerable congressional infighting as funds appear to have been allocated to feed congressional appetites rather than in a systematic response to assessed needs.[38]

**Blame America.** A third pillar of U.S. strategy toward Mexico is to place greater emphasis on the correlation between U.S. domestic illegal drug consumption, gun laws, and economic openness and the violent cross-border consequences in Mexico. The Obama Administration's acceptance of "co-responsibility" for Mexico's drug crisis was articulated most forcefully during Secretary of State Clinton's March 2009 trip to Mexico, made primarily to highlight the Administration's response to the Mexico drug challenge. "Our insatiable demand for illegal drugs," the Secretary announced, "fuels the drug trade. Our inability to prevent weapons from being illegally smuggled across the border to arm these criminals causes the deaths of police, of soldiers and civilians." In other words, the U.S. has all the drug users and provides the guns. It's all our fault; we're sorry.

Setting aside the fact that those two propositions are wildly inaccurate, such admissions tend to make good headlines in the mainstream press and among the blame-America crowd. Further, they may temporarily moderate foreign criticism of the U.S. and its policies. However, they should also require that responsible political leaders deliver results and make serious changes in U.S. domestic policy.

Shortly after taking office, the Obama Administration signaled a new readiness to tackle issues such as U.S. gun exports, to push for treaty efforts to stem illegal trafficking in firearms, and to reassess domestic policies regarding drug consumption and drug law enforcement. Yet few issues aroused greater controversy in the past year than the debate regarding the scale and impact of the southward flow of firearms from the U.S. to Mexico and the importance of these arms in fueling Mexico's escalating violence.

Throughout 2009, leaders on both sides of the border made unsubstantiated statements blaming lax U.S. gun regulation for both the increase in deaths and the growing lethality of drug violence in Mexico. President Obama, as part of his blame-America crusade, claimed during his Mexico trip in April that "[m]ore than 90 percent of the guns recovered in Mexico come from the United States"—a claim that is simply not verifiable. Senior Mexican officials spoke of an "iron river of guns" drenching Mexico in blood and claimed that as many as 2,000 illegal arms crossed from the U.S. into Mexico every day.[39]

The media joined the chorus and focused on the proximity of 6,600 licensed gun dealers in border states, as well as on the frequent holding of gun shows and the alleged laxity with which high-powered weapons could be acquired. A senior U.S. official testified before Congress that the U.S. was essentially in the business of operating an unregulated arms bazaar at the easy disposal of the Mexican cartels.[40]

The Obama–Biden presidential election campaign promised to deliver major changes in U.S. gun laws.[41] Once in office, Attorney General Eric Holder and several Members of Congress issued fresh calls for renewing the 2003 expired ban on the sale of assault weapons, requiring background checks for buyers at gun shows, and greater law enforcement access to and sharing of gun ownership data. These trial balloons for more restrictive changes governing gun laws, however, encountered strong congressional and negative public reactions, raising numerous concerns about legitimate restrictions on Second Amendment rights. In mid-April 2009, President Obama stated that changes in gun laws would be placed on hold.[42]

[...]

Finally, stating that U.S. demand for cocaine, marijuana, and other illegal drugs is at the root of problems in Mexico and the rest of the region, including Colombia, Central America, and the Caribbean, plays well abroad. Most recently in Guatemala, in March 2010, Secretary of State Clinton proclaimed that:

[T]he United States under the Obama Administration recognizes and accepts its share of responsibility for the problems posed by drug trafficking in this region. The demand in the large market in the United States drives the drug trade. We know that we are part of the problem and that is an admission that we have been willing to make this past year.[52]

The claim that demand is the root cause of the drug crisis implies that the federal government is responsible for and prepared to assume new responsibilities for reducing the demand for drugs within the U.S. Although the President can try to set the tone in the country and ask his fellow citizens to reject illegal drugs, reducing the demand for illegal drugs is not and never has been primarily the responsibility of the federal government. Traditionally, it has been the responsibility of states, local governments, private and charitable organizations, religious organizations, and other entities. By stating that the United States "accepts its share of responsibility," the Administration may be raising expectations that the federal government has the primary responsibility for addressing the demand for illegal drugs by end users when in fact it has no such charter.

The Obama Administration's record on the domestic front also does not appear to match the blame-America rhetoric employed abroad. President Obama selected Seattle, Washington, Chief of Police Gil Kerlikowske to head the Office of National Drug Control Policy. In naming Kerlikowske, the White House decided that the ONDCP "drug czar" would no longer be considered a Cabinet-level position.[53] In a May interview with The Wall Street Journal, Kerlikowske raised eyebrows when he announced that the drug fight was actually a misnamed "war on a product." Kerlikowske insisted that "we should stop using the metaphor about war on drugs. People look at it as a war on them, and frankly we are not at war with the people of this country."[54]

The challenge for the Obama Administration is to combat drug cartels and redouble the government's efforts to contain the cross-border movement of drugs and guns. It must also resist the siren calls for decriminalization of marijuana and other dangerous drugs. President Vicente Fox's foreign minister Jorge Castañeda, a persistent commentator and skeptic regarding Mexico's current anti-drug strategy, succinctly captures the Administration's dilemma:

> If anything, the United States seems to be moving…toward decriminalization of marijuana, greater tolerance for safer forms of heroin, an effort to wean people off of methamphetamines, and in general the adoption of a far more relaxed attitude toward drugs….
>
> It is absurd for hundreds of Mexican soldiers, police officers, and petty drug dealers to be dying over the drug war in Tijuana when, 100 or so miles to the north in Los Angeles, there are… more legal and public dispensaries of marijuana than public schools.[55]

The Administration needs to resolve the dilemma by enforcing laws that prohibit sales to "recreational" users or that allow the establishment of dispensaries of dubious legality. It must also respond to individual state efforts such as the upcoming California referendum in November on marijuana legalization in the state.[56] For the moment, the Administration has reiterated that it has no intention of advocating national legalization of marijuana consumption, a measure that ONDCP Director Kerlikowske called a "nonstarter in the Obama Administration."[57]

Finally, it should be noted that after a year in office, President Obama has remained reticent about warning the American public of the dangers of drug abuse and has not clearly indicated that the medical, psychological, and economic harm done by drug abuse remains at the center of the debate about the quality and security of American lives.

## The Resource Vice

The Obama Administration's readiness to launch a major departure in its drug policy, either internationally or domestically, is severely circumscribed by current resource limitations. While the entire FY 2011 federal budget races toward record-setting spending levels and deficits, funding for drug-related efforts reflects either modest increases or, in certain cases, reductions in requests for funding. The Administration's budget proposal for the State Department, for example, specifies a reduction in overall support for international narcotics and law enforcement from $2.448 billion in FY 2010 to $2.136 billion in FY 2011. The FY 2011 budget proposal for the State Department calls for additional funding for Mérida Initiative programs of approximately $292 million, a 25 percent decrease from previous funding levels.[58]

The National Drug Control budget request for FY 2011 calls for $15.5 billion to reduce drug use and its consequences for the U.S.[59] This represents an increase of $521.1 million over FY 2010. The largest increase will be dedicated to prevention with an increase of more than $200 million, a 13.4 percent increase over FY 2010. A 3.7 percent increase will be allocated to treatment programs, while international programs are to be increased by a modest $20.1 million (0.9 percent).

According to ONDCP's budget account, approximately $6 billion will be spent in FY 2011 for interdiction and international law enforcement programs. The interdiction side of the ONDCP budget includes a recapitalization program for ships and aircraft for the Coast Guard. Within the international assistance component of the ONDCP-monitored budget, resources in international programs are being shifted to Department of Defense counternarcotics support in Central Asia. The ONDCP budget also carves out of the limited budget funding for the start-up of a new Caribbean Basin Security Initiative.

Overall, resource limitations will substantially constrain the capacity of the Administration to respond to the mounting challenges posed by Mexico's drug crises. In addition, they will leave the United States well short of the resources needed to wage an aggressive strategy that targets foreign producers, suppliers, and traffickers while making serious inroads against consumption and drug use here in the U.S.

[...]

If the Obama Administration wishes to pursue a bolder policy that does more than perpetuate the status quo and demonstrates a deeper commitment to leadership and a genuine, enduring commitment to work with regional partners, it should undertake the following:

- **Develop an integrated hemispheric drug strategy.** The U.S. cannot run separate drug strategies for the Andes, the Caribbean, and Mexico and Central America as a three-ring circus. Congress should move swiftly to set up a Western Hemisphere drug commission to review the totality of U.S. drug strategies.[60] While most commissions consume tax dollars and seldom produce more than large unread documents, a high-level commission offers an opportunity to recommend greater discipline and coherence in the United States' scattered drug policies.

- **Fulfill Mérida Initiative commitments and develop a robust follow-up strategy.** The Administration and Congress must redouble their efforts to speed delivery of promised assistance to Mexico. The Administration must also begin consultations with the Mexican government and key military and law enforcement agencies to develop programs that focus on enhanced, secure, multi-layered cooperation with the goal of providing adequate resources. Particular attention must be paid to building and strengthening federal law enforcement capabilities and judicial reform in Mexico, enhancing citizen security and community participation, and continued secure cross-border cooperation.

- **Build a cross-border anti-drug coalition.** The U.S. also needs to pursue a more aggressive public diplomacy that encourages citizen-to-citizen contacts and mobilizes Mexico's growing middle class and civil society to press for effective reform and anti-corruption measures.[61]

- **Strengthen military-to-military ties.** Congress should end its misapplied efforts to hold broad-based assistance and the provision of promised equipment hostage to alleged human rights abuses by Mexico's military. The Administration should, in fact, strengthen efforts aimed at cooperating with the Mexican armed forces. The U.S. should focus on targets such as human-rights training and military justice reform as well as training in intelligence collection and analysis and special operations needed to wage the fight the most violent elements in Mexico.

- **Invite Mexico to join NORAD.** The North American Aerospace Defense Command (NORAD) is a joint U.S.–Canadian command for monitoring air and sea approaches to the U.S. Extending participation to Mexico would augment "domain awareness" in North America and buttress continuing U.S.–Mexican cooperation.[62]
- **Maintain a sustained commitment to border security.** The Administration must continue to reaffirm its readiness to look for effective, cost-efficient strategies that draw on innovative technologies such as SBInet, unmanned aerial surveillance, and innovative, intelligence-driven partnerships forged by BEST teams.
- **Engage in responsible public diplomacy.** President Obama should employ his considerable communication skills in a revamped and realistic effort that addresses both the challenges and the limits that the U.S. government faces when approaching the drug issue both at home and abroad, perhaps in conjunction with Latin American presidents such as Calderón of Mexico and Alvaro Uribe of Colombia. The Obama Administration must make a greater effort to educate the American public about the domestic and foreign harm caused by drug consumption.

## Conclusion

From the domestic and foreign policy perspectives, there are no easy solutions to the nation's continued drug consumption habits, nor are there easy ways to respond to the mayhem created by powerful, nihilistic transnational criminal organizations with their nefarious, life-destroying businesses that capitalize on the weaknesses of individuals, law enforcement agencies, courts, and entire nations. U.S. drug policy must also answer to a chorus of domestic tinkerers, libertarians, and hedonists who believe in the necessity of a massive paradigm change away from the "failed drug war."

In the year ahead, the U.S. needs manpower, technology, intelligence—and public support—to break the will and organization of Mexico's criminal gangs. The U.S. must degrade them by preserving a broad international front while working diligently to lower the pool of consumers in the U.S. It must strengthen secure partnerships with honest officials abroad and link these partnerships for greater security in the Americas. It needs effective statistics and solid evidence that target the illicit sales and export of firearms and transfers of bulk cash. Despite the austere budget climate, the Administration and Congress must make adequate resources available for tough, intelligent cooperation and enforcement at home and abroad against violent trafficking organizations, coupled with more education, research, treatment programs, and intelligent punitive options, such as drug courts.

If the U.S. fails to take these measures, the cost will be far higher.

## Endnotes

1. Mary Beth Sheridan, "Clinton: U.S. Drug Policies Failed, Fueled Mexico's Drug Wars," The Washington Post , March 26, 2009 at http://www.washingtonpost.com/wp-dyn/content/article/2009/03/25/AR2009032501034.html (April 13, 2010).

2. U.S. Department of Justice, National Drug Intelligence Center, "Domestic Cannabis Cultivation Assessment," 2009, at http://www.justice.gov/ndic/pubs37/37035/37035p.pdf. The number one source for marijuana consumed in the U.S. is U.S.-based production, much of it run by Mexican DTOs.

3. Elliott Spagat, "Reputed Drug Lord Teodoro Garcia Simental Is Captured," The Washington Post , January 13, 2010, at http://www.washingtonpost.com/wp-dyn/content/article/2010/01/12/AR2010011203660.html (April 13 2010); José de Córdoba and Nicholas Casey, "Arrest Targets Drug Cartel," The Wall Street Journal, January 4, 2010, at http://online.wsj.com/article/SB126248870125713783.html?mod=WSJ_hpp_sections_world (April 13, 2010); and John Lyons and José de Córdoba, "Top Mexican Drug Lord Killed in Shootout," The Wall Street Journal, December 18, 2009, at http://online.wsj.com/article/SB126104630707195259.html?mod=WSJ_hpp_MIDDLENexttoWhatsNewsThird (April 13, 2010).

4. Extraditions, while an important weapon against traffickers, mask problems with the Mexican judicial system and the extent to which Mexican prisons are themselves

corrupted by traffickers or become breeding grounds for further recruiting and hardening of criminals as well as alternate centers for conducting criminal activity. Extraditions also leave dissatisfaction among the victims of crime, who seldom see justice in their own country against criminals who murdered or harmed loved ones.

5. Esther Sanchez, "Aumenta Nivel de Violencia del Narco," El Universal, January 1, 2010, at http://www.eluniversal.com.mx/primera/34184.html (April 13, 2010). Per capita murder rates in Mexico nevertheless still appear to be lower than those in many other violence-prone countries such as Brazil and South Africa. Reformed former Salvadoran guerrilla Joaquin Villalobos believes the overall murder rate in Mexico is 10 per 100,000 citizens, compared to 48 per 100,000 in Venezuela and more than 50 per 100,000 in Guatemala, Honduras, and El Salvador. Joaquin Villalobos, "Twelve Myths in the Fight Against Drug Trafficking," Nexos , January 1, 2010.

6. Useful studies that probe the growing challenge include H. L Brands, "Mexico's Narco-Insurgency and U.S. Counterdrug Policy," U.S. Army War College, Strategic Studies Institute, May 2009; George Grayson, Mexico's Struggle with Drugs and Thugs (New York: Foreign Policy Association, 2009); Max G. Manwaring, A "New" Dynamic in the Western Hemisphere Security Environment: The Mexican Zetas and Other Private Armies (Carlisle, Pa.: U.S. Army War College, Strategic Studies Institute, September 2009); and John P. Sullivan, "Future Conflict: Criminal Insurgencies, Gangs and Intelligence," Small Wars Journal, May 31, 2009, at http://smallwarsjournal.com/blog/journal/docs-temp/248-sullivan.pdf (April 20, 2010).

7. Stephanie Hanson, "Mexico's Drug War," Council on Foreign Relations Backgrounder, November 20, 2008, at http://www.cfr.org/publication/13689/ (April 13, 2010).

8. Steven Fainaru and William Booth, "Mexico's Drug Cartels Siphon Liquid Gold," The Washington Post, December 13, 2009, at http://www.washingtonpost.com/wp dyn/content/article/2009/12/12/AR2009121202888.html (April 13, 2010).

9. Villalobos, "Twelve Myths in the Fight Against Drug Trafficking."

22. Despite frequent criticism, the U.S., under the Bush Administration, was engaged in cooperative efforts with the Mexican government to construct a security framework for North America in the aftermath of 9/11. A key element of this was the Security and Prosperity Partnership of North America. See SPP.gov at http://www.spp.gov/ (April 14, 2010).

23. Claire Ribando Seelke, "Mérida Initiative for Mexico and Central America: Funding and Policy Issues," Congressional Research Service Report for Congress No. R40135, January 21, 2010, at http://www.wilsoncenter.org/topics/pubs/M%C3%A9rida%20Initiative%20for%20Mexico%20and%20Central%20America%20Funding%20and%20Policy%20Issues.pdf (April 14, 2010).

24. Thomas A. Shannon, Jr., Assistant Secretary of State, Bureau of Western Hemisphere Affairs, U.S. Department of State, testimony before the Subcommittee on the Western Hemisphere, Committee on Foreign Affairs, U.S. House of Representatives, May 28, 2008, at http://foreignaffairs.house.gov/110/sha050808.htm (April 14, 2010).

25. The promised aircraft include eight UH-60 Black Hawk helicopters, four Casa 235 Persuaders, and eight Bell 412 helicopters.

26. Executive Office of the President, Office of National Drug Control Policy, "National Drug Control Budget: FY 2011 Funding Highlights," February 2010, at http://www.ondcp.gov/pdf/FY2011_Drug_Control_Budget_Highlights.pdf (April 14, 2010).

29. For a discussion of the paradigm change concept, see Roger F. Noriega, "Helping Win the War on Our Doorstep," American Enterprise Institute Latin American Outlook No. 6, August 2007, at http://www.aei.org/outlook/26601 (April 14, 2010).

30. U.S. Government Accountability Office, Status of Funds for the Mérida Initiative, GAO-10-253R, December 3, 2009, at http://www.gao.gov/new.items/d10253r.pdf (April 14, 2010).

31. John Brennan, Assistant to the President for Homeland Security and Counter-Terrorism, speech at Helicopter Transfer Ceremony, Embassy of the United States, Mexico, December 15, 2009, at http://mexico.usembassy.gov/eng/texts/et091215Brennan.html (April 15, 2010).

32. Woodrow Wilson International Center for Scholars, "Southwest Border Security Initiatives," August 2009, at http://www.wilsoncenter.org/news/docs/SWB%20Fact%20Sheet1.pdf (April 15, 2010).

33. Congress mandated the National Southwest Border Counternarcotics Strategy in 2006 when it issued reauthorization for the ONDCP, thus making the strategy another legacy of the Bush Administration.

34. Office of National Drug Control Policy, "National Southwest Border Counternarcotics Strategy," June 2009, at http://www.whitehousedrugpolicy.gov/publications/swb_counternarcotics_strategy09/swb_counternarcotics_strategy09.pdf (April 15, 2010).

35. U.S. Department of Homeland Security, "Remarks by Secretary Napolitano at the Border Security Conference," University of Texas at El Paso, August 11, 2009, at http://www.dhs.gov/ynews/speeches/sp_1250028863008.shtm (April 15, 2010).

36. Matt A. Mayer, "U.S. Border Security: Realities and Challenges for the Obama Administration," Heritage Foundation Backgrounder No. 2285, June 17, 2009, at http://www.heritage.org/Research/Reports/2009/06/US-Border-Security-Realitiesand-Challenges-for-the-Obama-Administration.

37. Alice Lipowicz, "Napolitano Orders SBInet Reassessment, " Federal Computer Week, January 22, 2010, at http://fcw.com/Articles/2010/01/22/SBInet-Napolitano-reassessment.aspx (April 15, 2010).

38. Eileen Sullivan and Matt Apuzzo, "Hit and Miss on the Border," The Houston Chronicle , August 26, 2009, at http://www.chron.com/disp/story.mpl/metropolitan/6587768.html (April 15, 2010).

39. According to former Mexican Foreign Minister Jorge G. Castañeda, "A large proportion of the assault weapons used by the cartels do come from the United States, but the figure is far lower than the oft-quoted 90 percent (90 percent of the guns Mexican authorities give to U.S. authorities to trace turn out to be from the United States—but better estimates suggest 20 to 35 percent of guns in Mexico are American) or the also oft-quoted claim that 2,000 assault rifles cross into Mexico every day. If true, this would mean that more than 2 million weapons have entered Mexico just since Calderón has been in office. To put it into context, Mexico has an average of 15 guns per 100 inhabitants. Finland has 55." See Jorge G. Casteñada, "What's Spanish for Quagmire? Five Myths that Caused the Failed War Next Door," Foreign Policy , January/February 2010, at http://www.foreignpolicy.com/articles/2010/01/04/whats_spanish_for_quagmire (April 15, 2010).

40. "Arms purchased or otherwise acquired here [in the U.S.] and smuggled into Mexico equip the cartels with mines, antitank weapons, heavy machine guns, military hand grenades, and high-powered sniper rifles and high-tech equipment. Smuggling also equips the cartels with night-vision goggles, electronic intercept capabilities, encrypted communications, and helicopters." Testimony of David T. Johnson, Assistant Secretary, Bureau of International Narcotics and Law Enforcement Affairs, before the Subcommittee on State, Foreign Operations and Related Programs, Committee on Appropriations, U.S. House of Representatives, March 10, 2009.

41. Candidate Obama proposed to "repeal the Tiahrt Amendment, which restricts the ability of local law enforcement to access important gun trace information, and give police

officers across the nation the tools they need to solve gun crimes and fight the illegal arms trade." Candidate Obama also pledged to support "closing the gun show loophole and making guns in this country childproof. They also support making the expired federal Assault Weapons Ban permanent." Office of the President-Elect, "Urban Policy Agenda," 2008, at http://www.barackobama.com/issues/urban_policy/index_campaign.php (April 19, 2010).

42. Jake Tapper, "President Obama Suggests Pushing for 'Assault Weapon' Ban Not in the Cards," ABC News, April 16, 2009, at http://blogs.abcnews.com/politicalpunch/2009/04/president-ob-17.html (April 15, 2010).

52. Matthew Lee, "Clinton Admits U.S. Demand Fuels Drug War," Associated Press, March 6, 2010, at http://news.theage.com.au/breaking-news-world/clinton-admits-us-demand-fuels-drug-war-20100306-pp8c.html (April 19, 2010).

53. John P. Walters, "Up in Smoke," The Daily Standard , March 17, 2009, at http://www.hudson.org/index.cfm?fuseaction=publication_details&id=6095 (April 15, 2010).\

54. Gary Fields, "White House Czar Calls for End to 'War on Drugs,'" The Wall Street Journal , May 14, 2009, at http://online.wsj.com/article/SB124225891527617397.html (April 15, 2010), and Andy Sullivan, "U.S. Drug Czar Calls for End to War on Drugs," Reuters, June 8, 2009.

55. Castañeda, "What's Spanish for Quagmire?"

56. Peter Hecht, "California Sets Marijuana Legalization Vote for November," The Miami Herald , March 25, 2010, at http://www.miamiherald.com/2010/03/25/1546385/california-sets-marijuana-legalization.html (April 15, 2010).

57. "Marijuana Legalization? A White House Rebuttal, Finally," The Christian Science Monitor, March 12, 2010, at http://www.csmonitor.com/Commentary/the-monitors-view/2010/0312/Marijuana-legalization-A-White-House-rebuttal-finally (April 15, 2010).

58. U.S. Department of State, Executive Budget Summary: Function 150 and Other International Programs, Fiscal Year 2011, at http://www.state.gov/documents/organization/135888.pdf (April 15, 2010).

59. Office of National Drug Control Policy, "National Drug Control Budget: FY 2011 Funding Highlights," February 2010, at http://www.ondcp.gov/pdf/FY2011_Drug_Control_Budget_Highlights.pdf (April 15, 2010).

61. O'Neil, "The Real War in Mexico." O'Neil highlights the growing importance of Mexico's emerging middle class as a critical weapon in the fight for democratic reform, good governance, and anti-corruption measures.

62. Craig A. Deare, "U.S.–Mexico Defense Relations: An Incompatible Interface," National Defense University, Institute for National Strategic Studies, July 2009, at http://www.dtic.mil/cgi-bin/GetTRDoc?AD=ADA504170&Location=U2&doc=GetTRDoc.pdf (April 15, 2010), and James Carafano, "Let Mexico Join NORAD," The Examiner (Washington, D.C.), December 7, 2009, at http://www.washingtonexaminer.com/opinion/columns/Let-Mexico-join-NORAD-8634584-78643172.html (April 15, 2010).

> *"The experiences of these states reinforce that criminal justice policies, and not crime rates, are the prime drivers of changes in prison populations."*

# The Relationship Between Incarceration and Crime Is Limited

*Marc Mauer and Nazgol Ghandnoosh*

*In the following viewpoint, Marc Mauer and Dr. Nazgol Ghandnoosh examine three states that reduced their prison populations during a set time period. They explore the effect on rates of various crime types, as well as the potential for substantially reducing prison populations. The authors conclude the threat to public safety that might be anticipated does not exist, or is so slight that the benefits outweigh the risks. Mauer is an expert on sentencing policy, race, and the criminal justice system. He is the author of the book* Race to Incarcerate *and was a co-editor for a collection of essays titled* Invisible Punishment. *Ghandnoosh is a research analyst at The Sentencing Project.*

"Fewer Prisoners, Less Crime: A Tale of Three States," by Marc Mauer, The Sentencing Project, November, 2011. Reprinted by Permission.

As you read, consider the following questions:

1. According to the authors, why has the federal prison population grown?
2. What effect did the U.S. Supreme Court's decision in *Brown v. Plata* have on the California prison system?
3. What factors do Mauer and Ghandnoosh discuss in explaining why a prison population decline may not equate to higher levels of crime?

Although the pace of criminal justice reform has accelerated at both the federal and state levels in the past decade, current initiatives have had only a modest effect on the size of the prison population. But over this period, three states—New York, New Jersey, and California—have achieved prison population reductions in the range of 25%. They have also seen their crime rates generally decline at a faster pace than the national average.

## Key findings:

- New York and New Jersey led the nation by reducing their prison populations by 26% between 1999 and 2012, while the nationwide state prison population increased by 10%.
- California downsized its prison population by 23% between 2006 and 2012. During this period, the nationwide state prison population decreased by just 1%.
- During their periods of decarceration, violent crime rates fell at a greater rate in these three states than they did nationwide. Between 1999-2012, New York and New Jersey's violent crime rate fell by 31% and 30%, respectively, while the national rate decreased by 26%. Between 2006-2012, California's violent crime rate drop of 21% exceeded the national decline of 19%.
- Property crime rates also decreased in New York and New Jersey more than they did nationwide, while California's reduction was slightly lower than the national average. Between 1999-2012, New York's property crime rate fell by

29% and New Jersey's by 31%, compared to the national decline of 24%. Between 2006-2012, California's property crime drop of 13% was slightly lower than the national reduction of 15%.

These prison population reductions have come about through a mix of changes in policy and practice designed to reduce admissions to prison and lengths of stay. The experiences of these states reinforce that criminal justice policies, and not crime rates, are the prime drivers of changes in prison populations. They also demonstrate that it is possible to substantially reduce prison populations without harming public safety.

## A Decade of Evolving Criminal Justice Reform

For more than a decade the political environment shaping criminal justice policy has been evolving in a direction emphasizing "smart on crime" and evidence-based approaches to public safety. This has involved growing bipartisan campaigns at both the federal and state levels to promote more strategic sentencing and reentry policies, and to address the unprecedented growth and cost of the corrections system created over the past several decades.

The changing climate can be seen in a variety of legislative, judicial, and policy changes during this period of time. At the federal level, this has included the Fair Sentencing Act of 2010 which reduced the disparity in sentencing between crack and powder cocaine offenses; the adoption of the Second Chance Act in 2008 which currently funds about $67 million in reentry services annually; and the U.S. Supreme Court's 2005 Booker decision making the Federal Sentencing Guidelines advisory and thereby restoring a greater degree of sentencing discretion to federal judges.

At the state level, 29 states have adopted reforms designed to scale back the scope and severity of their mandatory sentencing policies over the past decade.[1] Voters in California approved a ballot initiative in 2012 that curbed the scope of the state's notoriously broad "three strikes and you're out" law and policymakers around the country have become increasingly supportive of Justice

Reinvestment initiatives, reducing parole revocations, establishing treatment courts, and developing alternatives to incarceration.

## Limited Impact on Incarceration to Date

The impact of these various initiatives on incarceration has been mixed. At the federal level the prison population has continued its more than three-decade historic rise, driven in large part by the ongoing effect of mandatory penalties for many drug and gun crimes, and increasing incarceration for immigration offenses.[2]

At the state level there has been more of a shift in prison population trends. The number of people incarcerated in state prisons has declined for three years since 2010, and in 2012 (the most recent year for which data are available) 27 states experienced a reduction in their population.

While these trends are encouraging it is also important to note that the overall scale of change has been quite modest. The national prison population has only declined by less than 2% annually in recent years, and a disproportionate amount of that decline is due to California's "Realignment" policy. In 2012, the prison population reduction of 15,000 in California accounted for half of the national decline for all states that year.

## Substantial Prison Population Declines in Three States

The exceptions to the modest scale of decarceration can be seen in three states—New York, New Jersey, and California—each of which has reduced its prison population in the range of 25% over the past decade.

While New York and New Jersey reduced their prisoner counts by 26% between 1999 and 2012, the nationwide state prison population increased by 10%. While California downsized its prison population by 23% between 2006 and 2012, the nationwide level decreased by just 1%.[3] Six other states achieved double-digit reductions during varying periods within these years, though of a lesser magnitude: Colorado, Connecticut, Hawaii, Michigan,

Rhode Island, and Vermont. Coming after a nearly four-decade historic rise in imprisonment, the substantial and sustained reductions in New York, New Jersey, and California should be particularly instructive for all concerned with excessively high prison populations.

Because incarceration is ostensibly designed to support public safety, in this analysis we review how prisoner reductions in these three states impacted crime control. While some political leaders warn of a "crime wave" when prison population reductions are considered, such talk ignores the complexity of how public safety is produced. Incarceration is a limited factor among many that shape public safety. Further, in the era of mass incarceration, there is a growing consensus that current levels of incarceration place the nation well past the point of diminishing returns in crime control.

## Impact of Prison Population Reductions on Crime

The periods in which New York, New Jersey, and California significantly decreased their prison populations were ones in which crime rates were declining around the country.[4] Yet in these states, crime rates generally fell at a faster pace than in the country as a whole. In all three states, violent crime rates decreased more than they did nationwide. Property crime rates decreased in New York and New Jersey more than they did nationwide, while California's property crime reduction was slightly lower than the national average.

### All Three States Experienced Violent Crime Drops That Exceeded the National Average

The violent crime rate measures the incidence of four crime categories (murder, forcible rape, robbery, and aggravated assault) per 100,000 residents. Between 1999-2012, the nationwide violent crime rate decreased by 26%. New York and New Jersey outpaced this decline, with reductions of 31% and 30%, respectively. California's violent crime drop of 21% between 2006-2012 also exceeded the national decline of 19% during this period.

New York and California's violent crime reductions have exceeded nationwide trends despite recent upticks. Between 2010 and 2012, while the nationwide violent crime rate slowed its decline, New York's violent crime rate increased each year – by 3.7% between 2010 and 2012. Because this uptick has only brought the state back to its 2007 level, New York maintains its historically low violent crime rate.

California's violent crime drop between 2006 and 2012 also exceeded the national average. Its rate in 2012 was 21% lower than in 2006 despite an increase of 2.9% in 2012.

Magnus Lofstrom and Steven Raphael's analysis of county-level variation in crime and incarceration rates has shown that California's violent crime uptick in 2012 was unlikely to have been related to the prison downsizing achieved through Realignment, a policy that went into effect in October 2011.[5] Lofstrom and Raphael compared monthly changes in crime rates with changes in jail and prison incarceration rates in each California county in the twelve months before and after Realignment. "There is no evidence that realignment resulted in an increase in murder or rape, with the estimates near zero and statistically insignificant," they concluded. When they examined California crime data without controlling for broader regional trends, they found that Realignment had a small and marginally significant effect on robbery and aggravated assault. But "all evidence of an effect of realignment on violent crime vanishes," they noted, when broader regional trends are incorporated into the analysis.

## All Three States Experienced Substantial Declines in Property Crime Rates, and Two Exceeded the National Average

The property crime rate measures the incidence of four crime categories (burglary, larceny-theft, motor vehicle theft, and arson) per 100,000 residents. While the national property crime rate decreased by 24% between 1999 and 2012, New York's rate dropped by 29% and New Jersey's by 31%. Between 2006 and 2012,

California's property crime rate decreased significantly, but at a slightly lower rate than the national average. While California's property crime rate fell by 13% during this period, the nationwide property crime rate fell by 15%.

New York and New Jersey have outpaced the national decline in property rates since 1999 even while experiencing modest upticks in some years. Both nationwide and in New York and New Jersey, property crime rates have been falling at a slower rate since 2009.

While California's property crime rate decreased by 13% between 2006 and 2012, the state experienced a 6.8% uptick in 2012. That increase, the first since 2003, brought the state's property crime rate back to its 2009 level.

Lofstrom and Raphael's analysis of California's monthly crime data at the county level presents evidence that the small uptick in property crimes, particularly auto thefts, was related to Realignment.[6] "The start of the increase in motor vehicle theft coincides exactly with the implementation of realignment in October 2011," they write, and there was a statistically significant relationship between decarceration and motor vehicle theft at the county level even after incorporating broader regional trends. But, as the authors note, the post-Realignment uptick in car thefts only brought the state's auto theft rate back to 2009 levels. Given Realignment's modest impact on property crimes, Lofstrom and Raphael's cost-benefit analysis leads them to conclude that Realignment's "benefits in terms of prison expenditure savings outweigh the costs in terms of somewhat higher property crimes."

## Policies and Practices that Reduced Prison Populations in Three States

The declining prison populations of New York, New Jersey, and California were not simply the result of falling crime rates; rather, prisons were downsized through a mix of policy and practice changes designed to reduce admissions to prison and lengths of stay. While crime rates were declining nationally during this period, other states either experienced continued increases in their prison populations, or only modest declines. Following is a brief overview of the key reforms that produced these outcomes.

## New York

New York's prison population peaked in 1999, with 72,896 prisoners. Mandatory penalties created by the passage of Rockefeller Drug Laws and related legislation, along with the intensification of street drug enforcement in the 1980s and 1990s caused the state's prison population to balloon in size with lowerlevel drug offenders.[7] Other "get-tough" measures, such as limitations on parole, also added to the state's prison population. Through a combination of changes in policy and practice that largely affected enforcement and sentencing for drug offenses in New York City, the state's 2012 prison population was 26% smaller than its 1999 peak.

Felony drug arrests began their sharp decline in New York City beginning in 1999, following a widely- publicized poll showing that the public had grown critical of mandatory drug sentencing.[8] The decline in arrests was driven largely by a shift in enforcement priorities in the New York City Police Department. During the 1990s, there were generally over 40,000 felony drug arrests per year in New York City.[9] By 2003, there were only 23,711 felony drug arrests, and that figure had fallen to 19,680 by 2012.[10]

At the same time, misdemeanor drug arrests had increased dramatically in New York City—doubling between 1986 and 2008—in part because of the broader growth in controversial police policies to target misdemeanor crimes under "broken windows" and "stop and frisk" strategies.[11] James Austin and Michael Jacobson have argued that "NYPD's shifting resources toward misdemeanor arrests as part of the 'broken windows' policing model contributed to the decrease in the felony arrests" (emphasis added).[12] Given the disproportionate influence of prison admissions from New York City, policing changes in that jurisdiction played a significant role in the state's prison decline.

Prison disposition rates also fell, with a growing number of people with felony drug arrests being diverted to alternative sentences, enabled by the growth in treatment programs and their demonstrated efficacy. Initiatives such as the Drug Treatment Alternative to Prison program, pioneered by the Brooklyn District Attorney's Office, provided high quality substance abuse treatment services to an otherwise prison-bound population, and have since been replicated in a number of other jurisdictions. Statewide, the proportion of people with felony drug arrests who were sentenced to prison declined from 23.3% during the 1990s to 13.2% in 2012.[13] Recently, the city and state have also curbed prison admissions through probation revocations by shortening probation terms, thereby reducing unnecessary supervision of low-risk individuals.[14]

The state also implemented a "Merit Time Program," signed into law by Governor George Pataki in 1997. This program enabled people serving prison sentences for a nonviolent, non-sex crime to earn reductions in their minimum term and become eligible for parole consideration sooner by completing educational, vocational, treatment, and service programs.

Finally, between 2003-2005 the state made substantial revisions to the mandatory sentences stipulated by the Rockefeller Drug Laws, and in 2009 largely repealed the provisions of the policy. Mandatory minimum terms were eliminated or reduced in 2009, and the revisions were made retroactive for persons still incarcerated under the old law.

### New Jersey

New Jersey reached its peak prison population in 1999, with 31,493 prisoners, and reduced its size by 26% by 2012. The state downscaled its prisons through both front-end reforms affecting the number of admissions and sentence lengths, and back-end reforms that increased rates of parole and reduced parole revocations.

In 2001, the state settled a lawsuit accusing the Parole Board of failing to meet deadlines required by state law to prepare pre-parole reports and hold timely hearings.[15] The parole board agreed to conduct more timely hearings to prevent a future backlog as part of the settlement, and it enhanced decision- making tools and supervision. Parole approval rates rose dramatically, from 30.1% in 1999 to 51.0% the following year, and have sustained elevated rates since.[16] The state also reduced the rate at which people who violate the technical terms of their parole are readmitted to prison.

New Jersey's drug policy reforms also contributed to its decarceration. State legislators established a sentencing commission in 2004 that first investigated the state's "drug free zone law," concluding that the law created unwarranted racial disparity among people incarcerated for drug offenses. The New Jersey Office of the Attorney General issued guidelines to exempt the lowest level of drug offenders from the law and increase judicial discretion in sentencing. The state also passed Senate Bill 1866 to give judges discretion to sentence individuals below the mandatory minimums of the school zone law, and made this retroactive with a companion bill.

## California

Since California reached its peak prison population in 2006, with 173,942 men and women, prisoner counts have fallen every year. The rate of decline was small at first: the size receded by 5.6% between 2006 and 2010. But between 2010 and 2012, the prison population decreased by 18.3%. This dramatic change was primarily driven by the state's efforts to comply with a court order to reduce prison overcrowding.

In a significant 2011 decision, the U.S. Supreme Court in *Brown v. Plata* found the provision of health care in the California prison system to be constitutionally inadequate due to the severe overcrowding in the system.[17] Noting that California prisons had been operating at around 200% of their design capacity for at least 11 years, the Court ruled that the state was required to reduce this figure to 137.5% of design capacity within two years. This meant an additional reduction of 37,000 prisoners. Through "Realignment," described next, the state has made significant reductions in its prison population but has yet to reach the court-stipulated level.

In order to substantially reduce prison overcrowding, the California Legislature enacted a "Realignment" policy (Assembly Bill 109) in October, 2011.[18] Key elements of the legislation included: 1) individuals with non-violent, non-sex-related, and non-serious (referred to as "non-non-non") current and prior convictions could be incarcerated in county jails but no longer in state prisons; 2) released prisoners with "non-non-non" offenses would be supervised for a shorter period of time and released to county probation supervision instead of to state parole supervision, and; 3) individuals who violated the technical terms of their probation or parole (i.e., did not commit a new crime) could only be sentenced to jail rather than prison, and for a shorter length of time. Prior to Realignment, the state had also passed legislation in 2009 to limit parole supervision for lowrisk individuals, with the intention of reducing the number of people returning to prison for violating the technical terms of their parole.[19]

Realignment has increased county jail populations while reducing the state's prison population. But the net effect has been to reduce the total incarcerated population (in jail and prison combined). The best estimates show that: "Realignment increased the average daily jail population by roughly one inmate for every three fewer offenders going to state prison."[20]

## The Limited Relationship Between Incarceration and Crime

While it might seem intuitive that reducing prison populations would negatively impact public safety—or conversely, that declining crime rates would drive down levels of incarceration—such a relationship has generally been shown to be relatively weak. This is because just as forces beyond crime rates affect incarceration levels, forces beyond incarceration affect crime.

During the near four-decade continuous rise in incarceration since 1972, crime rates increased in some periods and declined in others. Most notably, during the period 1984-1991 the incarceration rate increased by more than 5% each year, reaching a peak increase of 12.8% in 1989 alone. Yet despite this significant rise in the number of imprisoned individuals, crime rates also rose substantially during this time.

Conversely, one might expect that trends in rates of crime might affect the size of the prison population, but there is little evidence for this assertion. As described in the comprehensive 2014 report of the National Research Council, The Growth of Incarceration in the United States: Exploring Causes and Consequences:

> Over the four decades when incarceration rates steadily rose, U.S crime rates showed no clear trend: the rate of violent crime rose, then fell, rose again, then declined sharply. The best single proximate explanation of the rise in incarceration is not rising crime rates, but the policy choices made by legislators to greatly increase the use of imprisonment as a response to crime.[21]

Even to the extent that changes in crime rates might contribute to a rise or decline in prison populations, the experience of the three states analyzed in this report demonstrates that such a relationship is very much a secondary explanation. During the period that the prison population was declining in these states, crime rates were declining not only in these states but in virtually all states. Yet despite a slowing of incarceration growth, most states nevertheless experienced an increase in their prison populations, and in some cases, very substantial increases. Policy decisions, and not levels of crime, have been the main determinant of the scale of incarceration.

Finally, many studies have asked how one approach to decarceration, shortening prison sentences, affects recidivism. Data on recidivism rates have the advantage of linking crime to convicted individuals, but they are also impacted by changing police and court practices towards people under parole or probation supervision. Yet studies quite consistently find that expediting prisoners' release from prison has no or a minimal impact on recidivism rates. This pattern has been true among federal prisoners whose sentences were shortened,[22] California prisoners re-sentenced under the state's reform to the "three strikes and you're out" law,[23] and released

## THE IMPACT OF PRISON EXPERIENCE ON RECIDIVISM

NIJ [National Institute of Justice] researchers examined the impact of the rate of crime prior to prison and how prison affected crime post release. The method was applied to the same datasets used by the Bureau of Justice Statistics for its special report, *Recidivism of Prisoners Released in 1994*. NIJ's researchers found that—

Criminal history prior to incarceration reliably predicted whether or not incarceration would deter reoffending within three years after release.

For 56 percent of the offender sample, incarceration had the predicted deterrent effect (that is, they did not recidivate within the three-year period).

Forty percent of the sample reoffended as predicted from their criminal history before incarceration.

For a small percentage of offenders (4 percent), incarceration had a criminogenic effect, increasing the rate of crime after release from prison.

Supervision after release did not seem to lower likelihood of re-arrest.

These findings suggest that an analysis of criminal history prior to incarceration may help corrections practitioners identify who is and is not likely to be deterred from post-release reoffending. (Studying the Effects of Incarceration on Offending Trajectories: An Information-Theoretic Approach, by A.S. Bhati, July 2006, NCJ 216639.)

**"Impact of Prison Experience on Recidivism," National Institute of Justice, October 3, 2008.**

California prisoners who did not face imprisonment for technical parole violations after Realignment.[24]

A number of factors are key to understanding why a declining prison population might not produce higher rates of crime. These include:

- The number of individuals released from prison in a given year represents a relatively small proportion of the overall "at risk" population of young males.

- The crime-reducing effect of incarcerating certain groups of offenders—particularly for drug offenses and youth crimes, which are often committed in groups—is relatively modest since such offenders are frequently replaced on the streets by others seeking to gain income.
- To some extent prison may produce criminogenic effects; that is, longer stays in prison may lead to higher rates of recidivism, in part due to the challenges of maintaining ties with family and community. A 1999 meta-analysis of offender studies over four decades found that longer prison sentences were associated with a modest increase in recidivism.[25] So reductions in the length of prison terms may contribute to public safety, or at least produce fewer negative consequences.

## International Experience in Prison Population Reduction

The experience of the three states described in this report is mirrored in other nations as well, with policymakers and practitioners abroad enacting a range of measures that have substantially reduced prison populations. The Canadian province of Alberta significantly decreased its prison population in the 1990s. The decline was not produced by a government committed to a reduced use of imprisonment, but rather a newly elected provincial premier committed to balancing the budget through sharp cuts in government expenditures, including corrections. As a result there was a sharp decline in the number of people sentenced to provincial prisons for less serious crimes (persons convicted of serious crimes continued to be sentenced to federal prisons). By closing two provincial prisons, diverting minor cases from the justice system, and expanding the use of alternative sentencing, the province was able to reduce prison admissions by 32% between 1993 and 1997. Researchers have found that the decline was not due to changes in reported crime and also that reduced incarceration "had no obvious important negative impacts on offenders."[26]

In Europe, governments in Germany and Finland embarked on ambitious campaigns to reduce prison populations in the 1960s and 1970s, the effects of which can still be seen today.[27] In Germany officials concluded that short prison terms served little crime control purpose, but significantly affected offenders' relationships with families and communities, and so substituted a range of community penalties instead. In Finland policymakers became concerned that though their crime rates were similar to those of other Scandinavian nations their rate of incarceration was two to three times higher. Through a series of sentencing and programmatic shifts over a number of years the country was able to reduce its imprisonment rate to become comparable to neighboring nations. By contrast, Italy's 2006 prison downsizing through commutation proved shortlived.[28] The large-scale parliamentary commutation cut the country's prison population by one-third. But the legislation did not reform sentences for future convictions and in fact enhanced prison terms for released individuals who recidivated. Consequently, the country's incarceration rate returned to its pre-pardon high within two and half years.

## Potential for Substantial Prison Population Reductions

The experience in New York, New Jersey, and California over more than a decade demonstrates that substantial reductions in prison populations can be achieved without adverse effects on public safety. It is also important to note that prior to embarking on these population reductions these states did not have excessive rates of incarceration by U.S. standards. In 1999, New Jersey and New York had incarceration rates of 384 and 400 per 100,000 population respectively, compared to a national rate for all states of 434 per 100,000. California's rate of 475 per 100,000 when it began its reduction in 2006 was just 7% above the national rate of 445 per 100,000.

In contrast, 14 states had rates of incarceration in excess of 450 per 100,000 as of 2012. Given the relatively modest relationship between crime rates and incarceration rates we can therefore surmise that the degree of "excessive" imprisonment in these states is likely to be substantial. Such a finding helps to provide context for recent population reductions in states like Texas. During 2012 the state experienced a reduction of nearly 6,000 people in its prison population. This shift built on bipartisan initiatives designed to reduce parole revocations and enhance treatment programming. But even with this recent population reduction the state's incarceration rate declined only to 601 per 100,000, a dramatic rate of imprisonment even by the standards of a nation of mass incarceration. Such an observation does not diminish the significance of these changes or suggest that changing a political climate on criminal justice policy is a simple matter, but it does tell us that there is potential for more substantial change in many states.

Further, we note that in the three states under review continuous prison population reductions were achieved during a mix of Democratic and Republican gubernatorial terms. As can be seen nationally, increasingly issues of criminal justice reform are being viewed as bipartisan initiatives designed to produce better public safety outcomes and reduced reliance on incarceration.

## Expanding the Agenda for Prison Population Reduction

In seeking to take advantage of the changing climate for reform, policymakers would be well advised to prioritize several goals:

### Focus on Long-term Prisoners

Much of the reform activity of recent years has centered around lower-level drug offenders, with increasing support for diverting such people to treatment programs rather than prisons, as well as reducing excessively severe mandatory minimum sentencing provisions. While these initiatives have produced significant results in many cases, they represent only one aspect of a broader strategy for prison population reduction. This can be seen by examining the composition of prison populations today.

Among the population in state prisons nationally half (53.5% as of 2011) were incarcerated for a violent offense and a declining proportion, now 16.6%, for a drug offense (with the remainder having been convicted of property and public order offenses). While persons convicted of a violent offense clearly raise significant concerns for public safety, in far too many cases such concerns have led to excessively lengthy prison terms. Through policies and practices such as "life means life" and "no parole for violent offenders," parole boards and governors in many states have adopted across-the-board policies that fail to distinguish among individual offense circumstances, accomplishments in prison, or degree of risk to public safety. Research over many years has shown that older offenders have much lower rates of recidivism than younger ones, and so such limitations on release both lack compassion and are counterproductive in allocating public safety resources.

### Address Racial/Ethnic Disparities in Prison Population

As policymakers reduce prison populations in the coming years, it will be important to assess how those initiatives affect the racial composition of incarcerated persons. Reductions in populations overall may or may not affect existing disparities in imprisonment depending on the strategies and criteria employed for such change.

For example, in New York State the prison population reduction of recent years has also produced a significant decline in racial disparity among women.[29] Most of this decline has come about through a substantially reduced number of persons serving sentences for drug offenses. Since that population was about 90% African American or Hispanic, the declines almost inevitably led to a reduction in overall disparity as well.

But in situations where policymakers restrict sentence reductions for persons convicted of a serious offense and/or with a prior criminal record, population reductions may then exacerbate racial disparities. This is because African Americans in particular are more likely to fall in these categories, either due to greater involvement in offending and/ or greater attention from law enforcement agencies. Unless there is a sustained focus and attention to this issue, racial disparities may be compounded even as overall populations decline.

### Reinvest in Communities

Mass incarceration has been produced by the combined impact of a broad range of law enforcement, sentencing, and corrections policies. But ultimately, it stems from a substantial shift in the balance of approaches to public safety in disadvantaged communities. Whereas public safety is produced by a complex mix of family and community support, education and economic opportunity, and social interventions to address individual deficits, as well as criminal justice responses, over the past several decades policymakers have created a severe imbalance in these approaches. Rather than preventing or addressing crime through job creation, mental health and substance abuse treatment and other interventions, far too often arrest and incarceration have become the preferred options.

As a means of remedying this imbalance, savings achieved through reductions in prison populations should be targeted to those communities most heavily affected by mass incarceration. As originally conceptualized in Justice Reinvestment, targeting such savings to high incarceration neighborhoods would both address the harms created by mass incarceration as well as promote public safety in a proactive manner.[30]

## Conclusion

At least in three states we now know that the prison population can be reduced by about 25% with little or no adverse effect on public safety. Individual circumstances vary by state, but policymakers should explore the reforms in New York, New Jersey, and California as a guide for other states.

There is also no reason why a reduction of 25% should be considered the maximum that might be achieved. Even if every state and the federal government were able to produce such reductions, that would still leave the United States with an incarceration rate of more than 500 per 100,000 population—a level 3-6 times that of most industrialized nations.

In recent years a broader range of proposals has emerged for how to reduce the prison population and by various scales of decarceration. In a recent right/left commentary Newt Gingrich and Van Jones describe how they will "be working together to explore ways to reduce the prison population substantially in the next decade."[31] The experiences of New York, New Jersey, and California demonstrate that it is possible to achieve substantial reductions in mass incarceration without compromising public safety.

## Endnotes

1. Ram Subramanian & Ruth Delaney, Playbook for Change? States Reconsider Mandatory Sentences (Vera Institute of Justice 2014), available at http://www.vera.org/sites/default/files/resources/downloads/mandatory-sentences-policy-report-v3.pdf.
2. All prison population data taken from various corrections reports of the Bureau of Justice Statistics.
3. California's Realignment policy has produced a concomitant increase in the jail population, although of a much smaller magnitude than the prison decline, as described later in the report.
4. All crime data are offenses known to law enforcement, taken from the Federal Bureau of Investigation's Crime in the United States series.
5. Magnus Lofstrom & Steven Raphael, Public Safety Realignment and Crime Rates in California (Public Policy Institute of California 2013), available at http://www.ppic.org/content/pubs/report/R_1213MLR.pdf.
6. Id.
7. Judith Greene & Marc Mauer, Downscaling Prisons: Lessons from Four States, The Sentencing Project (2010), http://www.sentencingproject.org/ doc/publications/publications/inc_DownscalingPrisons2010.pdf.
8. Id.
9. James Austin & Michael Jacobson, How New York City Reduced Mass Incarceration: A Model for Change? (Vera Institute of Justice 2012), available at http://www.brennancenter.org/sites/default/files/publications/How_NYC_Reduced_Mass_Incarceration.pdf
10. Computerized Criminal History System: Adult Arrests 2004-2013, New York State Division of Criminal Justice Services (Feb. 25, 2014), http://www. criminaljustice.ny.gov/crimnet/ojsa/arrests/Allcounties.pdf; Greene & Mauer, supra note 10.
11. Austin & Jacobson, supra note 9.
12. Id.
13. Computerized Criminal History System: Adult Arrests Disposed, New York State Division of Criminal Justice Services (Apr. 22, 2014), http://www. criminaljustice. ny.gov/crimnet/ojsa/dispos/nys.pdf; Computerized Criminal History System: Adult Arrests Disposed, New York State Division of Criminal Justice Services (June 23, 2014) (unpublished) (on file with author).

14. Vincent Schiraldi & Michael Jacobson, Could Less Be More When it Comes to Probation Supervision?, American City & County Viewpoints (June 4, 2014), http://americancityandcounty.com/blog/could-less-be-more-when-it-comes-probation-supervision.

15. Greene & Mauer, supra note 7.

16. Id.; New Jersey State Parole Board, 2013 Annual Report (2013), available at http://www.state.nj.us/parole/docs/reports/AnnualReport2013.pdf.

17. *Brown v. Plata*, 131 S. Ct. 1910 (2011).

18. Joan Petersilia & Jessica Greenlick Snyder, Looking Past The Hype: 10 Questions Everyone Should Ask About California's Prison Realignment, 5 California Journal of Politics and Policy 266 (2013), http://www.bscc.ca.gov/downloads/Looking_Past_The_Hype_Petersilia.pdf. This is part of an ongoing series of analyses conducted and produced at Stanford Law School, see Stanford Law Sch., California Realignment, http://www.law.stanford.edu/organizations/programs-and-centers/stanford-criminal-justice-center-scjc/california-realignment.

19. CDCR Implements Public Safety Reforms to Parole Supervision, Expanded Incentive Credits for Inmates, Inside CDCR News (Jan. 25, 2010), http://www. insidecdcr.ca.gov/2010/01/cdcr-implements-public-safety-reforms-to-parole-supervision-expanded-incentive-credits-for-inmates.

20. Magnus Lofstrom & Steven Raphael, Impact of Realignment on County Jail Populations (Public Policy Institute of California 2013), available at http://www.ppic.org/content/pubs/report/R_613MLR.pdf.

21. National Research Council, The Growth of Incarceration in the United States: Exploring Causes and Consequences 3 (The National Academies Press 2014), available at http://www.nap.edu/openbook.php?record_id=18613.

22. U.S. Sentencing Commission, Recidivism Among Offenders Receiving Retroactive Sentence Reductions: The 2007 Crack Cocaine Amendment (2014), available at http://www.ussc.gov/sites/default/files/pdf/research-and-publications/research-projects-and-surveys/miscellaneous/20140527_ Recidivism_2007_Crack_Cocaine_Amendment.pdf.

23. Proposition 36 Progress Report: Over 1,500 Prisoners Released Historically Low Recidivism Rate, Stanford Law School Three Strikes Project & NAACP Legal Defense and Education Fund (2014), https://www.law.stanford.edu/sites/default/files/child-page/595365/doc/slspublic/ ThreeStrikesReport.pdf.

24. Magnus Lofstrom, Steven Raphael, & Ryken Grattet, Is Public Safety Realignment Reducing Recidivism in California? (Public Policy Institute of California 2014), available at http://www.ppic.org/content/pubs/report/R_614MLR.pdf.

25. Paul Gendreau, Claire Goggin, & Francis T. Cullen, The Effects of Prison Sentences on Recidivism (Public Works and Government Services Canada 1999), available at http://www.prisonpolicy.org/scans/e199912.htm.

26. Cheryl Marie Webster & Anthony N. Doob, Penal Reform 'Canadian style': Fiscal Responsibility and Decarceration in Alberta, Canada, 16 Punishment and Soc'y 3, 23 (2014).

27. Michael Tonry, Thinking About Crime: Sense and Sensibility in American Penal Culture 29-34 (Oxford University Press 2004).

28. Paolo Buonanno & Steven Raphael, Incarceration and Incapacitation: Evidence from the 2006 Italian Collective Pardon, 103 Am. Econ. Rev. 2437, 2442 (2013).

29. Marc Mauer, The Changing Racial Dynamics of Women's Incarceration, The Sentencing Project (2013), http://sentencingproject.org/doc/publications/ rd_Changing%20Racial%20Dynamics%202013.pdf.

30. Susan B. Tucker & Eric Cadora, Ideas for an Open Society: Justice Reinvestment, Open Society Institute (November 2003) http://www.opensocietyfoundations.org /sites/default/files/ideas_reinvestment.pdf.
31. Newt Gingrich & Van Jones, Prison System is Failing America, CNN Opinion (May 22, 2014 5:23PM EDT), http://tyger.ac/posts/4036/frame.

# Periodical and Internet Sources Bibliography

*The following articles have been selected to supplement the diverse views presented in this chapter.*

Jason Furman and Douglas Holtz-Eakin, "Why Mass Incarceration Doesn't Pay," The New York Times, April 21, 2016. https://www. nytimes.com/2016/04/21/opinion/why-mass-incarceration-doesnt-pay.html

Adam Gopnik, "The Caging of America: Why do we lock up so many people?" The New Yorker, Jan. 30, 2012. http://www.newyorker. com/magazine/2012/01/30/the-caging-of-america

Marie Gottschalk, "It's Not Just the Drug War," Jacobin, March 5, 2015. https://www.jacobinmag.com/2015/03/mass-incarceration-war-on-drugs/

Elizabeth Gudrais, "The Prison Problem," Harvard Magazine, March-April 2013. http://harvardmagazine.com/2013/03/the-prison-problem

Chris Hedges, "Why Mass Incarceration Defines Us As a Society," Smithsonian Magazine, Dec. 2012. http://www.smithsonianmag. com/people-places/why-mass-incarceration-defines-us-as-a-society-135793245/

Sean McElwee, "America's Awful, Terrible, No Good, Very Bad Prison System," The Huffington Post, July 1, 2013. http:// www.huffingtonpost.com/sean-mcelwee/incarceration-america_b_3528901.html

Doug Noonan, "Want to Reduce Crime? End mass incarceration," Washington Examiner, Nov. 2, 2016. http://www. washingtonexaminer.com/want-to-reduce-crime-end-mass-incarceration/article/2606209

Tom Risen, "White House: America's Prisons More Costly Than Helpful," U.S. News and World Report, Apr. 28, 2016. http://www. usnews.com/news/blogs/data-mine/articles/2016-04-28/white-house-americas-prisons-more-costly-than-helpful

Audrey Williams, "Prison Overcrowding Threatens Public Safety and State Budgets," ALEC (American Legislative Exchange Council),

Apr. 8, 2014. https://www.alec.org/article/prison-overcrowding-threatens-public-safety-state-budgets/

Grace Wyler, "The Mass Incarceration Problem in America," Vice News, July 26, 2014. https://news.vice.com/article/the-mass-incarceration-problem-in-america

# CHAPTER 2

# What Are the Societal Effects of Incarceration?

# Chapter Preface

An individual behind bars is not the only person affected by mass incarceration; consequences exist for children and family members as well. Mass incarceration brings with it effects on America's society, including breakup of the family unit, a cycle of poverty, and disenfranchisement. Research shows that having a family member sent to prison can negatively affect both the physical and mental health of the people back at home. A household has one fewer person to contribute and maintain that family's livelihood when a family member is incarcerated. This means not only less economic security but also more stress.

Some people argue that a cyclical relationship exists between poverty and mass incarceration and that the criminal justice system unfairly targets minorities. Within the last decade cases have been coming to light that expose the injustice of the criminal justice system. This anecdotal evidence illustrates how a simple traffic violation for a poor person, especially a person of color, can spiral out of control, leading to fees and fines that grow quickly and that if left unpaid, can lead to arrest and time in jail. In this true cycle of poverty, simply being poor can bring criminal charges due to unpaid debts and eventual incarceration because the debts cannot be paid.

At the heart of this poverty question lies the issue of wages for prison inmates. The issue is controversial—should convicted criminals be paid the minimum wage for their work inside prison walls? While incarcerated, inmates can perform jobs such as maintenance, cleaning, and kitchen duties; prisoners might also build furniture, or making clothing or license plates. However, in most cases those incarcerated workers earn far less than the minimum wage.

The question then remains, how do we hold people accountable for criminal behavior, yet minimize the effect punishment—in the form of incarceration—has on an offender's family and, ultimately, the community at large. Indeed, the pitfalls of having a criminal record are numerous. The following chapter examines some of the societal issues tied to mass imprisonment including cyclical poverty, similarities to now-outlawed debtors' prisons, livable wages, and more.

"*Prison 'has become a routine event for poor African-American men and their families, creating an enduring disadvantage at the very bottom of American society.*'"

# Prison Is the New Poverty Trap

*Friends Committee on National Legislation*

*In the following viewpoint, the Friends Committee on National Legislation reflects on the pitfalls that can occur for people with a criminal record. The article focuses on consequences after release from prison, such as the ability to receive government assistance, housing issues, interference with getting ahead, and the ability to contribute to one's own family. The authors argue that mass incarceration ultimately crushes the human soul. The Friends Committee on National Legislation was founded by individuals from the Religious Society of Friends (Quakers). The group works to lobby Congress in order to advance issues related to peace, justice, opportunity, and the environment.*

"Mass Incarceration: Long-Term Effects," Friends Committee on National Legislation, April 2015. Reprinted by Permission of Friends Committee on National Legislation (fcnl.org).

As you read, consider the following questions:

1. According to the article, what obstacles to personal advancement do former inmates face?
2. Why is there a cyclical relationship between poverty and mass incarceration according to the author?
3. What is the statistical chance that an African American child has a parent in prison?

Ending mass incarceration means working to close the front door of prisons, preventing nonviolent offenders from being incarcerated in the first place. It also means opening doors for people after release.

Today, the effects of mass incarceration permeate and reverberate. This society's choices about who is sent to prison, for what reason, and for how long affect people for years or even decades. It affects all of society as well. We will never know how much talent and potential our country has wasted because of unnecessarily long, destructive prison sentences.

People and communities of color particularly feel these effects. Although people of color do not commit crimes or use drugs at any higher rate than whites, they are more likely to face prosecution, and they make up the majority of the prison population.

## No Helping Hand, Few Opportunities

Everyone in the United States should be able to live a life of dignity, with access to basic necessities. Recognizing this, advocates have worked hard to ensure that the U.S. government offers some assistance for people who have difficulty meeting these needs. Food, housing and income support can give people a platform from which they can escape from poverty.

But what if someone doesn't have income because he or she has just been released from prison? Depending on the reason he or she was sent to prison, both the U.S. and many state governments may deny help.

For example, federal law permanently bans people with felony drug convictions from receiving welfare (TANF) or food stamps (SNAP). Some states have changed their laws to limit these bans, but the TANF restrictions are still fully or partially in effect in 38 states and the District of Columbia, and 9 states have SNAP restrictions. Many released prisoners are banned from public housing, which can separate them from their families and lead to homelessness.

There are also obstacles to personal advancement, such as finding work or going to school. Formerly incarcerated people can be automatically banned from driving or getting professional licenses, for example as accountants, nail technicians, hair stylists or barbers. Even though some inmates can receive specialized training in these fields while in prison, they may be unable to use these skills upon release.

The repercussions of a criminal conviction make it harder for people to fully re-enter society upon release, which can increase recidivism. If people can't work or obtain food and shelter legally, their options are severely limited. More than two-thirds of former prisoners will be arrested again within three years of release. More than half will re-enter the prison system.

## "Prison is the new poverty trap"

The so-called "collateral consequences" of criminal convictions affect the families and communities of offenders as well as the individuals themselves.

There is a cyclical relationship between poverty and mass incarceration. Villanova sociologists Robert DeFina and Lance Hannon estimate that, without the mass incarceration epidemic, five million fewer people would be living in poverty. Harvard sociologist Bruce Western calls prison "the new poverty trap." He states that prison "has become a routine event for poor African-American men and their families, creating an enduring disadvantage at the very bottom of American society."

Examining pre-existing social and economic conditions in black communities reveals an even bleaker picture of incarceration's long-term effects. Today, 1 in 28 children in the United States has a parent in prison. For African-American children, the statistics are 1 in 4. These children are more likely to live in or fall into poverty.

Once people leave prison, the combined stigma of race and a criminal record can keep formerly incarcerated individuals from contributing economically to their families. A criminal record reduces wages significantly. According to a January 2015 National Employment Law Project report, almost 1 in 3 adults in the United States has a criminal record, and black men with a conviction are 40 percent less likely than whites to receive a job call-back, creating significant barriers that lead to poverty.

Civic participation can also be denied to formerly incarcerated people. An estimated 5.85 million people in the United States cannot vote because of a felony conviction. Because of racial disparities in the criminal justice system, this leaves 1 in 13 African Americans unable to vote.

## Fulfilling Potential

The U.S. criminal justice system has removed millions of people from their communities, often for non-violent offenses, and locked them away for significant portions of their lives. Even when they are released, they find the door to opportunity and advancement barred at every turn. Mass incarceration goes far beyond a concern for community safety to create a soul-crushing system of hopelessness.

We can end mass incarceration and stop this cycle. Our communities and families will be strengthened by a system that embraces restorative justice and seeks to return offenders to society with their full rights and obligations. Congress should exercise its ability to change laws, put fewer people in prison, and remove the barriers that prevent them from reclaiming a productive place in their community upon release.

> *"People of color are more likely to become entangled in the criminal justice system. Among black males born in 2001, one in three will go to prison at some point during their lifetimes…"*

# The Criminal Justice System Is Stacked Against People of Color

*Jamal Hagler*

*In the following viewpoint, Jamal Hagler provides eight facts to support his belief that our current system of justice disproportionately affects African Americans and Hispanics. In his argument, incarceration rates, arrests, drug convictions, sentence lengths, and even traffic stops are all skewed in how they're carried out when comparing whites and people of color. He also addresses differences in school punishments and the juvenile justice system, as well as the effect on voting rights. Hagler is research assistant for Progress 2050 at the Center for American Progress. He has a degree in economics and also served as an intern at the progressive think tank the Institute for Wisconsin's Future.*

"8 Facts You Should Know About the Criminal Justice System and People of Color," by Jamal Hagler, Center for American Progress, May 28, 2015. Reprinted by Permission.

As you read, consider the following questions:

1. What setting does the author provide to introduce his facts and statistics?
2. What are the comparisons Hagler draws regarding sentences for white and black men?
3. According to Hagler, what happens more often to blacks and Latinos during traffic stops than to whites?

The nation's criminal justice system is broken. People of color, particularly African Americans and Latinos, are unfairly targeted by the police and face harsher prison sentences than their white counterparts. Given the nation's coming demographic shift, in which there will be no clear racial or ethnic majority by 2044, the United States cannot afford for these trends to continue. Not only could the money spent on mass incarceration—$80 billion in 2010—be put to better use, but the consequences for people who become entangled in the criminal justice system are also lifelong, leading to barriers to employment and housing, among many other things.

The shocking deaths at the hands of police in New York City; Ferguson, Missouri; North Charleston, South Carolina; and Baltimore, to name a few, have awakened the nation to the criminal justice system's disparate impact on people of color. Tensions have flared throughout the country as news stories about how people of color are targeted and mistreated have come to light. As Americans reflect on the devastating recent events and as momentum builds to reform the U.S. criminal justice system, it is important to take note of the many ways in which the current system disproportionately affects people of color and creates significant barriers to opportunity for people with criminal records. Consider the following eight facts:

- People of color are significantly overrepresented in the U.S. prison population, making up more than 60 percent of the people behind bars. Despite being only 13 percent of the overall U.S. population, 40 percent of those who are incarcerated are black. Latinos represent 16 percent of the overall population but 19 percent of those who are incarcerated. On the other hand, whites make up 64 percent of the overall population but account for only 39 percent of those who are incarcerated.

- People of color are more likely to become entangled in the criminal justice system. Among black males born in 2001, one in three will go to prison at some point during their lifetimes; one in six Latino males will have the same fate. By contrast, only 1 out of every 17 white males is expected to go to prison. A similar pattern exists among women: 1 in 111 white women, 1 in 18 black women, and 1 in 45 Latina women will go to prison at some point. Furthermore, African Americans are 2.5 times more likely to be arrested than whites.

- The so-called War on Drugs has disproportionately affected people of color. Despite using and selling drugs at rates similar to those of their white counterparts, African Americans and Latinos comprise 62 percent of those in state prisons for drug offenses and 72 percent of those sentenced for federal drug trafficking offenses, which generally carry extreme mandatory minimum sentences.

- People of color, particularly black males, face longer sentences than their white non-Hispanic counterparts for similar crimes. According to the U.S. Sentencing Commission, between 2007 and 2011, sentences for black males were 19.5 percent longer than those for whites. Furthermore, black men were 25 percent less likely to receive sentences below the sentencing guidelines for the crime of which they were convicted.

- During traffic stops, people of color are more likely to be searched than their white counterparts. National survey data show that blacks and Latinos are three times more likely to be searched than whites. Blacks are searched in 6 percent of traffic stops and Hispanics are searched in 7 percent of stops, whereas whites are searched only 2 percent of the time.

- Students of color continue to face harsher punishments at school than their white non-Hispanic counterparts. A 2010 study found that more than 70 percent of students who are "involved in school-related arrests or referred to law enforcement" are black or Latino. Furthermore, black students are three times more likely to be suspended or expelled than white students. During the 2011-12 school year, 16 percent of black K-12 students were suspended, compared with 7 percent of Latino students and 5 percent of white students.

- People of color are extremely overrepresented in the juvenile justice system. According to a 2014 report on racial discrimination in America, juveniles of color represented 67 percent of "juveniles committed to public facilities nationwide," nearly twice their share of the juvenile population. Despite comprising only 15 percent of the juvenile population, black juveniles were arrested two times more often than their white counterparts.

- Voting restrictions on the formerly incarcerated have disenfranchised millions of voters, particularly African Americans. Today, approximately 5.9 million people are not able to vote due to felony convictions. While laws vary from state to state—with some allowing for restoration of voting rights—1 in 13 blacks nationwide are disenfranchised due to felony convictions. In Florida, Kentucky, and Virginia, more than one in five black adults are denied the right to vote.

These glaring disparities in the application of justice have real consequences for the nation as a whole. Mass incarceration is not sustainable, and evidence does not support the theory that harsh punishments effectively reduce crime or recidivism rates. Recent events have brought this issue to the forefront, and reform has garnered support along the ideological spectrum. It is time to take steps to reduce the disparate impact that the American criminal justice system has on people of color and institute reforms that apply justice fairly and equitably for all.

# THE SCHOOL-TO-PRISON PIPELINE

Under international law, children's human rights are underpinned by the fundamental principle that all decisions relating to children should be guided by the best interests. Yet current school educational and disciplinary policies in the U.S. are dovetailing to create an environment that funnels youth into the criminal justice system at an unprecedented rate. Zero-tolerance discipline policies have resulted in skyrocketing rates of suspensions, expulsions and school-based arrests. These policies disproportionly affect children of color and those living in poverty or with a disability, gravely undermining all children's rights to education, to be free from discrimination, and to the highest standard of health and well-being.

Discrimination in school discipline contributes to disparities in incarceration rates, with African Americans comprising only 12% of the US population but 44% of its incarcerated. The U.N. Committee on the Elimination of Racial Discrimination has expressed concern about the "school-to-prison pipeline" and called on the United States to intensify its efforts to address racial disparities in the application of disciplinary measures.

Amnesty International calls on the U.S. Government to investigate and work to end racial, ethnic, and disability disparities in school discipline and to promote and invest in positives model of improving school safety, attendance, and environment.

Incarceration triggers a cascade of imperiled rights not only for former prisoners, who face disenfranchisement, denial of housing, the inability to find work and food insecurity, but also for their dependents. The U.N. Committee on the Elimination of Racial Discrimination has expressed concern about the impact of parental incarceration on children from racial and ethnic minorities and urged the U.S. to ensure that the impact of incarceration on children and/or other dependents is taken into account when sentencing an individual convicted of a nonviolent offence and promoting the use of alternatives imprisonment.

"Mass Incarceration in the USA," ©2016 Amnesty International USA.

> "Most people, regardless of their poverty or race, resist the temptation to commit crimes. Cotton is not a helpless victim just like his ancestors, and it demeans the free will of poor black men to suggest otherwise."

# Poverty and Racism Are Not Excuses for Breaking the Law

## Stephanos Bibas

*In the following viewpoint, Stephanos Bibas argues that racism and drug crime cannot be blamed for America's increasing prison population. He points to black communities that have wanted improved law enforcement, as well as black leaders that have pushed for stronger drug laws. He also lays out a plan for holding people accountable for their actions, while also minimizing the effects punishment can have on communities and families. Bibas is a professor of law and criminology and a former federal prosecutor. He is author of the book* The Machinery of Criminal Justice.

"The Truth about Mass Incarceration", by Stephanos Bibas, National Review Online, September 16, 2015. Reprinted by Permission.

As you read, consider the following questions:

1. What does Bibas attest is the true reason for prison growth?
2. Why does the author refer to criminals as "gamblers"?
3. What does Bibas believe should be the cornerstone when it comes to a conservative agenda for criminal justice?

America has the highest incarceration rate in the world, outstripping even Russia, Cuba, Rwanda, Belarus, and Kazakhstan. Though America is home to only about one-twentieth of the world's population, we house almost a quarter of the world's prisoners. Since the mid 1970s, American prison populations have boomed, multiplying sevenfold while the population has increased by only 50 percent. Why?

Liberals blame racism and the "War on Drugs," in particular long sentences for nonviolent drug crimes. This past July, in a speech to the NAACP, President Obama insisted that "the real reason our prison population is so high" is that "over the last few decades, we've also locked up more and more nonviolent drug offenders than ever before, for longer than ever before." The War on Drugs, he suggested, is just a continuation of America's "long history of inequity in the criminal-justice system," which has disproportionately harmed minorities.

Two days later, Obama became the first sitting president to visit a prison. Speaking immediately after his visit, the president blamed mandatory drug sentencing as a "primary driver of this mass-incarceration phenomenon." To underscore that point, he met with half a dozen inmates at the prison, all of whom had been convicted of nonviolent drug offenses. Three days earlier, he had commuted the federal prison terms of 46 nonviolent drug offenders, most of whom had been sentenced to at least 20 years' imprisonment.

The president is echoing what liberal criminologists and lawyers have long charged. They blame our prison boom on punitive, ever-longer sentences tainted by racism, particularly for drug crimes. Criminologists coined the term "mass incarceration" or "mass imprisonment" a few decades ago, as if police were arresting and herding suspects en masse into cattle cars bound for prison. Many blame this phenomenon on structural racism, as manifested in the War on Drugs.

No one has captured and fueled this zeitgeist better than Michelle Alexander, an ACLU lawyer turned Ohio State law professor. Her 2010 book, *The New Jim Crow: Mass Incarceration in the Age of Colorblindness*, is, as Cornel West put it, "the secular bible for a new social movement in early twenty-first-century America." She condemns "mass incarceration . . . as a stunningly comprehensive and well-disguised system of racialized social control that functions in a manner strikingly similar to Jim Crow." Ex-felons, like victims of Jim Crow, are a stigmatized underclass, excluded from voting, juries, jobs, housing, education, and public benefits. This phenomenon "is not—as many argue—just a symptom of poverty or poor choices, but rather evidence of a new racial caste system at work," like Jim Crow and slavery before it. She even implies that this system is just the latest manifestation of whites' ongoing racist conspiracy to subjugate blacks, pointing to the CIA's support of Nicaraguan contras who supplied cocaine to black neighborhoods in the U.S.

Like President Obama, Alexander blames mass incarceration on the racially tinged War on Drugs. "In less than thirty years, the U.S. penal population exploded from around 300,000 to more than 2 million, with drug convictions accounting for the majority of the increase." And the War on Drugs was supposedly driven by coded racial appeals, in which elite whites galvanized poor whites to vote Republican by scapegoating black drug addicts. The fault, she insists, does not lie with criminals or violence. "Violent crime is not responsible for the prison boom. . . . The uncomfortable reality is that convictions for drug offenses—not violent crime—are the single most important cause of the prison boom in the

United States," and minorities are disproportionately convicted of drug crimes.

Alexander's critique is catnip to liberals. *The New Jim Crow* stayed on the New York Times best-seller list for more than a year and remains Amazon's best-selling book in criminology. And it dovetailed with liberal and libertarian pundits' calls to legalize or decriminalize drugs, or at least marijuana, as the cure for burgeoning prisons.

President Obama's and Alexander's well-known narrative, however, doesn't fit the facts. Prison growth has been driven mainly by violent and property crime, not drugs. As Fordham law professor John Pfaff has shown, more than half of the extra prisoners added in the 1980s, 1990s, and 2000s were imprisoned for violent crimes; two thirds were in for violent or property crimes. Only about a fifth of prison inmates are incarcerated for drug offenses, and only a sliver of those are in for marijuana. Moreover, many of these incarcerated drug offenders have prior convictions for violent crimes. The median state prisoner serves roughly two years before being released; three quarters are released within roughly six years.

For the last several decades, arrest rates as a percentage of crimes—including drug arrests—have been basically flat, as have sentence lengths. What has driven prison populations, Pfaff proves convincingly, is that arrests are far more likely to result in felony charges: Twenty years ago, only three eighths of arrests resulted in felony charges, but today more than half do. Over the past few decades, prosecutors have grown tougher and more consistent.

Nor is law enforcement simply a tool of white supremacy to oppress blacks. As several prominent black scholars have emphasized, law-abiding blacks often want more and better law enforcement, not less. Harvard law professor Randall Kennedy emphasized that "blacks have suffered more from being left unprotected or underprotected by law enforcement authorities than from being mistreated as suspects or defendants," though the latter claims often get more attention. Most crime is intra-racial, so black victims suffer disproportionately at the hands of black criminals. Yale law professors Tracey Meares and James Forman Jr. have observed that minority-neighborhood residents often want tough enforcement of drug and other laws to ensure their safety and protect their property values. The black community is far from monolithic; many fear becoming crime victims and identify more with them than they do with victims of police mistreatment. There is no racist conspiracy, nor are we locking everyone up and throwing away the key. Most prisoners are guilty of violent or property crimes that no orderly society can excuse.

Black Democrats, responding to their constituents' understandable fears, have played leading roles in toughening the nation's drug laws. In New York, black activists in Harlem, the NAACP Citizens' Mobilization Against Crime, and New York's leading black newspaper, the Amsterdam News, advocated what in the 1970s became the Rockefeller drug laws, with their stiff mandatory minimum sentences. At the federal level, liberal black Democrats representing black New York City neighborhoods supported tough crack-cocaine penalties. Representative Charles Rangel, from Harlem, chaired the House Select Committee on Narcotics Abuse and Control when Congress enacted crack-cocaine sentences that were much higher than those for powder cocaine. Though many have come to regret it, the War on Drugs was bipartisan and cross-racial.

More fundamentally, The New Jim Crow wrongly absolves criminals of responsibility for their "poor choices." Alexander opens her book by analogizing the disenfranchisement of Jarvious Cotton, a felon on parole, to that of his great-great-grandfather (for being a slave), his great-grandfather (beaten to death by the Ku Klux Klan for trying to vote), his grandfather (intimidated by the Klan into not voting), and his father (by poll taxes and literacy tests).

But Cotton's ancestors were disenfranchised through violence and coercion solely because of their race. Cotton is being judged not by the color of his skin, but by the content of his choices. He chose to commit a felony, and Alexander omits that his felony was not a nonviolent drug crime, but murdering 17-year-old Robert Irby during an armed robbery. All adults of sound mind know the difference between right and wrong. Poverty and racism are no excuses for choosing to break the law; most people, regardless of their poverty or race, resist the temptation to commit crimes. Cotton is not a helpless victim just like his ancestors, and it demeans the free will of poor black men to suggest otherwise.

So the stock liberal charges against "mass incarceration" simply don't hold water. There is no racist conspiracy, nor are we locking everyone up and throwing away the key. Most prisoners are guilty of violent or property crimes that no orderly society can excuse. Even those convicted of drug crimes have often been implicated in violence, as well as promoting addiction that destroys neighborhoods and lives.

But just because liberals are wrong does not mean the status quo is right. Conservatives cannot reflexively jump from critiquing the Left's preferred narrative to defending our astronomical incarceration rate and permanent second-class status for ex-cons. The criminal-justice system and prisons are big-government institutions. They are often manipulated by special interests such as prison guards' unions, and they consume huge shares of most states' budgets. And cities' avarice tempts police to arrest and jail too many people in order to collect fines, fees, tickets, and the like. As the Department of Justice found in its report following the Michael Brown shooting in Missouri, "Ferguson's law enforcement practices are shaped by the City's focus on revenue rather than by public safety needs." That approach poisons the legitimacy of law enforcement, particularly in the eyes of poor and minority communities.

Conservatives also need to care more about ways to hold wrongdoers accountable while minimizing the damage punishment does to families and communities. Punishment is coercion by the state, and it disrupts not only defendants' lives but also their families and neighborhoods. Contrary to the liberal critique, we need to punish and condemn crimes unequivocally, without excusing criminals or treating them as victims. But we should be careful to do so in ways that reinforce rather than undercut conservative values, such as strengthening families and communities.

Historically, colonial America punished crimes swiftly but temporarily. Only a few convicts were hanged, exiled, or mutilated. Most paid a fine, were shamed in the town square, sat in the stocks or pillory, or were whipped; all of these punishments were brief. Having condemned the crime, the colonists then forgave the criminal, who had paid his debt to society and the victim.

That was in keeping with the colonists' Christian faith in forgiveness, and it meant there was no permanent underclass of ex-cons. Preachers stressed that any of us could have committed such crimes, and we all needed to steel ourselves against the same temptations; the message was "There but for the grace of God go I." The point of criminal punishment was to condemn the wrong, humble the wrongdoer, induce him to make amends and learn his lesson, and then welcome him back as a brother in Christ. The punishment fell on the criminal, not on his family or friends, and he went right back to work.

Two centuries ago, the shift from shaming and corporal punishments to imprisonment made punishment an enduring status. Reformers had hoped that isolation and Bible reading in prison would induce repentance and law-abiding work habits, but it didn't turn out that way. Now we warehouse large numbers of criminals, in idleness and at great expense. By exiling them, often far away, prison severs them from their responsibilities to their families and communities, not to mention separating them from opportunities for gainful work. This approach is hugely disruptive, especially when it passes a tipping point in some communities and exacerbates the number of fatherless families. And much of the burden falls on innocent women and children, who lose a husband, boyfriend, or father as well as a breadwinner.

Even though wrongdoers may deserve to have the book thrown at them, it is not always wise to exact the full measure of justice. There is evidence that prison turns people into career criminals.

On the one hand, it cuts prisoners off from families, friends, and neighbors, who give them reasons to follow the law. Responsibilities as husbands and fathers are key factors that tame young men's wildness and encourage them to settle down: One longitudinal study found that marriage may reduce reoffending by 35 percent. But prison makes it difficult to maintain families and friendships; visiting in person is difficult and time-consuming, prisons are often far away, and telephone calls are horrifically expensive.

On the other hand, prison does much to draw inmates away from lawful work. In the month before their arrest, roughly three quarters of inmates were employed, earning the bulk of their income lawfully. Many were not only taking care of their children but helping to pay for rent, groceries, utilities, and health care. But prison destroys their earning potential. Prisoners lose their jobs on the outside. Felony convictions also disqualify ex-cons from certain jobs, housing, student loans, and voting. Michigan economics professor Michael Mueller-Smith finds that spending a year or more in prison reduces the odds of post-prison employment by 24 percent and increases the odds of living on food stamps by 5 percent.

Conversely, prisons are breeding grounds for crime. Instead of working to support their own families and their victims, most prisoners are forced to remain idle. Instead of having to learn vocational skills, they have too much free time to hone criminal skills and connections. And instead of removing wrongdoers from criminogenic environments, prison clusters together neophytes and experienced recidivists, breeding gangs, criminal networks, and more crime. Thus, Mueller-Smith finds, long sentences on average breed much more crime after release than they prevent during the sentence. Any benefit from locking criminals up temporarily is more than offset by the crime increase caused when prison turns small-timers into career criminals. So conservatives' emphasis on retribution and responsibility, even when morally warranted, can quickly become counterproductive.

Another justification for prison is that the threat of punishment deters crime. The problem with deterrence, however, is that we overestimate prospective criminals' foresight and self-discipline. At its root, crime is generally a failure of self-discipline. Conservative criminologists such as the late James Q. Wilson and Richard Herrnstein pin primary blame for crime on criminals' impulsively satisfying their immediate desires. They are short-sighted gamblers; who else would risk getting shot or arrested in order to steal $300 and a six-pack of beer from a convenience store?

Impulsiveness, short-sightedness, and risk-taking are even more pronounced among the very many wrongdoers whose crimes are fueled by some combination of drugs, alcohol, and mental illness. But those very qualities make it hard to deter them. We naïvely expect to deter these same short-sighted gamblers by threatening a chance of getting caught, convicted, and sent to prison for years far off in the future. Of course, optimistic, intoxicated risk-takers think they will not be caught. And if they have cycled through the juvenile-justice system and received meaningless probation for early convictions, the system has taught them exactly the wrong lessons.

To deter crime effectively, punishment must speak to the same short-sighted wrongdoers who commit crime — not primarily through threats of long punishment far off in the future, but more through swift, certain sanctions that pay back victims while knitting wrongdoers back into the social fabric. If we make punishments immediate and predictable, yet modest, even drug addicts respond to them. Hawaii's Opportunity Probation with Enforcement (HOPE) is an intensive-probation program that has the hardest-core drug users face random urinalysis one day each week; violators immediately go off to a weekend in jail. Though the Left paints drug addiction as a disease requiring costly medical intervention, drug addicts can in fact choose to stop using drugs. Under HOPE, even habitual drug users usually go clean on their own when faced with the immediate threat of two days in jail. Well over 80 percent stop using drugs right away and remain clean, without any further treatment.

The contrast with ordinary probation is stark. Probation officers juggle hundreds of cases, rarely see their clients, and routinely ignore multiple violations until they unpredictably send a client back to prison at some point in the future. Probation thus teaches probationers exactly the wrong lesson: that they are likely to get away with violations. It is no wonder that HOPE succeeds where ordinary probation fails.

Applying the same insight to prisons could revolutionize them. UCLA professor Mark Kleiman notes that most inmates could be released early and watched round the clock with webcams, drug and alcohol testing, and electronic ankle bracelets via GPS. They could live in government-rented apartments, see their families, and work at public-service jobs, all at much less expense than prison. These surveillance methods could enforce rules such as strict curfews, location limits, and bans on drug and alcohol use, with swift penalties for noncompliance. But the Left hates the idea, in part because its critics blame crime on society rather than on wrongdoers who need to be held accountable, disciplined, and taught structure and self-control.

States like Texas and Georgia have already been experimenting with alternatives to endlessly building more prison cells. They have dramatically expanded inpatient and outpatient drug treatment as well as drug courts, diverted more minor offenders out of prison, kept juveniles out of state prison, and set up cheaper diversion beds for inmates who do not need to be in regular prison. For instance, Texas has begun creating special substance-abuse cells, so that repeat drunk drivers can get treatment instead of being housed with murderers and rapists. Risk-assessment tools can help to identify the sliver of recidivists and predators who pose the greatest danger and need long-term confinement.

Most of all, the government needs to work on reweaving the frayed but still extant fabric of criminals' families and communities. Both excessive crime and excessive punishment rend communal bonds, further atomizing society. The more that punishment exacerbates the breakdown of families and communities, the more the overweening state and its social services and law enforcement grow to fill the resulting void.

The cornerstone of a conservative criminal-justice agenda should be strengthening families. More than half of America's inmates have minor children, more than 1.7 million in all; most of these inmates were living with minor children right before their arrest or incarceration. Inmates should meet with their families often. They should be incarcerated as close to home as possible, not deliberately sent to the other end of the state. Visitation rules and hours need to be eased, and extortionate collect-call telephone rates should come down to actual cost.

We should also pay more attention to the victims of crime. Victims are often friends, neighbors, or relatives of the wrongdoers who must go back to living among them. Though victims want to see justice done — including appropriate punishment — that does not generally mean the maximum possible sentence. In surveys, victims care much more about receiving restitution and apologies. So prison-based programs should encourage wrongdoers to meet with their victims if the victims are willing, to listen to their stories, apologize, and seek their forgiveness. Having to apologize and make amends makes most wrongdoers uncomfortable, teaching them lessons that they must learn.

Another important component of punishment should be work. It is madness that prisoners spend years in state-sponsored idleness punctuated by sporadic brutality. It is time to repeal Depression-era protectionist laws that ban prison-made goods from interstate commerce and require payment of prevailing-wage rates to prisoners (making prison industries unprofitable). All able-bodied prisoners should have to complete their educations and work, learning good work habits as well as marketable skills. One could even experiment with sending able-bodied prisoners without serious violent tendencies to enlist in the military, as used to be routine (think of the movie The Dirty Dozen). Some of prisoners' wages could go to support their families, cover some costs of incarceration, and make restitution to their victims.

Finally, inmates need religion and the religious communities that come with it. Most prisoners are eventually released, and we do almost nothing to help them reenter society, simply providing a bus ticket and perhaps $20. But faith-based programs like Prison Fellowship Ministries can transform cell blocks from wards of idleness or violence to orderly places of prayer, repentance, education, and work. After inmates are released, these faith-based groups can also perform much of the oversight, community reintegration, fellowship, and prayer that returning inmates need. Inmates must accept their responsibility, vow to mend their ways, and have fellow believers to hold them to those promises. Having a job, an apartment, and a congregation waiting for them after release from prison offers ex-cons a law-abiding alternative to returning to lives of crime.

American criminal justice has drifted away from its moral roots. The Left has forgotten how to blame and punish, and too often the Right has forgotten how to forgive. Over-imprisonment is wrong, but not because wrongdoers are blameless victims of a white-supremacist conspiracy. It is wrong because state coercion excessively disrupts work, families, and communities, the building blocks of society, with too little benefit to show for it. Our strategies for deterring crime not only fail to work on short-sighted, impulsive criminals, but harden them into careerists. Criminals deserve punishment, but it is wise as well as humane to temper justice with mercy.

> "Jailing the indigent for their failure to meet contractual obligations was considered primitive by ancient Greek and Roman politicians, and remains illegal and unheard of in most developed countries."

# Mass Incarceration Has Helped Bring Back Debtors' Prisons

*Eli Hager*

*In the following viewpoint, Eli Hager writes to demonstrate that debtors' prisons are alive and well even though ruled unconstitutional by the Supreme Court. He uses examples and a short history to show that this jailing of debtors unfairly stacks the deck against the indigent. Hager examines their outlaw and return, and also delves into the differences between private and criminal-justice debt. In addition, he explores the nuances between civil and criminal matters related to the issue. Hager works as a writer for The Marshall Project. His work has also been featured in the Washington Post.*

As you read, consider the following questions:

1. Why does the author claim that putting people in jail for debt is an American tradition?

2. During the 20th Century, what has been the Supreme Court's view on matters related to debtors' prisons?

3. According to the article, what are some of the items deemed "criminal-justice financial obligations"?

In 2011, Robin Sanders was driving home when she saw the blue and red lights flashing behind her. She knew she had not fixed her muffler, and believed that was why she was being pulled over. She thought she might get a ticket.

Instead, Sanders, who lives in Illinois, was arrested and taken to jail.

As she was booked and processed, she learned that she had been jailed because she owed debt—$730 to be precise, related to an unpaid medical bill. Unbeknownst to her, a collection agency had filed a lawsuit against her, and, having never received the notice instructing her to appear, she had missed her date in court.

Debra Shoemaker Ford, a citizen of Harpersville, Ala., spent seven weeks in the county jail without ever appearing in court. Her crime was a failure to pay the monthly fees mailed to her by a private probation company, called Judicial Correction Services. She was on probation because of a traffic violation.

In Benton County, Wash., a quarter of those in jail are there because they owe fines and fees. And in Ferguson, Mo., simmering anger with the police and court system has given rise to a pair of lawsuits aimed at the local practice of imprisoning indigent debtors.

The American tradition of debtors' imprisonment seems to be alive and well. But how could that be? Jailing the indigent for their failure to meet contractual obligations was considered primitive by ancient Greek and Roman politicians, and remains illegal and unheard of in most developed countries. Under the International

Covenant of Civil and Political Rights, the practice is listed as a civil-rights violation.

In the United States, debtors' prisons were banned under federal law in 1833. A century and a half later, in 1983, the Supreme Court affirmed that incarcerating indigent debtors was unconstitutional under the Fourteenth Amendment's Equal Protection clause. Yet, citizens like Sanders and Ford are, to this day, routinely jailed after failing to repay debt. Though *de jure* debtors' prisons are a thing of the past, *de facto* debtors' imprisonment is not. So what do we really know about modern-day debtors' imprisonment – how it returned, when, and where? Below, seven frequently asked questions about the history and abolition of debtors' imprisonment, and its under-the-radar second act. [Debtor's imprisonment went largely unnoticed until after the financial crisis of 2008, when investigative reporting in the Minneapolis Star Tribune and elsewhere began to expose the trend.]

## What is a debtors' prison?

A debtors' prison is any prison, jail, or other detention facility in which people are incarcerated for their inability, refusal, or failure to pay debt.

## What is the history of debtors' prisons in the United States?

From the late 1600s to the early 1800s, many cities and states operated actual "debtors' prisons," brick-and-mortar facilities that were designed explicitly and exclusively for jailing negligent borrowers – some of whom owed no more than 60 cents. These dungeons, such as Walnut Street Debtors' Prison in Philadelphia and the New Gaol in downtown Manhattan, were modeled after debtors' prisons in London, like the "Clink" (the origin of the expression "in the clink").

Imprisonment for indebtedness was commonplace. Two signatories of the Declaration of Independence, James Wilson, an associate justice of the Supreme Court, and Robert Morris, a close friend of George Washington's, spent time in jail after neglecting loans.

But for those without friends in high places, debtors' imprisonment could turn into a life sentence. In many jurisdictions, debtors were not freed until they acquired outside funds to pay what they owed, or else worked off the debt through years of penal labor. As a result, many languished in prison – and died there – for the crime of their indigence.

## But that was outlawed, right?

Yes, technically.

After the War of 1812, a costly stalemate, more and more Americans were holding debt, and the notion of imprisoning all these debtors seemed increasingly "feudal." Moreover, America was seen as a country of immigrants, and many European immigrants had come here to escape debt.

So, in 1833, Congress abolished the practice under federal law. Between 1821 and 1849, twelve states followed suit.

Meanwhile, with the advent of bankruptcy law, individuals were given a way out of insurmountable debt, and creditors were made to share some of the risk inherent in a loan transaction. Legislation passed in 1841, 1867, and 1898 replacing a system that criminalized bankruptcy with one designed to resolve as much debt as the debtor could afford, while absolving the remainder.

During the 20th century, on three separate occasions, the Supreme Court affirmed the unconstitutionality of incarcerating those too poor to repay debt. In 1970, in *Williams v. Illinois*, the high court decided that a maximum prison term could not be extended because the defendant failed to pay court costs or fines. A year later, in *Tate v. Short*, the justices ruled that a defendant may not be jailed solely because he or she is too indigent to pay a fine.

Most importantly, the 1983 decision in *Bearden v. Georgia* compelled local judges to distinguish between debtors who are too poor to pay and those who have the financial ability but "willfully" refuse to do so.

# When (and why) did the courts revert to jailing debtors?

Experts say that the trend, though ongoing, coincided with the rise of "mass incarceration."

Alec Karakatsanis, a lawyer who last year brought one of the only lawsuits to successfully challenge a local court system for jailing indigent debtors, says that the first step was the normalization of incarceration.

"In the 1970s and 1980s," he says, "we started to imprison more people for lesser crimes. In the process, we were lowering our standards for what constituted an offense deserving of imprisonment, and, more broadly, we were losing our sense of how serious, how truly serious, it is to incarcerate. If we can imprison for possession of marijuana, why can't we imprison for not paying back a loan?"

As a result of the greater reliance on incarceration, says Karin Martin, a professor at John Jay College and an expert on "criminal justice financial obligations," there was a dramatic increase in the number of statutes listing a prison term as a possible sentence for failure to repay criminal-justice debt.

"In the late 80s and early 90s," she says, "there was a major uptick in the number of rules, at the state level but also in the counties, indicating jail time for failure to pay various fines and fees."

Next came the fiscal crisis of the 2000s, during which many states were contending with budget deficits and looking for ways to save. [According to CBS MoneyWatch and the ACLU, the cost to taxpayers of arresting and incarcerating a debtor is generally more than the amount to be gained by collecting the debt.] Many judges, including J. Scott Vowell, a circuit court judge in Alabama, felt pressured to make their courts financially self-sufficient, by using the threat of jail time—established in those statutes—to squeeze cash out of small-time debtors.

Finally, in only the last several years, the birth of a new brand of "offender-funded" justice has created a market for private probation companies. Purporting to save taxpayer dollars, these outfits force the offenders themselves to foot the bill for parole, reentry, drug rehab, electronic monitoring, and other services (some of which are not even assigned by a judge). When the offenders can't pay for all of this, they may be jailed—even if they have already served their time for the offense.

## What are some types of debt that people are sent to jail for not paying?

There are two types: private debt, which may lead to involvement in the criminal justice system, and criminal-justice debt, accrued through involvement in the criminal justice system.

In the first category are credit card debt, unpaid medical bills and car payments, and payday loans and other high-interest, short-term cash advances, which indigent borrowers rely on but struggle to repay.

In these cases, the creditor—a predatory lender, a landlord, or a utility provider—or a debt collector (hired by the creditor) may bypass bankruptcy court and take the debtor straight to civil court. If the debtor fails to show up, or if the judge deems that the debtor is "willfully" not paying the debt, the judge may write a warrant for the debtor's arrest on a charge of "contempt of court." The debtor is then held in jail until he or she posts bond or pays the debt, in a process known as "pay or stay."

The second category, termed "criminal justice financial obligations," actually consists of three sub-categories: fines, i.e. monetary penalties imposed as a condition of a sentence, including, say, a traffic ticket; fees, which may include jail book-in fees, bail investigation fees, public defender application fees, drug testing fees, DNA testing fees, jail per-diems for pretrial detention, court costs, felony surcharges, public defender recoupment fees, and on and on and on; and restitution, made to the victim or victims for personal or property damage. Also in this category are costs of imprisonment (billed to inmates in 41 states), and of parole and probation (44 states).

If an offender or ex-offender fails to pay any of this debt, the court will outsource the debt to a private debt collector, and the process of taking the debtor to court, described above, begins all over again.

## I'm confused, is this a civil or a criminal matter? Is this debt private or public?

That's confusing for debtors, too. For indigent people, a civil proceeding regarding private debt—say, an unpaid payday loan—may have criminal ramifications; conversely, involvement in a criminal case may create debt, causing a new civil proceeding.

According to Martin, this ambiguity has grave consequences. For one, indigent debtors do not know whom to negotiate with—the DMV, which mailed the speeding ticket, or the debt collector that now seems to be pursuing the matter. Also, criminal-justice debt affects private creditworthiness and eligibility for a driver's license, making it harder to get a job, get a home, get a loan, or otherwise find a way to avoid jail, repay the debt and regain solid economic footing.

Most importantly, explains John Pollock, the coordinator of the National Coalition for a Civil Right to Counsel, indigent defendants have a right to counsel in criminal cases, but not in civil ones. Yet, as noted, they may be jailed for failing to show up at a civil hearing or for not resolving civil debt. In other words, poor people with debt face criminal consequences but without the Constitutional protections afforded to criminal defendants.

## If debtors' imprisonment is unconstitutional, why does it happen?

It happens for two reasons. The first is that judges may incarcerate debtors who fail to show up at debt-related proceedings.

In these cases, the crime is not failure to pay, but rather "failing to appear in court," "disobeying a court order," or "contempt of court."

The second is that the Supreme Court, in Bearden, did not define two key terms: "indigent" and "willful." How are judges supposed to decide whether a debtor is "indigent" or, rather, is "willfully" refusing to pay?

By leaving this *mens rea* determination to individual judges, rather than providing bright-line criteria as to how to make the distinction, the justices left open the possibility that a local judge with high standards for "indigence" could circumvent the spirit of Bearden and send a very, very poor debtor to jail or prison.

In practice, different judges have different criteria for deciphering whether a debtor is "indigent." Some judges will determine how much money a debtor has by having him or her complete an interview or a short questionnaire. Some judges will rule that the debtor is not "legitimately" indigent and is, instead, "willfully" neglecting the debt – because the debtor showed up to the courtroom wearing a flashy jacket or expensive tattoos.

And other judges will consider all nonpayment to be "willful," unless or until the debtor can prove that he or she has exhausted absolutely all other sources of income – by quitting smoking, collecting and returning used soda cans and bottles, and asking family and friends for loans.

> "*Consider how important it is that inmates maintain or develop a productive work ethic prior to being released back into society.*"

# Prison Inmates Should Earn a Living Wage

## Shafaq Hasan

*In the following viewpoint, Shafaq Hasan presents a case for paying prisoners a reasonable wage for work by providing instances in which prison labor has been used and the wages paid in return. She compares today's prison labor to that of the past. In her piece, Hasan also poses questions about how to determine what the right wage is and how to balance that with the reality of raising that dollar amount. Hasan is a writer for Nonprofit Quarterly. She also served as a research assistant for the Justice Brandeis Law Project at the Schuster Institute for Investigative Journalism.*

As you read, consider the following questions:

1. What amount does the article say can be a lot of money per day for someone in prison?
2. According to the author, how does convict-leasing of the past compare to prison work today?
3. What is the much larger problem that Hasan mentions at the end of her piece?

"Should Inmates in Prison Earn a Living Wage?" by Shafaq Hasan, Nonprofit Quarterly, April 8, 2015. Reprinted by Permission.

Yes, yes, we have all heard. This past winter in Boston was a doozy—apparently so much so that before the second of the four blizzards in February, the Massachusetts Bay Transportation Authority (MBTA) "hired" inmates to help dig out train stations. A public records request from ThinkProgress revealed that more than 90 inmates worked through subzero temperatures and earned between to $3 to $4 a day.

Although the news of inmates shoveling MBTA stops broke back in February, emails and MBTA internal documents recently retrieved by ThinkProgress revealed the details of the collaboration between the MBTA and the Massachusetts Department of Corrections (DOC), including who would be funding the equipment, protective wear, and the "daily inmate wage" for the inmates. In one of the emails, Michelle Goldman from the Homeland Security department relayed questions about getting the inmates better snow gear.

According to a spokesman for the DOC, regardless of the conditions and concerns expressed in the emails, the "equipment did not change depending on the day, location, or availability." Back in February, Suffolk County inmates from a minimum-security prison volunteered as part of the Community Work Program, an initiative allows inmate nearing the end of their sentence to work to help finish neighboring community projects.

The idea came from Mayor Marty Walsh's office as a way of using resources more efficiently. A note from February on the Suffolk County Sheriff's Office website quoted Walsh:

"Creating opportunities for our inmates to give back to our community is an important component in successful re–entry," said Mayor Walsh. "I am thrilled that the City is able to partner with the Suffolk County Sheriff's Office to assist in snow removal in areas critical to the safety of our residents."

The DOC spokesman also told ThinkProgress that inmates voluntarily opted into the program and that they were earning their daily inmate wage, which ranges from $3 to $4.

Now, don't be fooled by these numbers; three or four dollars per day can be a lot of money by prison standards. There hasn't been a significant amount of research, but numbers from 2002 indicate the average American inmate in a state prison could make anywhere from $0.30 to $7.00 an hour. Federal inmates have a more narrow range, from $0.18 to $1.15 per hour. These numbers haven't changed a lot in the last 13 years. Of course, compared to the $30 that the MBTA was offering everyone else, it's not much at all.

The concept of prison labor dates back to the Reconstruction and Jim Crow eras, spanning the late 1800s and the early 20th century, where prison work was essentially "slavery by another name," according to historian Douglas Blackmon. "Convict-leasing," as it was known, allowed mostly black inmates to be leased out involuntarily to private companies to work in coalmines, plantations, and factories. While the inmates were treated horribly and worked in terrible conditions, it was incredibly profitable for the states and private companies.

According to Blackmon, inmates "were compelled to labor without compensation, were repeatedly bought and sold, and were forced to do the bidding of white masters through the regular application of extraordinary physical coercion." While today prisoners work voluntarily rather than being forced, the parallels are hard to ignore, especially given the extremely low wages as compared to outside society.

Should inmates be paid more? What is the proper wage to pay inmates? How are these wages to be calculated—state by state? By the inmate? By the job they are assigned? Inmates don't necessarily need much money, as they're not paying taxes or for their room and board. Aside from items they can buy within the prison system, what purpose is served by paying a more significant wage?

Consider how important it is that inmates maintain or develop a productive work ethic prior to being released back into society. For the for-profit industries that invest in prison labor, consider how inmates could be motivated with a more reasonable salary. Earning a living would be particularly important for any inmate who enters without a support system or any kind of savings to help them adjust once they are released. We already know the impact that an incarceration record can have on a former inmate's job prospects, but how do these low wages factor into their post-release attitude?

All of this must be balanced with the realities of paying inmates more. A past study by the U.S. Government Accountability Office from 1993 entertained the idea of paying prison labor minimum wage. Although perhaps too old a study to be relevant, the report did predictably find a significant difference between what prisons were paying at the time for prison labor and what they would have to pay with a minimum wage—a difference of millions of dollars. To the extent that it's possible to pay inmates more, however, hinges at least in part on whether it's a worthwhile venture.

The unfortunate truth is that the system knows that once stripped of their basic freedom, it does not take much money to employ inmates and give them a glimpse of civilized society. These considerations come back to whether we as a society want to invest and reform the prison system, rather than using the facilities as temporary solutions to a much larger problem.

# Periodical and Internet Sources Bibliography

*The following articles have been selected to supplement the diverse views presented in this chapter.*

Sasha Abramsky, "Toxic Persons: New research shows precisely how the prison-to-poverty cycle does its damage," Slate.com, Oct. 8, 2010. http://www.slate.com/articles/news_and_politics/ jurisprudence/2010/10/toxic_persons.html

Sarah Barth, "What Are Societal Costs Associated With Mass Incarceration?" Newsmax, Dec. 11, 2016. http://www.newsmax. com/FastFeatures/mass-incarceration-voting-rights/2015/05/26/ id/646830/

Ta-Nehisi Coates, "The Black Family in the Age of Mass Incarceration," The Atlantic, Oct. 2015. http://www.theatlantic. com/magazine/archive/2015/10/the-black-family-in-the-age-of-mass-incarceration/403246/

Tim Hrenchir, "5 Reasons Prisoners Should Not Be Paid Minimum Wage," Newsmax, April 15, 2015. http://www.newsmax.com/ FastFeatures/minimum-wage-reasons-prisoners/2015/04/15/ id/638626/

Trymaine Lee, "The City: Prison's Grip on the Black Family: The spirals of poverty and mass incarceration upend urban communities," MSNBC.com, 2016. http://www.nbcnews.com/ specials/geographyofpoverty-big-city

Nicholas Kristof, "Mothers in Prison: 'Prison got me sober, but it didn't get me anywhere,'" The New York Times, Nov. 25, 2016. http://www.nytimes.com/2016/11/25/opinion/sunday/mothers-in-prison.html

Robin Moroney, "How Prisons Affect Society," The Wall Street Journal, March 26, 2007. http://blogs.wsj.com/ informedreader/2007/03/26/how-prisons-affect-society/

Caroline Simon, "There is a stunning gap between the number of white and black inmates in America's prisons," Business Insider, June 16, 2016. http://www.businessinsider.com/study-finds-huge-racial-disparity-in-americas-prisons-2016-6

Emily von Hoffmann, "How Incarceration Infects a Community," The Atlantic, March 6, 2015. http://www.theatlantic.com/health/archive/2015/03/how-incarceration-infects-a-community/385967/

Heather Ann Thompson, "Inner-City Violence in the Age of Mass Incarceration," The Atlantic, Oct 30, 2014. http://www.theatlantic.com/national/archive/2014/10/inner-city-violence-in-the-age-of-mass-incarceration/382154/

John Tierney, "Prison and the Poverty Trap," The New York Times, Feb. 18, 2013. http://www.nytimes.com/2013/02/19/science/long-prison-terms-eyed-as-contributing-to-poverty.html?pagewanted=all&_r=0

Kanyakrit Vongkiatkajor, "Why Prisoners Across the Country Have Gone on Strike: Activists say the prison labor system needs an overhaul," Mother Jones, Sept. 19, 2016. http://www.motherjones.com/politics/2016/09/prison-strike-inmate-labor-work

# Are There Problems with Our Prison System?

# Chapter Preface

The word *prisons* seems simple enough to understand—they are places for a society to hold those who have broken the rules of that society. But in the United States, prisons are comprised of several different types: there are federal and state prisons and local jails. Private prisons are also a factor. In general, regardless of type, most prisons today are overcrowded—some to the point of bursting—and dangerous because of it.

Reasons behind this population growth and the resulting issues it has created are as varied as the types of prisons themselves. It's been argued that mandatory minimums, most notably for drug crimes, have led to a marked population growth in federal prisons. State incarceration rates for drug crimes increased tenfold between 1980 and 2010, and in federal prisons, the increase was a staggering twentyfold. Mandatory minimums were intended to expedite criminal sentencing and create a fairer system by limiting judicial discretion and the possibility of uneven outcomes. However, some argue other factors have nullified the good intentions behind mandatory minimums.

As a result, a movement has grown to decrease harsh penalties for drug crimes, and in turn, the ever-expanding prison population. In some instances, people are even voicing arguments regarding the overpunishment of violent crime.

Prison privatization is another area people point to as ripe for system improvements. Some say such facilities are economical and provide quality care for inmates, while others say these institutions are mismanaged, interested only in profit, and that they actually exacerbate crime within prison walls and out of them, the latter shown by the rate of recidivism.

And while the focus seems to stay on prisons themselves when it comes to reform, other arguments have been made that the problem actually begins with our approach to policing and punishment. Regardless of fault, there is no doubt that something must be done to fix the current system. The following chapter examines our current system, including overcrowding, the prison industrial complex, and the way we police. The authors of the viewpoints presented offer opinions on the actions they believe are needed to solve this problem of prison overpopulation.

> "*Prison reform advocates say the commission's proposal is an incremental step, but an important one.*"

# Reforming Drug Offenses Can Curb Mass Incarceration

**Sarah Childress**

*In the following viewpoint, Sarah Childress explores movement among various governmental bodies to reconsider the harsh penalties for federal drug offenses. Childress argues that these one-size-fits-all punishments are ineffective, and they have a devastating effect on mainly African American communities. Statistics provided show how current mandatory minimums would be affected by pending legislation and other attempts at reform. Childress is a digital reporter for Frontline. She has also done reporting for Newsweek and The Wall Street Journal and her writing has appeared in The New York Times and The Washington Post.*

"Feds to Reconsider Harsh Prison Terms for Drug Offenders," by Sarah Childress, Frontline, April 09, 2014. Reprinted by Permission.

As you read, consider the following questions:

1.  Why are the guidelines for drug-trafficking offenses currently set at even higher levels than mandatory minimum sentences?
2.  Why would the U.S. Sentencing Commission's amendment have little effect on the majority of the country's prison population?
3.  What increase was there in the number of penalties that carried mandatory minimum sentences over the last two decades?

The federal prison population has expanded by nearly 800 percent in the past 30 years, spurred in part by the increasing use of tougher sentences applied to nonviolent drug crimes.

Now there's a growing movement to scale it back. On Thursday, the U.S. Sentencing Commission, an independent federal agency, plans to vote on an amendment to sentencing guidelines that could ultimately begin to winnow the federal prison population, nearly half of whom are people convicted of drug offenses.

The amendment is part of a bipartisan push away from America's addiction to incarceration, which prison reform experts say costs far too much, not only in dollars—$80 billion a year in 2010—but also in the devastation primarily of African-American communities, who have been disproportionately caught up in the system.

The commission's proposal would lower the sentencing guideline levels for drug-trafficking offenses, allowing judges to impose reduced sentences by about 11 months, on average, for these crimes. The guidelines are the range between which a judge can sentence an offender. Currently, those guidelines are set higher even than mandatory minimum sentences—the lowest possible sentence a judge could impose—to give prosecutors bargaining power. The amendment would set the upper and lower guideline limits around the mandatory minimums, leading to lower sentences for nearly 70 percent of drug-trafficking offenders, the commission said.

If it passes, the amendment would take effect Nov. 1 and reduce the federal population by 3 percent over the next five years. But it won't impact the bulk of the prison population, estimated at about 2.2 million in 2012, which is locked up mainly in state prisons and jails.

The amendment would make a difference for people like Dana Bowerman, a Texas honor student who developed a meth addiction at 15, under her father's influence. When she was 30 years old, Bowerman was arrested with her father and several others and convicted of drug conspiracy charges. Because of the stiff sentencing guidelines, she was sentenced to 19 years and seven months.

Bowerman had committed no violent crimes. She's since kicked her habit and wants a second chance, according to Families Against Mandatory Minimums, an advocacy group that documented her story. Under the proposed amendment, she would serve 15 years and six months, Julie Stewart, FAMM's president, said in testimony before the Sentencing Commission.

Prison reform advocates say the commission's proposal is an incremental step, but an important one. "When you're serving 10 years, six months can make a difference," said Jesselyn McCurdy, an attorney with the ACLU's Washington legislative office. "It's incremental, but it's all important because it sends the larger message that we have to do something about the harsh sentencing in the federal system."

Should the Sentencing Commission's amendment pass, it will be sent to Congress, which will have 180 days to make any changes. If it does nothing—which is the likely outcome given bipartisan Congressional support for the proposal—the resolution will take effect on Nov. 1.

## Model States

For years, states, which carry the bulk of U.S. prisoners, have taken the lead on sentencing reform—largely out of necessity.

Struggling with stretched budgets and overflowing prisons, 40 states have passed laws that ease sentencing guidelines for drug crimes from 2009 to 2013, according to a comprehensive analysis by the Pew Research Center. Seventeen states have invested in reforms like drug treatment and supervision that will save about $4.6 billion over 10 years, according to the Justice Department.

Such reforms also have gained popular public support. According to Pew's own polling, 63 percent of Americans say that states moving away from mandatory minimum sentencing is a "good thing," up from 41 percent in 2001. Even more—67 percent—said that states should focus on treatment, rather than punishment, for people struggling with addiction to illegal drugs.

## Federal Intervention

In recent years, the Obama administration has also made moves towards sentencing reform.

In August 2013, Attorney General Eric Holder announced a change in the charging policy for federal prosecutors, instructing them not to charge low-level, non-violent drug crimes with offenses that would trigger a mandatory minimum sentence.

Mandatory minimums offer a one-size-fits-all sentencing. They eliminate the discretion that a prosecutor or judge might otherwise use in determining how to punish an offender based on mitigating circumstances, such as a first-time offender or a low-level, non-violent offense. The number of penalties that carry mandatory minimum sentences has nearly doubled from 98 to 195 over the last 20 years, according to the Sentencing Commission.

There are no proposals to alter mandatory minimums that address violent crimes, such as kidnapping and crimes against children. But a significant number of mandatory minimum sentences involve nonviolent, drug-related offenses, which advocates for reform, and now even some members of Congress, argue end up sending too many first-time offenders to prison for too long.

"Many of those mandatory minimums originated right here in this committee room," said Sen. Patrick Leahy (D-Vt.), at a recent Judiciary Committee hearing last year. "When I look at the evidence we have now, I realize we were wrong. Our reliance on a one-size-fits-all approach to sentencing has been a great mistake. Mandatory minimums are costly, unfair, and do not make our country safer."

## Prospects for Congressional Reform

The Sentencing Commission itself notes that substantial reform requires action by Congress. "Our proposed approach is modest," said Patti Saris, the commission's chairwoman. "The real solution rests with Congress, and we continue to support efforts there to reduce mandatory minimum penalties, consistent with our recent report finding that mandatory minimum penalties are often too severe and sweep too broadly in the drug context, often capturing lower-level players."

There has been some movement toward reform on both sides of the aisle.

In 2010, Congress passed the Fair Sentencing Act, which reduced the sentencing disparity between crack and powdered cocaine, which had been at about 100 to 1—meaning people, mostly African-Americans, served significantly more time for crack possession than those arrested for possessing the same amount of powdered cocaine. The disparity's now at 18 to 1.

The Senate is currently considering a bill called the Smarter Sentencing Act, a bipartisan bill introduced in July 2013 by Sen. Richard Durbin (D-Ill.) and Sen. Mike Lee (R-Utah). It wouldn't abolish mandatory minimums, but it would allow judges to impose more lenient sentences for certain non-violent drug offenses.

"Our current scheme of mandatory minimum sentences is irrational and wasteful," Lee said when introducing the bill, adding that the act "takes an important step forward in reducing the financial and human cost of outdated and imprudent sentencing policies."

It would also allow the Fair Sentencing Act to be applied retroactively to some prisoners, a move that could affect an estimated 8,800 people currently in federal prisons, according to the ACLU. The law would also lower certain mandatory minimum sentences.

But the bill, which even the senators acknowledged as "studied and modest" on their website, doesn't have great odds of passing. According to govtrack.us, a nonpartisan website that tracks congressional legislation, the Smarter Sentencing Act has only a 39 percent chance of being enacted.

> *"This progress on rolling back some use of prison for drug crimes will not, by itself, end mass incarceration in America. Instead, we need to turn to a topic that has lot less appeal than criticizing the war on drugs: the overpunishment of violent crime."*

# A Drugs-First Strategy Cannot Solve the Prison Problem

*Jonathan Simon*

*In the following viewpoint, Jonathan Simon argues that over-incarceration, an embarrassment to our nation, should not start with drug-sentencing reform, but instead with reform in the overpunishment of violent crime. He states that only through a new view on murder in its varying degrees, will other necessary changes occur to end structural racism in the United States. Simon is the author of* Governing through Crime: How the War on Crime Transformed American Democracy and Created a Culture of Fear.

As you read, consider the following questions:

1. What example does Simon give regarding deep racialization of drug crimes?
2. According to the author, how do sentences for murder in other countries compare to those in the U.S.?
3. What are the cascades of positive and negative effects that Simon discusses?

## Drugs Are Not the (Only) Problem: Structural Racism, Mass Imprisonment, and the Overpunishment of Violent Crime

The huge scale and racial disproportionality of America's prison population seem an increasing problem for the nation, an embarrassment in the eyes of a world quite interested in our penal practices generally. Indeed, for perhaps the first time in our history, our penal system is clearly a good deal more racist than the society it purports to represent. Events like the grotesque murder of James Byrd some years back tell us more about the racial climate in Texas prisons (where both Byrd and his white attackers had spent time) than in Jasper, Texas, where the murder occurred—just as the outrageous overprosecution of the six black teenagers convicted of beating a white student in Jena, Louisiana, is a story more about the prosecution complex in America than about traditional southern racial conflict.

State legislatures seem to be getting it. New York managed to repeal the Rockefeller drug laws (a name that linked the great pro–civil rights Republican of his generation to the harshest penal laws of its time, telling us a lot about the complexity of race and this issue). California voters even rejected an artfully worded crime initiative that promised community safety through long prison terms for gang members and larger police budgets.

Much of the progress in recent years has come from a strategy aimed at delegitimizing the incarceration approach to drug crime, especially for drug possession and use. The "drugs-first" approach has a lot of appeal. Harsh punishment for drug crime runs into several powerful critiques that are gaining traction with many Americans:

- Prison for drug crime is distinctively associated with racial disparity. The whole selection of drugs deemed illegal in the United States is deeply racialized from the start. Drug enforcement policy and the harshest prison sentences seem focused on the drugs most associated with minorities and especially African Americans (e.g., crack cocaine).
- For many drug users, treatment seems a more humane and effective approach,
- while other drugs, particularly marijuana, could well be handled through a muscular civil regulatory approach.
- When people consider drug crime on its own terms, they do not consider it an inherently serious crime. Fear of drug crime is mostly associated with violence generated either by the drug trade or by the actions of drug-addicted users.

But this progress on rolling back some use of prison for drug crimes will not, by itself, end mass incarceration in America. Instead, we need to turn to a topic that has lot less appeal than criticizing the war on drugs: the overpunishment of violent crime.

I have come to believe that our approach to punishing violent crime is the hardened back of mass imprisonment (to use an unusual metaphoric contrast to the soft underbelly) in America. We cannot extricate ourselves from mass imprisonment with a strategy exclusively based on moving drug offenders out of prison.

As Marie Gottschalk argues in her very fine book on mass imprisonment and the death penalty:

> While the drug and sentencing ballot initiatives vary greatly, they share some common features. They risk reinforcing a disturbing distinction between deserving and undeserving offenders. Many of these initiatives sanction throwing the book at drug dealers, recidivists, and violent offenders, thus reinforcing powerful stereotypes about crime and criminals that may help bolster the fundamental legitimacy of the carceral state.[1]

At its best, the drugs-first strategy will produce an incarceration rate in America that is 25 to 45 percent lower than it is now but that remains two or three times the norm for the twentieth century. This prison population will be just as concentrated with people of color[2] and from neighborhoods (now often rural as well as urban) of multiple disadvantages.

At worst, given our current practice of excessively punishing violent crime, a drugs-first strategy may only anchor a sensibility that will lock us into mass imprisonment and distort the way America rebuilds its urban landscape over the coming decades. "Violence" is a fuzzy category—for example, Is emotional abuse violence? Does threat of violence constitute violence?—and one highly prone to racial stereotyping.[3] Through four decades of a war on crime, we have lost the capacity to judge appropriate punishment, and we must confront our fears rather than avoid them. Only by confronting our fear of violent crime can we hope to frame a sustainable scale of punishment that ceases to exacerbate structural racism in America.

In the remainder of this chapter, I consider one category of violent crime that is relatively free from classification problems and racialized stereotypes: murder.

I suggest that the political expediency of focusing justice reform on drug users and other, less-frightening prisoners will ultimately fail, and that we need instead to find a politically viable way to question the overpunishment of violent crime, beginning with murder.

## Murder by Degrees

The law of murder is one of the great innovations in American jurisprudence. English common law considered all criminal homicides, except for a few narrow categories treated as manslaughter, to be murder, and they carried a mandatory death sentence. In the United States, beginning in Pennsylvania in 1794, murder was early on divided into two levels: first and second degree. Capital punishment was available only for first-degree murder, and then only at the discretion of the jury. This became the near-universal rule in the United States, until it was complicated by the U.S. Supreme Court's death-penalty decisions in the 1970s.[4] (England did not follow this path until the Homicide Act of 1957 created a category of less serious homicide, for which a life sentence in prison was the normal punishment.)

Americans also innovated in manslaughter jurisprudence. While common law only permitted the mitigation of murder down to manslaughter in a narrow set of categories (the most famous being "sight of adultery"), American judges began to broaden these categories. In the twentieth century, following the Model Penal Code, most states made manslaughter open to any killing done under circumstances likely to create an extreme emotional disturbance in ordinary people. [5]

Ever a magnet for public attention, homicides in the nineteenth century became a major topic that helped sell the first mass-market newspapers. This helped murder to emerge as the dominant crime in the public imagination around the middle of the nineteenth century.[6] A wave of efforts to abolish the death penalty in the early nineteenth century left murder practically the only crime punishable by death on a regular basis.[7]

In the twentieth century, murders similarly preoccupied radio, television, and the Internet. Mass-media coverage of homicide helps to inform the public understanding of serious crime and drives campaigns for harsher punishment. The structure of modern homicide law was well adapted to addressing the media's demand for harsh punishment. The death penalty was available (and widely used in the first half of the twentieth century) to address those killings that most alarmed the public. The vast majority of other people convicted of murder received either a very long term of years in prison or, often, a life sentence. Few served such long times, because the parole process—largely invisible to the public—

favored an eventual release date for all life-sentenced prisoners who avoided trouble and actively sought rehabilitative programming.

Criminology, which has always enjoyed a popular as well as elite following in America, also played a role in elevating murder in the public imagination. Criminology has long viewed murder as the ultimate expression of a criminality that shows its early presence in delinquency and minor criminality.[8] Burglary, robbery, or rape may constitute serious violations of the victims' rights, but they are also feared because they could result in a murder (which is why the latter two remained capital crimes even in the twentieth century).

The modern law of murder and manslaughter can be considered, in some respects, a triumph of progress. For much of the twentieth century, the law of murder as it existed in the larger industrialized states played an important role in containing demand for severe punishment and in regulating the overall scale of punishment. (This is a theoretical assertion on my part, but the logic of this claim can be outlined.) The law limited the field of convicted killers exposed to the death penalty and gave juries discretion to decide imprisonment for life, even in aggravated cases. The length of punishment for those people not sentenced to death for murder was largely transferred to administrative agencies often known as "parole boards," which had authority to decide when imprisoned killers could be released (usually after a minimum term of years).[9]

It is difficult to assess empirically how effective this legal and administrative structure was at dissipating populist demands for severe punishment. While homicide is not one of the most frequent reasons for committing a person to prison, homicide sentences wield a disproportionate impact on prison populations because of the relatively long sentences. The parole board was generally an excellent administrative solution to extend the punishment-limiting capacity of laws for murder and manslaughter, because it moved a decisive portion of the punishment decision to a point in time quite distant from the crime or even the trial and set it apart from the public eye, in the inner workings of a (supposedly) expert-based administrative agency.[10] However, the war on crime and the politicization of parole decisions that it produced have fundamentally transformed this modern structure into a monolithic edifice of extreme punishment.

Prison sentences for murder have escalated dramatically in the United States since the 1970s, and they are markedly and more generally harsher than punishment for homicide almost anywhere else in the world.[11] Even where capital punishment is practiced, few of those people who are not executed are subjected to more than a decade or two in prison. In the United States, however, punishments of three or more decades for even the least aggravated murders are becoming common (and may reflect the minimum punishment, as many murder convicts seem likely to die in prison).

## Why Degrees of Murder Matter: The California Example

In California, someone guilty of criminal homicide of another person faces—in theory—very different punishments depending on what grade of murder or manslaughter he or she is convicted of.[12] At the top of the punishment scale is the death penalty, or life in prison without possibility of parole for first-degree murder with special circumstances. First degree generally means that the killing was either planned or took place during one of a list of dangerous felonies.[13] Special circumstances include killing a police officer, multiple victims, and so on.

Next down is first-degree murder without special circumstances. The penalty for this is twenty-five years to life, meaning that parole eligibility begins after twenty-five years. California considers a killing that was not planned (but also not mitigated by some extreme emotional provocation) or was carried out in the course of another felony (but not the listed ones in the first-degree statute) to be second-degree murder, which carries a term of fifteen years to life. Finally, if the judge or jury finds that the defendant killed in the "heat of passion" (extreme emotional disturbance), the offender will face a determinate sentence of three, six, or eleven years.

As every first-year law student learns, the concepts that separate first- and second-degree murder (premeditation and deliberation) or murder and manslaughter (heat of passion) are notoriously ambiguous and dependent on cultural logics.

With so much at stake, the law can seem inherently arbitrary and capricious—or, even worse, predictably disfavorable to minorities and the poor. However, few courses in criminal law dwell on the fact that only the bottom line between murder and manslaughter really matters today.

In California, the death penalty is rarely carried out and, due to the politicization of parole, very few paroles are ever granted. Tough-on-crime governors have appointed to the parole board (known as the Board of Prison Terms) mostly former law enforcement officials or crime victims, who are unlikely to be sympathetic to life prisoners. Few lifers who have served their minimum sentence, and thus are eligible to have a parole release date set by the board, actually get such a date.

Moreover, since 1988 California law has required the governor to review each parole release granted and either approve or disapprove it. Recent governors have rejected more than 98 percent of parole releases approved by the board. Thus, a mere fraction of 1 percent of the thousands of eligible lifers gets an approved release datein a typical year. In other words, while more than one thousand new life prisoners arrive in California prisons every year, and more than ten thousand are eligible for parole each year, only an average of about twenty-three actually get released.[14] There are now more than thirty-seven thousand life prisoners in California.[15]

**This situation creates a monolith of extreme punishment that constitutes an increasingly large and indigestible block of prisoners in California prisons.** At the top end of the spectrum, legal challenges and lack of sufficient lawyers to represent the prisoners sentenced to death mean that executions are extremely rare. While nearly seven hundred prisoners are on death row, only thirteen executions have occurred since they resumed in the early 1990s.[16] Thus the complex legal distinctions that separate special circumstances, first-degree murder, and second-degree murder have come to mean relatively little in terms of the quantity of punishment faced (although the quality of punishment is probably more severe for death row inmates, due to a security regime that keeps most of them locked in a cell twenty-three hours a day). For all practical purposes, anyone sent to prison in California for murder is likely to die there—and not at the hands of the state.[17]

**Punishment for murder has become the remainder of the prisoners' natural life, which is extreme** compared to past policies and to most of the rest of the world. In the 1970s, for example, a first-degree murderer in California who played the rehabilitation game behind bars and avoided serious disciplinary problems could expect to be paroled in as little as ten or fifteen years (five less for second degree).In most of the rest of the world, murderers serve fewer than twenty years. (In Finland, most life prisoners are released after ten years.) Yet today, California prisons are full of men and women who have spent twenty-five, thirty, or thirty-five years constructing meticulous rehabilitation records with virtually no chance of getting out of prison before they die. This situation is not only unjust—at least in the minimalist sense that it renders meaningless the distinctions that the law explicitly draws—it also plays a significant role in anchoring the larger structure of overpunishment and mass imprisonment in America.

Many of us who want to wean America from its addiction to prisons have focused on drug users and other minor and nonviolent offenders. Indeed, this approach often contrasts nonthreatening offenders with dangerous and violent offenders who belong in prison for long terms. Wasting prison space on "druggies" and minor offenders, the argument goes, makes it harder to keep violent offenders in prison. I believe that we need to combine this reform with a serious effort to question and reverse the overpunishment of violent crime, especially murder. I am deeply sympathetic to the view that drug users, low-level drug sellers, and minor violators of property and public order do not belong in prison. However, a strategy that focuses only on minor criminality is limited in how far it can reverse the level of imprisonment (e.g., we might end up with only three times, rather than six times, the prison population of the 1970s). Indeed, an emphasis only on the shallow end of the punishment spectrum may counterproductively reinforce the tendency to overpunish—so that, in the long run, any reductions gained through alternatives to incarceration for the shallow end may be modest.

## Homicide as a Regulator of Punishment

**If murder anchors one end of a continuum, with delinquency and minor crime at the other end, two interrelated implications arise:** (1) Murderers are the ultimate criminals who are capable of and likely to engage in crime of all sorts; and (2) minor offenders may seem relatively harmless now, but they may be on their way up the continuum toward murder. American criminology and criminal law have long positioned homicide as the principal crime against the modern legal subject, one that reveals the threat to life that is intrinsic in all crime.[18] The focus on minor delinquency as a starting point for intervention has been the primary lesson of criminology as public policy since the turn of the past century. The notion is that the juvenile delinquent who skips school and commits acts of vandalism is manifesting underlying criminalizing tendencies that, left unchecked, could escalate up the chain of crime all the way to murder.

Against this background, we can see that the overpunishment of murder may have effects all the way down the range of crimes. Three kinds of effects stand out in particular: prospect theory, loss aversion, or reference effects; the net-widening effects of "dangerousness"; and the racialization of punishment.

## Prospect theory, loss aversion, or reference effects

A well-known result in behavioral economics is that when consumers assess the reasonableness of an item's price, they are influenced by the price of another item that serves as the reference point or price. The so-called reference price establishes a level below which consumers feel that they are getting a good deal, and above which they feel they are experiencing a loss. So, for example, the high price tag on a $40 surf-and-turf special probably makes it more likely a diner will spend $29 on a steak or $19 on a pasta dish without complaining about the cost.

Similarly, natural life sentences for even nonaggravated murder set a reference price for crime that makes extreme but less-severe punishments for other crimes seem appropriate. Decades in prison for crimes like robbery, burglary, and drug dealing may not seem disproportionate when compared to the severity of execution or life in prison without parole.[19]

## Net-widening effects of dangerousness

Severe punishment reinforces the view that murderers are permanently dangerous. This perception can extend to include minor criminality, given the common view that there is a continuum of criminality to which both murderers and minor criminals belong. In practice, this means that reductions in the use of imprisonment for drug users, public order violators, minor property crime offenders, and other less-serious offenders may easily be reversed if a more serious crime is committed by someone on parole or probation for a less serious crime—something likely to occur, visions, opportunities, and challenges for justice reformers given the large number of people on parole or probation nationwide.

## Racialization of punishment

Criminologists and many policymakers recognize that the War on Drugs has contributed to the enormous racial disproportionality of the American penal population. Drug use is distributed quite evenly across major demographic groups, while punishment for drug crimes is radically skewed toward African Americans and

Latinos.[20] But the racialization of the drug war is intertwined with the racial coding of violence in America. High levels of violence in the African American community have been a criminological topic since the nineteenth century. While the causes of this are many, rooted in poverty and discrimination, the strong association between African Americans and homicide that has developed since the 1960s (with a pattern emerging then of approximately half of all homicide victims and perpetrators being African American) contributes mightily to racial disproportionality in the punishment of drug crimes. The well-documented police focus on young black men is driven by ecological presumptions about the presence of guns, the potential for violence, and the pressure to drive down homicide rates, but the immediate result of such policing tactics generally is more drug arrests and convictions.[21]

**These effects suggest that a strategy of reducing the level of punishment at the high end for murderers is an essential component of any approach to substantially reducing our use of imprisonment.** If we attack the mass-imprisonment problem by reducing the punishment of murderers, we can create a cascade of positive effects leading to more reductions in punishment.

Consider, for instance, what could happen if we reset the "reference price" for non-homicide sentences. If murder were punished at twenty years (the global norm), there would be no property offenders serving life terms, as there are now under California's three-strikes law. Indeed, the entire hierarchy of punishments would require dramatic reduction in order to avoid violating strong popular beliefs that some crimes are more deserving of punishment than others and that murder is the most deserving.[22]

Reducing the length of murder sentences would help diminish public belief in the permanent dangerousness of murderers, because the low rate of recidivism among released prisoners would become more widely known.[23] Criminologists have long documented the fact that prisoners who are released after serving time for homicide crimes have among the lowest recidivism rates, both for other homicides and crimes generally.[24] Such a demonstration of redemption will reduce the temptation to incapacitate minor criminals out of fear they are on a trajectory toward murder. (There may be risk factors that can help predict when a pattern of lawless behavior is likely to become violent, such as mental illness combined with a history of previous violence, or an escalating pattern of domestic violence, but they do not apply to the vast majority of people convicted of minor drug, public order, or property crimes. The public's legitimate desire to prevent homicide can be more effectively served through interventions targeted at these well-defined cases, including a more assertive civil commitment system for the mentally ill.)

The up-front political costs of reducing homicide penalties are likely to be large, but once the changes are made the virtuous circle of positive effects will reduce the public's propensity to fall back on long, incapacitative sentencing as a panacea for unfathomable risks. In contrast, the politically expeditious path we are on now—trying to separate low-end crimes from those involving violence, especially homicide—has tremendous risk of collapsing; indeed, quieter efforts have regularly done so in recent years.

**If we continue to attack mass imprisonment by focusing on removing drug users and low-level offenders, we may achieve some reduction in the prison population—but unless we do it very carefully, we may create a cascade of negative effects.** The most consequential one will be to reinforce the message that we need to rededicate prisons to incapacitating people convicted of murder and other violent crimes. At present, we already do so, and the argument that we need more prison space for this purpose implies that current levels of punishment for violent crimes are too low.

By failing to diminish public fear of violence linked to the category of crime, this strategy leaves its own modest reforms vulnerable to sudden reversals if, as is inevitable, a person on parole who is kept out of prison for a minor crime goes on to commit a violent crime. After such an event, the media and politicians will focus on the fact that under previous policies the minor offender would have been in prison at the time of the violent crime and thus safely incapacitated (ignoring, of course, the fact that the offender would have been released at some point). When that happens, demand will build to reverse policies of limited decarceration, even for nonviolent offenders.

## Additional Comments from the Public Forum

**JONATHAN SIMON:** I attack what I think has become a sacred cow for those of us in the anti-incarceration movement: an agenda or a strategy that I will call "drugs first." The essence of this strategy is to say to the public that too many druggies are in the prison system. So let's pass a law mandating treatment, not jail, and move some of those people out into the community.

Much of the "drugs-first" strategy has had the perverse consequence of actually reinforcing the public's belief that there's an enormous problem with violent crime in America, and that only mass incarceration can solve it. So a tag line that is becoming typical is, "Let's get the druggies out of prisons so we'll have more room to punish violent criminals."

Now, first of all, the sentences for violent crime, and murder especially—although this runs the gamut—have gone up. Nationwide, something like around 40 percent of the overall growth in incarceration since the 1970s is represented by this violent crime problem. So if all we're doing is chipping away the druggies first and leaving that violent block in there, we'd still be left with a disproportionately large prison system.

But the problem becomes worse because the focus on drugs falls prey to two things I want to highlight. One is the enormous popularity of criminology in American culture, which from the nineteenth century on has viewed murder as the only ultimate outcome of a criminal career that begins with minor crime and delinquency. That is sort of the story of criminology. Criminology wants to show you that this wayward youth, who could be intervened on now, could become a murderer if allowed to continue on this path. Probably the most famous example is Lee Harvey Oswald who, when he was arrested for truancy as a fourteen-year old, had a probation officer predict on paper that "someday he'll murder someone if we don't do something about this."

Now, many Americans have come to accept the premise that minor crime is important because it's on a path that leads to violent crime, which means that a strategy of decriminalizing violent behavior has a natural backlash tendency to it. As soon as something happens—like the home invasion in Connecticut a couple of summers ago, where a couple of minor criminals took over a home, raped and murdered the kids, and set fire to it—that's seen as a poster child for the death penalty. It also reinforces the idea that it's worth keeping relatively minor criminals in prison for a long, long time.

The other feature that I think is particularly important is the racialization of violence. From the nineteenth century on, homicide actually has been a disproportionately black crime in America. There are a lot of good explanations for it, but the bottom line is when we overpunish violent crime, we are by nature selectively picking out a population of color to punish harshly.

Second, because our laws have gotten so extreme (and California may be the extreme case) we have created an "indigestible block" of prisoners. In California, anything from first-degree murder with special circumstances down to second-degree murder—which is basically spousal killing, impulsive killing that's not mitigated down to manslaughter, a lot of road rage cases, etc.—basically, all of those folks are going to serve natural life in prison. Even if you're sentenced to death, you are almost certain not to be executed in California. Currently, there are about thirty thousand prisoners in the California prison system in that life status. California law requires the governor to personally approve every parole of a lifer, which means that none happened under Gray Davis, none happened under Pete Wilson. A handful have happened under Arnold Schwarzenegger. Approximately a thousand lifers come to California prisons every year; approximately five leave. So you can see how the math works.

Right now, it's very hard for me to imagine how to start the sound-bite campaign that says, "Let's be nicer to murderers." It's a really hard political sell, but consider he benefits of it.

**Q:** What is the way to introduce this issue of overpunishment of violent crime? Also, who is supposed to bring that message? It's not going to be any elected official, and the public isn't going to listen to academics. Is it ministers? Is it philosophers? Is it some sort of expert? Do we medicalize the question and have somebody wearing a white coat and a stethoscope say, "We've done lots of public health studies, and it turns out that breaking a window when you're fourteen does not indicate that you're going to become a murderer"?

**SIMON:** I'm dubious, because criminologists have known for years that essentially once you cross forty your chances of ever committing a crime of any sort again, let alone a violent crime, go down astronomically. Yet we keep people decades past that birthday. And I don't know that repeating that will make any difference.

If television networks like MSNBC are going to devote so much broadcast time to prisons, maybe they could do life histories in the nineteenth-century way where you actually tell stories about people in prisons, because they're often very sympathetic folks. Now, obviously there is a murder victim family out there somewhere whose pain is unending. We also have to understand the importance of violence in our society as a driver of this. A lot of us who oppose mass incarceration have been in denial about the role that high violent crime rates in the '60s and '80s played in driving home the message that this is an appropriate kind of governmental response. So since we have a gift in the recent crime decline—and you 145in New York City may have the greatest opportunity of all, because your crime decline was roughly twice what the rest of the country experienced—that creates an opportunity to begin to individualize these cases and to tell stories about people's lives.

A lot of Americans believe that a black version of Hannibal Lector is most of what is locked up in the murder wards of our prisons. Again, this feeds into this criminological cultural heritage we have. One of our strategies has to be to become "anticriminologists" in this sense. Murder and most violent crimes should not be seen as the developmental outcome of some kind of criminality track, in the way a polyp becomes a cancer. It's much more like an accident. People commit violent acts through a lot of combinations of circumstance, through situational factors. Background obviously can play a role, but the idea that the person who commits a murder is therefore the sort of supercriminal who can commit any crime if you let them out is widely believed by Americans. But when you meet people in San Quentin who killed their partner or got in a road rage incident on the highway and are now twenty years older than that event, they're not really frightening people. And by and large they've done a lot of good work on themselves.

The current pessimism about the fiscal crisis might offer another opportunity to communicate this—although as long as people believe that violent crime is what's being contained by mass incarceration, the price point at which it becomes too expensive is very high. I don't know how high it has to get before people will be open to reversing things.

**Q:** This proposal clashes somewhat with a lot of people's ideas about individual responsibility. How do we change that popular understanding?

**SIMON:** I teach criminal law, and our modern, contemporary criminal law is already shockingly indifferent to individual responsibility in a lot of ways. Accompliceliability has been enormously expanded to sweep up all kinds of people for violent and drug crimes. The proliferation of crimes that are essentially systemic—such as being a felon in possession of a weapon, regardless of why you were in possession of that weapon—has moved us away from this nineteenth-century notion of individual responsibility.

Now, there may be a lot of twenty-first century reasons to not be stuck on individual responsibility, but it seems to me that some return to a serious discussion about whether our criminal justice system actually does honor individual responsibility would be in keeping. And, in fact, when you meet some of the lifers that I have in San Quentin, what strikes you is that these people have taken responsibility for their crimes. They've spent decades working on themselves, trying to seek redemption to whatever extent they can from their victims, to get educations. They are really impressive stories, and yet they're being told by the system, "You'll never get out because we think even an eighty-nine-year-old man might, you know, hit somebody over the head with their crutch or something, there maybe some risk involved." That's all about risk and very nonfocused on individual responsibility.

**Q:** I've got a fact question for you, Jonathan. You said that since the nineteenth-century murder has been mostly a black affair and that there are reasons for that. The thing that came to my mind was the drug trade, but are there other factors involved you want to tell us about?

**SIMON:** Since the nineteenth century, criminologists have been aware of the disproportionately high rate of blacks both as victims of murder and perpetrators of it. As we know, homicide is overwhelmingly an intraracial experience in America. I think it's really been exacerbated since the '60s. Approximately half of all homicide victims in America are black, and we assume that about half of the perpetrators are black as well.

As for explanations, criminologists in the '80s looking at the crack epidemic pointed to proliferation of guns among young people. The increase in gun ownership by a certain number of young people made other young people feel that they had to have those guns in order to play peer roles. And once guns are introduced into an essentially adolescent society, you are going to have a lot of homicides. That's one of the reasons why this developmental model of crime that views the murderer as the sort of superpredator is so wrong. Any fourteen- or fifteen-year-old will do unbelievably horrible things, given the right circumstances and the right equipment, but that doesn't mean that for the rest of their lives they need to be in a cage.

## Notes

1. M. Gottschalk, *The Prison and the Gallows: The Politics of Mass Incarceration in America* (Cambridge: Cambridge University Press, 2001), 258.

2. For instance, in 2004, non-Hispanic blacks constituted 41 percent of all state prisoners serving time for murder, compared to 33 percent of all state prisoners serving time for burglary and 45 percent of all state prisoners serving time for drug offenses. See Sourcebook of Criminal Justice Statistics Online, http://www.albany.edu/sourcebook, table 6.001.2004.

3. Several cognitive science experiments available online provide tests of implicit bias in the assignment of dangerousness based on race. See https://implicit.harvard.edu for a test associating weapons with African American and white faces.

4. *Furman v. Georgia*, 408 U.S. 238 (1972); *Gregg v. Georgia*, 428 U.S. 153 (1976); F. Zimring and G. Hawkins, *Capital Punishment and the American Agenda* (Cambridge: Cambridge University Press, 1989).

5. C. Lee and A. Harris, *Criminal Law: Cases and Materials*, 2nd ed. (St. Paul, Minn.: Thomson/West, 2009).

6. K. Halttunen, *Murder Most Foul: The Killer and the America Gothic Imagination* (Cambridge, Mass.: Harvard University Press, 1998).

7. S. Banner, *The Death Penalty: An American History* (Cambridge, Mass.: Harvard University Press, 2002).

8. Lots of criminological research has suggested that murder is frequently a highly contingent event that reflects not an escalating degree of criminality but the intersection of multiple factors.

9. D. Rothman, *Conscience and Convenience: The Asylum and Its Alternatives in the Progressive Era* (Boston: Little, Brown, 1980).

10. S. L. Messinger et al., "The Foundations of Parole in California," Law & Society Review 19 (1985): 69.

11. The most recent estimate of the length of prison sentences for murder comes from an analysis of felony sentences in the seventy-five largest counties in the United States between 1990 and 2002, published in 2006. According to this analysis, the median sentence for murder is now 20 years (240 months) and the mean sentence is 25.6 years (308 months). See B. A. Reaves, Violent Felons in Large Urban Counties, Bureau of Justice Statistics Special Report (Washington, D.C.: U.S. Department of Justice, Office of Justice Programs, 2006), 8.

12. California Penal Code §187 (a): Murder is the unlawful killing of a human being, or a fetus, with malice aforethought.

13. California Penal Code §189: All murder which is perpetrated by means of a destructive device or explosive, a weapon of mass destruction, knowing use of ammunition designed primarily to penetrate metal or armor, poison, lying in wait, torture, or by any other kind of willful, deliberate, and premeditated killing, or which is committed in the perpetration of, or attempt to perpetrate, arson, rape, carjacking, robbery, burglary, mayhem, kidnapping, train wrecking, or any act punishable under Section 206, 286, 288, 288a, or 289, or any murder which is perpetrated by means of discharging a firearm from a motor

vehicle, intentionally at another person outside of the vehicle with the intent to inflict death, is murder of the first degree. All other kinds of murders are of the second degree.

14. J. Irwin, *Lifers: Seeking Redemption in Prison* (New York: Routledge, 2009), 2.

15. A. Nellis and R. S. King, *No Exit: The Expanding Use of Life Sentences in America* (Washington, D.C.: Sentencing Project, 2009), 7.

16. See http://www.deathpenaltyinfo.org/executions.

17. This sets a huge premium on getting murder down to manslaughter because it guarantees a release at the end of a fixed sentence. The legal doctrine of heat of passion, which distinguishes manslaughter from murder, is probably the most culturally determined of all, but I'll leave that problem for another time.

18. H. Wechsler and J. Michael, "A Rationale of the Law of Homicide, Part I," Columbia Law Review 37 (1937): 729.

19. David Garland raises the question of whether it is not escalation in the punishment of these serious-but-not-homicide crimes that drives increases in the severity of punishment for murder. It is true that some of the first extreme sentences arose in antinarcotics crimes. For example, the infamous Rockefeller drug law of 1973 made the sale of two ounces or more of a controlled substance (including marijuana) punishable by fifteen years to life in prison. The Rockefeller laws permitted parole. Even more severe antidrug laws have been adopted in Michigan, many other states, and under the federal sentencing guidelines, resulting in decades of imprisonment for sufficiently large quantities of drugs. The sequencing of homicide penalties and drug laws in the various states should be carefully examined. As a whole, drugs (at least "hard" drugs) came to be linked to the possibility or even likelihood of death during the 1970s and 1980s; selling large quantities of drugs in this respect might be seen as a kind of murder. Indeed, the Rockefeller laws explicitly linked the penalties for drugs to the penalties for second-degree murder.

20. M. Tonry, *Malign Neglect: Race, Crime, and Punishment in America* (New York: Oxford University Press, 1995).

21. Recent empirical research provides some support for the theory that racialized policing of drugs in Seattle is driven by a police emphasis on crack cocaine. More than any other recent drug, crack and its distribution have been associated with gun violence and homicide. See K. Beckett et al., "Drug Use, Drug Possession Arrests, and the Question of Race: Lessons from Seattle," Social Problems 52 (2005): 419–41.

22. A. Ristroph, "Desert, Democracy, and Sentencing Reform," Criminal Law & Criminology 96 (2006): 1293.

23. This reflects several factors. Many second-degree murder convictions involve the killing of a close personal friend, intimate, or business associate. The circumstances that led to the killing may have built up over years and involved unique associations unlikely to repeat themselves. Also, where parole from a life sentence is involved, prisoners have powerful incentives to engage in therapy, education, and other practices held out as essential to a positive parole file. (For examples of many such transformations, see Irwin, Lifers .) With years to spend in prison under the best of circumstances, many people convicted of murder genuinely seek opportunities for repentance and self-knowledge, and they work to heal the world around them.

24. A. Roberts, K. Zgoba, and S. M. Shahidullah, "Recidivism among Four Types of Homicide Offenders: An Exploratory Analysis of 336 Homicide Offenders in New Jersey," Aggression & Violent Behavior 12 (2007): 493–507.

> "While some private prisons have experienced problems, not unlike government-run prisons, on the whole, private prisons have a better record of performance than do government-run facilities."

# Private Prisons Increase Capacity, Save Money, and Improve Service

*Nathan Benefield*

*In the following viewpoint, Nathan Benefield puts forth an argument that privately run prisons are the answer to Pennsylvania's growing need for correctional facilities. He says it's inaccurate to call this type of privatization risky and gives evidence to support his claim. According to Benefield, private prisons will not only offer saving for taxpayers, but a higher quality of care for those incarcerated. Benefield is vice president and COO for the Commonwealth Foundation. His work on public policy issues has been featured in the Philadelphia Inquirer, Pittsburgh Post-Gazette, Pittsburgh Tribune-Review, and Patriot News. He also provides testimony to Pennsylvania's House and Senate.*

"Private Prisons Increase Capacity, Save Money, Improve Service," by Nathan Benefield, Commonwealth Foundation, October 24, 2007. Reprinted by Permission.

As you read, consider the following questions:

1.  In Pennsylvania in 2006, how many beds existed in state prisons and how many prisoners were incarcerated?
2.  According to the author, what threat helps keep private prisons operating at an adequate level of service?
3.  Who does Benefield call out as those most likely to object to prison privatization?

Good Afternoon, my name is Nathan Benefield, I am the Director of Policy Research with the Commonwealth Foundation, a research and educational organization based in Harrisburg. I would like to thank Chairman Belfanti and the members of this committee for inviting me to share some of our thoughts on House Bill 1469 and prison privatization in general.

There are three types of privatization within prisons and correctional institutions in the US. The first involves contracting out food service, medical services, job training, alcohol and drug rehabilitation, and the like. The second involves publicly owned prisons, which contract out the management to a private firm. The final type of privatization involves fully privatized prisons—both owned and operated by a private firm—which contract with governments for the care of prisoners.

House Bill 1469 would only address (that is, prohibit) the third type, i.e. fully private prisons, so I will limit my testimony to privately run prisons, and not address issues of contracting out services.

We believe HB 1469 is a misguided attempt to—well I'm not really sure what HB 1469 is attempting to do, other than deprive elected officials of a good government management tool. Pennsylvania faces a prison crunch, as we expect far greater demands for prison space than we currently have available. Private prisons can help meet this need. Studies demonstrate that private prisons are much more efficient than government-run prisons, and typically save taxpayers 10-15% in per-prisoner costs. Studies also show that private prisons typically provide better quality service and lower incidents of violence than government run prisons.

## Pennsylvania Faces a Prison Crunch

Pennsylvania's correctional facilities are in crisis. A growing—and aging—prison population is putting a strain on the budget. In December 2006, the state housed 44,365 prisoners, despite an operational bed capacity of only 39,284, and annual admissions to Pennsylvania's state prisons have increased 53% since 2000 with no indication of abatement.[1] The Pennsylvania Department of Corrections anticipates accommodating 51,596 prisoners by the close of the year 2011—with an estimated 42,851 beds. This would entail operating at 120% capacity.

At $93.21 per inmate per day, Pennsylvania's prisons are also among the nation's most costly facilities.[2] Pennsylvania currently spends $1.6 billion on corrections annually, an increase of 55% (24% after adjusting for inflation) in the last ten years. The anticipated growth in prison population will add almost $250 million to that cost—assuming per inmate costs remains constant. The Commonwealth faces a looming prison crisis, and the privatization of prison construction, services and management, offers a cost-effective solution to these pressing concerns.

## Prison Privatization is Not New

Critics of prison privatization often call private correctional facilities risky, unproven, or experimental. Yet private prisons operate successfully across the US. Nationally, over 107,000 federal and state prisoners—about 7% of the inmate population—were housed in private facilities in 2005 (an additional 73,000 inmates were held in privately-run local jails). Privately-operated prisons are the most common in the south and west, with five western states—New Mexico (43.3%), Wyoming (41.3%), Hawaii (30.9%), Alaska (28.4%) and Montana (25.5%)—housing more than a quarter of their inmates in private facilities.[3]

Currently, Pennsylvania has only one privately-run prison facility—the Monshannon Valley Correctional Center. But the vast experience of other states with private prisons should serve as case studies for how Pennsylvania can lower costs and provide higher quality services, while also meeting the future demand for correctional services.

## Privatization Leads to Cost Savings for Taxpayers

By expanding competition, Pennsylvanians can expect anywhere from 5 to 20% savings in per-prisoner costs from private facilities. A wealth of studies, as demonstrated in an accompanying table, find significant cost-savings of prison privatization, most frequently in the range of 10-15% savings.[4]

Additionally, states that have introduced privatization in prisons have seen slower rates of growth in correctional costs. A 2003 study found that states with 20% of prisoners in private facilities saw per-prisoner cost grow 5.9% from 1999 to 2001, versus 18.9% in state with no private facilities (states falling in the middle in private prisoners also ranked in the middle in rate of cost growth).[5]

Based on these findings, if Pennsylvania were to place 30% of inmates in private facilities, taxpayers could save upwards of $100 million annually, with higher expected savings in the future.

## Private Prisons Offer Higher Quality Care

Critics of private prisons often allege that privatization leads to lower service quality and endangers public safety. In fact, the opposite appears to be true. While some private prisons have experienced problems, not unlike government-run prisons, on the whole, private prisons have a better record of performance than do government-run facilities.

Private prisons have many institutional, contractual and legal safeguards to ensure quality, and contractors have compiled an enviable record of providing secure, safe, humane and well-run correctional facilities. Privately-managed correctional facilities have contractual requirements and inherent financial incentives to maintain order and security, provide educational and rehabilitation programs, and respect inmates' civil liberties. A private prison that fails to provide an adequate level of service is likely to suffer contract revocation or the threat thereof, which adversely affects the corporation's ability to offer its services elsewhere and survive among it competitors.

All prisons—public and private—must deal with inmate fights, rapes and attacks on guards. But in the private sector, prison management and staff are held accountable for a failure to perform. The state can terminate a contract with a private prison for mismanagement; private managers and staff are much more likely to face penalties, or be fired, than are government workers; and private companies may go out of business if they don't perform adequately. When is the last time a government-run prison was shut down because of rioting, abuse, poor care, etc.?

But the performance of private prisons is not merely conjecture or theoretical—we have evidence from 34 states. Many studies show private prisons outperforming state-run facilities on quality and performance indicators. A review of prison performance studies found that nine out of the ten rigorous studies of quality found higher quality of service in private prisons, as did most of the less rigorous studies.[6]

The Arizona Department of Corrections reported that private prisons outperformed state-run institutions across the board in safety of the public, staff, and inmates and compliance with professional standards. A University of Florida comparative analysis found significantly lower recidivism rates among comparable inmates released from private prisons. An Urban Institute study reported that inmates and staff alike rated services and programs offered by private facilities as superior to those available in state-run prisons, and found fewer escapes and disturbances at private prisons.[7]

A survey of inmates in Tennessee's Silverdale Detention Center provides further evidence of the ability of private management to substantially improve service quality. Inmates rated the facility highly on most issues, almost invariably better than the facility under previous management, leading the author of the study to conclude that "the evidence is overwhelming that the private takeover of Silverdale has resulted in substantial improvements in the institution's physical conditions and upkeep, as well as several critical areas of inmate service and institutional procedure."[8]

A Bureau of Justice Assistance study found that private prisons have slightly higher rates of assault on inmate and staff, but substantially lower rates of riots and inmate death,[9] as illustrated in an accompanying chart.

It is also useful to note that private corrections facilities are more than four times more likely than state-run prisons to obtain accreditation with the American Correctional Association,[10] certifying compliance with that organization's standards for quality of operation, management, and maintenance. Part of this discrepancy may be related to private prisons' need to demonstrate quality, whereas public prisons face no such scrutiny.

## Prison Privatization does not Mean Lost Jobs

While the impact of prison privatization on prisoners and taxpayers are the focus of this testimony—and should be the primary focus of policy makers—unions and employees of public prisons tend to be those objecting most to prison privatization.

An analysis by the Reason Foundation indicates that privatization of existing prison results in a 93% retention of employees, and often involve mitigating the impact of those laid off (often with early retirement options).[11] Much of the employment impact is controlled by a contract between the state and a private provider.

Furthermore, private prisons typically offer comparable compensation. These usually involve defined contribution 401(k) plans that may be as generous as traditional defined benefit pensions. Private prisons also frequently offer employees stock options, to take some ownership in the company[12]—this should be viewed both in the light of employee benefits and incentive for quality assurance.

Finally, it should be noted that given Pennsylvania's need for new prison capacity, prison privatization is most likely to be in the form of new capacity. Thus, privatized prisons would likely be additions to current state prisons, rather than replacements for state prisons. Thus, the State Corrections Officers Association should have no fear of fewer prison jobs, AFSCME should have no worries of less union dues, and lawmakers need not to worry about losing control.

## Summary and Conclusion

In short, private prisons allow Pennsylvania to address its growing need for corrections facilities, at a lower cost to taxpayers, while providing as good or better quality of service as existing state facilities.

I thank you for the opportunity to testify. I will be happy to address any questions you have, though I think most of the concerns over privately run prisons would better be answered by those involved in private prison management, or even representatives of their trade associations. Unfortunately, none of these groups were able to testify today, so I will do my best to answer your questions as best I can.

### Endnotes

1. Pennsylvania Department of Corrections 2007 Budget Request Presentation. www.cor. state.pa.us/stats/lib/stats/Budget2007.pdf
2. Bureau of Justice Statistics, "Prisoners in 2005." www.ojp.usdoj.gov/bjs/
3. Ibid.
4. Segal, Geoffrey and Adrian Moore, "Weighing the Watchmen: Evaluation the Costs and Benefits of Outsourcing Correctional Services," Reason Foundation, www.reason.org
5. Blumstein, James F. and Mark A Cohen, "The Interrelationship between Public And Private Prisons: Does The Existence Of Prisoners Under Private Management Affect The Rate Of Growth In Expenditures On Prisoners Under Public Management?," Corrections Corporation of America, www.correctionscorp.com/media/blumstein-report.pdf
6. Segal, Geoffrey and Adrian Moore, "Weighing the Watchmen: Evaluation the Costs and Benefits of Outsourcing Correctional Services." Reason Foundation, www.reason.org
7. Ibid.
8. Ibid.

9. Bureau of Justice Statistics, "Emerging Issues on Privatized Prisons," www.ncjrs.gov/txtfiles1/bja/181249.txt

10. American Correctional Association, www.aca.org

11. Segal, Geoffrey, "Frequently asked Questions about Prison Privatization, Reason Foundation," www.reason.org

12. Ibid.

> "The need for bed space created by our nation's bloated prison population has outstripped existing capacity, leading states and the federal government to go on a prison-building binge..."

# Private Prisons Hinder Reform, Expose Prisoners to Violence, and Increase Recidivism

*Alex Friedmann*

*In the following viewpoint, Alex Friedmann details why he believes prison privatization is detrimental to the criminal justice system. He states that those who run private prisons have hindered reform in sentencing and prison release policies. He claims private facilities also result in higher levels of violence and recidivism rates. Most objectionable of all to Friedmann is that this type of privatization has made it acceptable both politically and socially to profit from others' imprisonment. Friedmann is associate director at the Human Rights Defense Center and managing editor of Prison Legal News. He was incarcerated for 10 years in Tennessee, during which time he served as resources editor for Prison Life magazine.*

"The Societal Impact of the Prison Industrial Complex, or Incarceration for Fun and Profit—Mostly Profit," by Alex Friedmann, Prison Legal News, January 15, 2012. Reprinted by Permission.

As you read, consider the following questions:

1. What makes up the "Prison Industrial Complex" the author discusses?
2. What does Friedmann say is the problem with the additional capacity private prisons provide?
3. According to the author, where do private prison firms cut costs in order to increase their profit?

A t the beginning of the 1980s there were no privately-operated adult correctional facilities in the United States. As of 2009, more than 129,300 state and federal prisoners were housed in for-profit lock-ups. Prison privatization has become an acceptable practice and the private prison industry is now a multi-billion dollar business. How did this drastic expansion of incarceration-for-profit occur, and more importantly how has it rearranged the criminal justice landscape?

The prison and jail population in the United States has increased exponentially over the past several decades, from 648,000 in 1983 to more than 2.3 million as of 2010. That doesn't include another 5 million people on parole and probation, plus millions more who were formerly incarcerated and are no longer under correctional supervision. Spending on prisons has outstripped expenditures on higher education in at least five states, including Michigan, Connecticut and California, as lawmakers engage in one-upmanship to prove who's tougher on crime.

Why has our nation's prison population grown to epic proportions, until the U.S.—with only 5 percent of the world's population—now has 25 percent of the world's prisoners?

The succinct answer is because imprisonment has become enormously profitable as a result of politically-influenced decisions as to who should be locked up and for how long. In the 1980s and 90s a series of tough-on-crime laws were enacted, spurred by the so-called War on Drugs and the corporate media's steady and often sensationalistic coverage of violent offenses. Such laws included mandatory minimums, truth-in-sentencing statutes and three-strikes laws, which required lengthy prison terms or life sentences for certain offenders.

Consequently, more and more people were arrested, prosecuted, convicted and sent to prison where they served longer periods of time under harsher sentencing statutes.

Concurrently, prison release policies became more restrictive; for example, parole in the federal prison system was abolished in 1987. With more people entering the prison system to serve longer sentences and fewer leaving, the U.S. prison population grew rapidly – increasing over 350 percent from 1983 to the present.

This prison population boom created a market for companies that found they could profit by providing correctional services, and a multi-billion dollar industry was born to capitalize on crime and punishment. The industry, commonly referred to as the "Prison Industrial Complex," is composed of a confluence of business, policy and special interest groups that collectively profit from incarceration. The most overt members include private prisons companies such as Corrections Corporation of America (CCA), GEO Group (formerly Wackenhut Corrections), Management and Training Corp. (MTC), Cornell Corrections (acquired by GEO in 2010) and a bevy of smaller firms that operate detention facilities.

Beyond companies that own or operate prisons there are a number of other businesses that benefit from the prison boom – ranging from corporations that provide prison and jail food services (Aramark, Canteen Services), prison medical care (e.g., Prison Health Services and Correctional Medical Services, now combined into one company, Corizon), privatized probation supervision (such as Sentinel Offender Services) and prisoner transportation (TransCor, PTS of America), to the banks and investment firms that provide bond financing for new prisons, the construction companies that build them, suppliers of razor wire, surveillance cameras and other security equipment, etc. In short, the expansion of the U.S. prison population created an enormously profitable market opportunity. CCA alone grossed $1.67 billion in revenue in 2010; its closest competitor, GEO Group, grossed $1.24 billion.

The private companies that comprise the Prison Industrial Complex have thus reaped substantial monetary benefits by surfing the wave of overincarceration that has swept over our nation's criminal justice system. They are the ones that most obviously benefit from putting more people in prison for longer periods of time. But what are the collateral consequences of for-profit incarceration as social policy?

## Frustrating Prison Reform Efforts

Criminal justice policies in the U.S. are based in large part on capacity – that is, the capacity of state and federal prison systems, as well as sentencing and parole policies that govern the number of people entering prison and being released. The need for bed space created by our nation's bloated prison population has outstripped existing capacity, leading states and the federal government to go on a prison-building binge and, when that solution failed to accommodate growing numbers of prisoners, to overcrowd correctional facilities by double- or triple-bunking cells and installing beds in prison gyms, classrooms and even chapels.

However, overcrowding—which leads to increased violence, decreased access to medical care for prisoners and a host of other problems—can only go so far. At some point it becomes impossible or impractical to cram more prisoners into already-packed cells, and too expensive to build more prisons. Enter CCA, GEO Group and other companies that finance and build their own correctional facilities, which provide public prison systems with supplemental bed space capacity. Notably, if private prison firms did not provide such additional beds, then state and federal governments would be forced to address the harsh sentencing laws and prison release policies that have resulted in overincarceration and prison overcrowding.

## LOCKED UP AND SHIPPED AWAY

The number of inmates transferred to private prisons outside their home states decreased by about 3,000 between 2013 and 2015, but for-profit prisons continue to delay prison reform, according to a report published by the advocacy group Grassroots Leadership.

The January 2016 brief, entitled "Locked Up & Shipped Away: Interstate Prisoner Transfers and the Private Prison Industry," is an update to a November 2013 report which found more than 10,500 inmates from Vermont, California, Idaho, and Hawaii were incarcerated outside their home states—a number which had declined to 7,300 by 2015 due to reforms implemented in some of the states. However, one additional state—Arkansas—started transferring inmates out-of-state within the last two years.

The decline in California prisoners being transferred out-of-state (a 37 percent drop over two years) can be attributed in part to the 2011 Public Safety Realignment, the author of the study, Holly Kirby, said in an email. She added that the decline in Vermont can be attributed in part to the work of advocacy groups such as Vermonters for Criminal Justice Reform.

"While decreasing the number of prisoners sent to for-profit prisons across state lines is a step in the right direction, work remains to reduce incarceration and end the practice entirely. States should also avoid building new prisons, utilizing beds in local jails, or contracting with public facilities in other jurisdictions as strategies for addressing prison overcrowding," Kirby writes in the conclusion. "These strategies do not aim to reduce reliance on criminalization and incarceration and they perpetuate the mass incarceration crisis, which disproportionately harms the poor and communities of color."

"Locked Up and Shipped Away," by Gabe, The Crime Report, February 2, 2016.

Thus the private prison industry – the moving force behind the Prison Industrial Complex – has served to stymie criminal justice reform efforts over the past several decades, particularly in terms of sentencing and release policies. Rather than being forced to deal with the repercussions of such policies, government officials have used private prisons as a safety valve. As an analogy, if our prison system was a bucket being filled to overflowing by a steady stream of prisoners, the extra bed space provided by the private prison industry allows prisoners to be siphoned off into another bucket. So long as this additional capacity is provided by private prisons, government officials can postpone having to deal with such politically-unpopular issues as sentencing reform or decreasing the prison population.

Indeed, more sensible, socially-beneficial criminal justice policies are considered a threat to private prison firms. According to CCA's 2010 annual report, "The demand for our facilities and services could be adversely affected by the relaxation of enforcement efforts, leniency in conviction or parole standards and sentencing practices or through the decriminalization of certain activities that are currently proscribed by our criminal laws.

For instance, any changes with respect to drugs and controlled substances or illegal immigration could affect the number of persons arrested, convicted, and sentenced, thereby potentially reducing demand for correctional facilities to house them."

Although private prisons hold only 8 percent of state and federal prisoners, that is an important 8 percent. In 2009, private prisons were utilized by the federal government and 32 states, of which some have become dependent on privatization to accommodate their prison population levels. As of the end of 2009, ten states had 20 percent or more of their prisoners in privately-operated facilities, including New Mexico (43.3 percent), Montana (39.8 percent), Vermont (30.1 percent) and Hawaii (28.0 percent). The federal Bureau of Prisons houses 16.4 percent of its population in for-profit facilities – which does not include thousands of detainees held by Immigration and Customs Enforcement (ICE) in private detention centers. By leveraging a relatively small number of beds nationwide, the private prison industry has managed to forestall much-needed criminal justice reform that would address the problems of overincarceration and overcrowding in the U.S. prison system.

## More Violence and Increased Recidivism

Another deleterious aspect of the private prison industry is that, contrary to the claims of for-profit prison companies, prisoners held in privately-operated facilities are subjected to higher levels of violence. Also, when prisoners are released from such prisons they are less likely to be rehabilitated and more likely to recidivate.

Realizing why private prisons have higher levels of violence requires an understanding of the business model of the private prison industry and how the industry generates profit. At a basic level, public and private prisons have many simi-larities; both require cell blocks, fences, security staff, medical units, etc. In terms of operating costs, approximately 70-80 percent of a prison's expenses are related to staffing. Specifically, how many staff members are employed, how much they are paid, what benefits they receive and the amount of training provided.

Since such a high percentage of operating expenses are related to staffing, that is where private prison firms cut costs to generate profit. On average, they employ fewer staff members than comparable public prisons; they pay less than in the public sector; they offer fewer (or less costly) benefits; and they provide less training. These tactics undeniably reduce expenses for private prison firms and boost their bottom line, but at what cost?

There is substantial evidence to support the business model of the private prison industry described above. For example, according to the 2000 Corrections Yearbook, the average starting salary for private prison guards was $17,628 while the average starting salary in public prisons was $23,002. More recently, when CCA announced plans not to renew its contract to operate the Hernando County Jail in Florida effective August 2010, the sheriff said he would resume control over the jail. He also said he would increase the salaries of qualified CCA employees retained at the facility by more than $7,000 annually, to bring them in line with the salaries of the county's corrections deputies – indicating the pay differential between the public and private sector.

In terms of training for corrections employees, CCA vice president Ron Thompson stated in June 2010 that the company provides "a minimum of 200 hours of initial training, along with at least 40 hours of annual training." However, this is significantly less than the training that employees in some state prison systems receive. California, for example, requires "a sixteen-week, formal, comprehensive training program" consisting of 640 hours. In Alabama, state prison guards must "successfully complete 480 hours of correctional officer training at an approved Academy." The New Jersey Dept. of Corrections requires a "14-week, in-residence NJ Police Training Commission course."

Less training allows private prison companies to cut costs, but at the expense of employing staff who are less prepared for work in a prison setting.

In regard to job benefits, private prison employees do not enjoy government retirement plans, civil service protection or generous health insurance available in the public sector.

As a result of paying lower wages, supplying less training and providing fewer benefits, private prisons have much higher staff turnover rates than their public counterparts.

According to the last self-reported data from the private prison industry, published in the 2000 Corrections Yearbook, the average turnover rate at privately-operated facilities was 53 percent. The average rate in public prisons was 16 percent. More recently, a Texas Senate Committee on Criminal Justice report released in December 2008 found that the "correctional officer turnover rate at the seven private prisons [in Texas] was 90 percent (60 percent for the five privately-operated state jails), which in either case is higher than the 24 percent turnover rate for [state] correctional officers during FY 2008."

High staff turnover rates, in turn, mean less experienced employees who lack institutional knowledge about the facilities where they work, which results in greater instability in private prisons. Higher turnover also leads to under-staffing, as employees who resign or are terminated leave vacant positions that are not immediately filled. The 2000 Corrections Yearbook found that public prisons had an average guard-to-prisoner ratio of 1 to 5.6, compared with a ratio of 1 to 8 in private prisons—which reflects significantly less staffing at privately-operated facilities. Private prison companies have a financial incentive to keep staff positions vacant, as vacant positions mean reduced payroll costs and thus higher profits.

Understaffing, instability and fewer experienced employees result in higher levels of violence. Several studies have shown that privately-operated prisons experience more violence, including a 2004 report in the Federal Probation Journal that found private prisons had over twice as many prisoner-on-prisoner assaults than in public prisons. A 2001 Bureau of Justice Assistance report found that private prisons had 65 percent more prisoner-on-prisoner assaults and 48 percent more prisoner-on-staff assaults than public prisons with comparable security levels. A more recent 2011 examination of private and public prisons in Tennessee revealed similar results, with privately-operated facilities having higher average numbers and rates of violent incidents than public prisons.

There is also anecdotal evidence that security problems and violence are more likely to occur at private prisons as a result of the industry's business model, which results in high staff turnover and thus inexperienced staff and greater institutional instability. As just one example, during a four-month period from May to September 2004, CCA experienced four major riots at prisons in Colorado, Oklahoma, Mississippi and Kentucky, plus a hostage-taking at a jail in Florida.

A Department of Corrections report following the uprising in Colorado found that just 33 CCA guards were watching over 1,122 prisoners at the time of the riot—a ratio 1/7th that at Colorado state prisons (which had an average guard-to-prisoner ratio of 1 to 4.7). Some CCA employees had literally been "on the job for two days or less." The CCA facility had a 45 percent staff turnover rate, and CCA guards were paid an average salary of

$1,818 per month compared with $2,774 for state prison officers. As indicated above, these deficiencies are a direct result of the business model of the private prison industry.

Certainly public prisons experience riots, violence and other problems, too—but the frequency and severity of such incidents in private prisons imply that those facilities are more prone to unrest and instability as a consequence of how the private prison industry cuts costs in order to generate profit.

A related issue concerns the rehabilitation of prisoners in privately-operated facilities. Consider that for-profit prison firms have a vested interest in maintaining—and increasing—the number of people behind bars. The sole purpose of companies like CCA and GEO Group is to generate profit, not to ensure public safety, aid in the rehabilitation of offenders or reduce recidivism and thus decrease the amount of crime and victimization in our communities.

During CCA's annual meeting on May 14, 2010, CCA vice president Dennis Bradby confirmed that the company had not conducted any studies to determine whether the rehabilitative programs offered at its for-profit prisons were effective in terms of reducing recidivism. Independent research, however, has found that prisoners released from privately-operated facilities may have a higher rate of reoffending.

A 2003 joint study by the Florida Dept. of Corrections, Florida State University and Correctional Privatization Commission found that while there were no significant differences in recidivism rates among prisoners in private and public facilities, "in only one of thirty-six comparisons was there evidence that private prisons were more effective than public prisons in terms of reducing recidivism." More tellingly, a research study published in Crime and Delinquency in 2008, which tracked over 23,000 prison releasees, found that "private prison inmates had a greater hazard of recidivism in all eight models tested, six of which were statistically significant."

Thus, another outcome of the private prison industry is that prisoners are subjected to higher levels of violence due to the way private prison firms cut staffing costs to generate profit. Further, while the private prison industry benefits by keeping prisoners behind bars, those same prisoners are more likely to reoffend following their release—resulting in greater societal costs in terms of a recurring cycle of crime and incarceration.

## Institutionalizing For-Profit Imprisonment

Perhaps the most deleterious effect of the private prison industry is that it has successfully legitimized the concept of for-profit incarceration. While people might question the notion of a privatized police force that benefits financially when people are arrested, allowing companies to profit from people's imprisonment has become an accepted and normalized part of our nation's criminal justice system.

Private prison companies and other members of the Prison Industrial Complex do not operate in a vacuum, of course, nor are they solely responsible for crafting an industry that profits from incarceration. They certainly contribute to that state of affairs, though—sometimes literally. As with many other industries, private prison companies make campaign contributions to lawmakers and engage in political influence-peddling through lobbyists.

CCA, the nation's largest private prison firm, spent about $1 million in both 2009 and 2010 on direct lobbying expenses on the federal level alone. The company and its Political Action Committee further gave over $812,000 in federal and state political donations in 2009 and more than $722,000 in 2010. And that is just one company among many that comprise the Prison Industrial Complex. Through such spending, the private prison industry is able to influence and obtain the support of politicians to further its goals of greater investment in incarceration and expanded privatization in the criminal justice system.

Private prison companies also wield influence by hiring former public officials, mainly from corrections and law enforcement agencies, who use their connections to grease the political wheels that drive the private prison industry machine. CCA's executives and board members include a former director of Ohio's prison system, the former chief of facility operations for the New York City Dept. of Corrections, two former directors of the federal Bureau of Prisons, a former deputy assistant secretary of the U.S. Department of Defense, a former U.S. Senator and Thurgood Marshall, Jr.—son of the late U.S. Supreme Court Justice, who served as Secretary to the Cabinet in the Clinton administration.

The private prison industry has further enlisted supposedly-impartial research allies to produce studies that laud the benefits of privatization. For example, the Reason Foundation, a Los Angeles-based libertarian think-tank that promotes privatization of governmental services, receives funding from private prison companies—which it conveniently neglects to mention in its research. GEO Group was listed as a Platinum-level supporter of the Reason Foundation in a 2009 donor report, while CCA was listed as a Gold-level supporter.

Discredited former University of Florida professor Charles Thomas, who operated an academic project that studied the private prison industry, also produced research favorable to private prison companies. It was subsequently discovered that Thomas owned stock in the companies he was studying, sat on the board of Prison Realty Trust (a CCA spin-off) and had been paid $3 million by Prison Realty/CCA. Thomas retired from his University position after those conflicts became known; he was fined $20,000 by the Florida Commission on Ethics.

Additionally, members of the Prison Industrial Complex have formed their own industry trade group, the Association of Private Correctional & Treatment Organizations. APTCO and CCA jointly funded a 2007 Vanderbilt University study that, not surprisingly, found benefits from prison privatization.

More disturbingly, private prison companies have been accused of working behind the scenes to promote harsh sentencing laws that result in more people going to prison for longer periods of time – which, of course, benefits the private prison industry. For instance, in the 1990s and early 2000s, CCA executives John Rees and Brad Wiggins served on the Criminal Justice Task Force of the American Legislative Exchange Council (ALEC). ALEC is a powerful free-market organization that describes itself as a "public-private partnership" between state lawmakers and private-sector businesses. ALEC claims almost 2,000 lawmakers as members—one-third of the nation's state legislators—plus over 250 private companies and foundation members, including Wal-Mart, ExxonMobil, the American Bail Coalition and the National Rifle Association.

ALEC produces model laws that are introduced by legislative members in their home states. The organization's Criminal Justice Task Force (which has since been folded into the Public Safety and Elections Task Force) has drafted tough-on-crime model legislation for mandatory minimum laws, truth-in-sentencing statutes, three-strike laws and habitual offender laws—all of which result in longer prison terms that directly contribute to overincarceration and prison over-crowding.

ALEC has further promoted model legislation to benefit the private prison industry, including the Private Correctional Facilities Act, which permits state governments to contract with private prison companies. CCA senior director of business development Laurie Shanblum served as a member of ALEC's Public Safety and Elections Task Force, and in 2010 CCA was tied to ALEC model legislation introduced in Arizona, SB 1070, that is expected to result in an increase in immigrant detention. CCA operates three facilities in Arizona that house ICE detainees.

CCA has denied that it influences legislation that results in more incarceration or longer sentences. However, why would a private prison firm participate in ALEC except to influence criminal justice policy and help craft legislation beneficial to the company? The nation's second-largest private prison operator, GEO Group, has also been a member of ALEC, though both GEO and CCA no longer have active memberships with the organization.

By currying political favor through lobbying and substantial campaign contributions, by funding academics who produce supposedly-independent private prison studies, and by hiring former public officials, creating its own industry trade group and influencing criminal justice policy-making though participation in ALEC, the private prison industry has established its own legitimacy and ensured that profit trumps public policy when it comes to our nation's criminal justice priorities.

## Conclusion

This, then, is the egregious and lasting legacy of the Prison Industrial Complex.

While private prisons companies comprise only a small part of the overall corrections system in the United States, they have managed to hinder much-needed criminal justice reform— particularly in the areas of sentencing and prison release policies—by supplying supplemental bed space for overcrowded public prisons.

Prisoners held in for-profit facilities are exposed to higher levels of violence due to the private prison industry's business model of reducing staffing costs, which results in higher staff turnover rates, understaffing and instability. Prisoners released from privately-run facilities have higher recidivism rates, thus endangering public safety.

But the most harmful consequence of the private prison industry is that it has made imprisonment-for-profit politically and socially acceptable, thereby perpetuating an insidious business model that benefits from incarceration while instilling the notion that justice literally is for sale and crime does in fact pay—for private prison firms and their shareholders.

Hopefully, at some point in the future we will look back on this time when private prisons were considered sensible and wonder how such a socially-destructive concept was allowed to exist, much as we now look back on the institution of slavery. For now, though, we must deal with the harsh realities of for-profit prisons and their role in the Prison Industrial Complex, including their many flaws and harmful effects on prisoners, our justice system and society as a whole.

> "*Mass incarceration took root because
> we have a government that invests
> in policing and prisons to deal
> with problems...*"

# Private Prisons Are Not the Problem

*Daniel Denvir*

*In the following viewpoint, Daniel Denvir acknowledges that the system of private prisons may not be ideal, but states that reform in that area will solve only a small fraction of the larger problem— mass incarceration. According to the author, our country's focus on policing and punishment has created the issue at hand. Instead, Danvir argues, anyone wanting true reform will have to decide what our democracy truly stands for and work for change. Denvir has been a writer for Salon, the Philadelphia City Paper, and the Atlantic's CityLab. His work has also been featured in The New York Times, The Nation, Al Jazeera America, VICE, and The New Republic.*

As you read, consider the following questions:

1. Who does the author say most federal inmates in private facilities were in December 2015?
2. What entities have vested interests in what is called the "carceral state"?
3. What does the author say is the problem with placing negative emphasis on privatization?

"Private Prisons Are Not the Problem: Why Mass Incarceration Is the Real Issue," by Daniel Denvir, Salon Media Group, Inc., August 24, 2016. Reprinted by Permission.

The generally horrible state of the world entices people to blow small pieces of good news entirely out of proportion. Such was the case last week, when the Department of Justice announced that it would phase out the use of private prisons to hold federal inmates. Contrary to popular belief, however, private prisons play a very small role in American mass incarceration, as Vox's Dara Lind explained in a corrective tweet.

> Most prisons aren't private.
> Most private prisons aren't federal.
> Most fed private prisons are run by DHS.
> New memo affects 13 prisons.

As of December 2015, just 12 percent of federal prisoners were in private facilities, most of them immigrants convicted of offenses like illegal reentry. What's more, immigrants detained in private facilities pending deportation are in Immigration and Customs Enforcement custody, and won't be affected by the DOJ announcement. Those detention centers can be a deadly nightmare for the hundreds of thousands held in the majority-private system each year, according to a July Human Rights Watch report.

It would be a good thing if other federal agencies like the Department of Homeland Security, under which ICE operates, followed Justice's lead, as Human Rights Watch and The New York Times have proposed. But even if they did, the core problem is that our society incarcerates too many people, not the details of who incarcerates them or how. Roughly 193,299 people are still imprisoned in federal facilities (including 16,262 convicted of immigration crimes), the vast majority of which are public rather than private. Another 1.2-odd million people are incarcerated in overwhelmingly public state prisons, plus hundreds of thousands more held in local jails.

As of the end of 2014, just 8.4 percent of federal and state prisoners were incarcerated in private prisons. It's revolting that private business turns a profit from mass incarceration. But the carceral state — meaning a government that in recent decades has been fundamentally organized to police and punish en masse —

is a political problem, a disaster created and perpetuated by the state. Cutting private companies out of the deal won't make things that much better.

Libertarians certainly shouldn't gloat over this public-sector disaster: Economics has played a key role in the rise and persistence of mass incarceration, which is a problem not of too much government, but the wrong kind of government. As Marie Gottschalk notes in her book *Caught: The Prison State and the Lockdown of American Politics*, "the prison boom created and empowered new political and economic interests that have a large stake in maintaining the carceral state," including "guards' unions, private prison companies, public bond dealers, and the suppliers of everything from telephone services to Taser stun guns."

More generally, mass incarceration arose to discipline and control a disproportionately black economic underclass largely excluded from the post-war economic boom and negatively affected by the transition to a post-industrial service economy that has followed. Mass incarceration took root because we have a government that invests in policing and prisons to deal with problems—economic marginalization, addiction, mental illness, domestic and gun violence—instead of social services and decent jobs to prevent and ameliorate them. It's not just a budgetary tradeoff: the government's role in perpetuating inequality and segregation produces criminality and the criminals for the government to lock up.

The idea that mass incarceration is driven by a conspiratorial pact between government and business, or a prison-industrial complex, is undeniably seductive. To borrow a seminal phrase from anthropologist Claude Lévi-Strauss, it is "good to think" with: the relationship between a rampantly exploitative private sector and a complicit state ruled by oligarchs makes sense of a carceral status quo that feeds off and enforces dispossession and exploitation. It also jibes with the ideology of leftists, who were willing to criticize policies of mass incarceration long before that became politically trendy. After all, so much wrong with our society, from worker exploitation to environmental degradation, derives in significant part from the insatiable corporate appetite for profits. It's not a bad hunch. Private prisons appear to be the apotheosis of a political and economic system that values certain human lives at almost nothing.

But emphasizing private malfeasance is also appealing because it pins the blame for mass incarceration on a diabolical force external to our body politic. It conceives of Americans as the victims of mass incarceration instead of its perpetrators. In reality, government actions can be plenty horrible without privatization. It is the federal Bureau of Prisons, after all, that runs a supermax prison in Colorado where inmates are kept in solitary confinement for 23 hours each day, an institution where one prisoner "cut off both earlobes, chewed off a finger, sliced through his Achilles tendon, pushed staples into his face and forehead, swallowed a toothbrush and then tried to cut open his abdomen to retrieve it and injected what he considered 'a pretty fair amount of bacteria-laden fluid' into his brain cavity after smashing a hole in his forehead."

The roots of mass incarceration lie in a systematically corrupt system managed by a tangled web of opportunistic politicians, some of them sincere and some utterly cynical. Elected officials have used the prison system to mollify real public fears about crime—which can be considerably exaggerated, especially in an era when rates of violent crime have precipitously declined—and also to exploit racist paranoia and anti-civil rights backlash politics. Ending mass incarceration requires much more than rejecting shady contracts with private operators. It requires transforming a social contract that has never included poor people, especially those who are black.

Michelle Alexander, criticizing the notion that there is a quick technical fix to American policing, wrote that a real solution requires that we "get honest with ourselves about who our democracy actually serves and protects." The same holds true for our bloated prison system, which is filled by police and prosecutors enforcing democratically approved criminal statutes as ordered by the elected officials who ultimately supervise them.

Black Lives Matter, Occupy Wall Street and a broader youthful revolt against a status quo of mass immiseration have forced some progress. The rate at which people are being incarcerated has already declined; it's just not declining fast enough, given the huge number of people serving incredibly long sentences, to render this country's prison population less outrageous anytime soon.

The bad news is that the state made mass incarceration, and fighting privatization and profiteering aren't enough to undo it. The good news is that we live in a democracy, however flawed, and through the hard work of organizing a transformative political movement, critics can take the state over. It won't be easy. But the past few years of mass mobilizations in the streets and at the ballot box suggest that it can be done.

# Periodical and Internet Sources Bibliography

*The following articles have been selected to supplement the diverse views presented in this chapter.*

Paul Barrett, "Private Prisons Have a Problem: Not Enough Inmates; Investors are fleeing, so private operators are diversifying with halfway houses and check-in centers for drug offenders," BloombergBusinessweek, September 8, 2016. https://www.bloomberg.com/news/articles/2016-09-08/private-prisons-have-a-problem-not-enough-inmates

David Brooks, "The Prison Problem," The New York Times, Sept. 29, 2015. http://www.nytimes.com/2015/09/29/opinion/david-brooks-the-prison-problem.html?_r=0

David Dayen, "The True Cost: Why the Private Prison Industry Is About So Much More Than Prisons," TalkingPointsMemo.com. http://talkingpointsmemo.com/features/privatization/two/

Pamela Engel, "John Oliver Brilliantly Tears Apart America's Broken Prison System," Business Insider, Jul. 21, 2014. http://www.businessinsider.com/john-oliver-explains-problems-with-americas-prison-system-2014-7

Elizabeth Gudrais, "The Prison Problem," Harvard Magazine, March-April 2013. http://harvardmagazine.com/2013/03/the-prison-problem

Carrie Johnson and Marisa Peñaloza, "Judge Regrets Harsh Human Toll of Mandatory Minimum Sentences," Morning Edition—NPR.org, December 16, 2014. http://www.npr.org/2014/12/16/370991710/judge-regrets-harsh-human-toll-of-mandatory-minimum-sentences

Andrea Jones, "The Nation's Shame: The Injustice of Mandatory Minimums," Rolling Stone, October 7, 2014. http://www.rollingstone.com/politics/news/the-nations-shame-the-injustice-of-mandatory-minimums-20141007

Joseph Margulies, "This Is the Real Reason Private Prisons Should Be Outlawed," Time, Aug. 24, 2016. http://time.com/4461791/private-prisons-department-of-justice/

Ben Notterman, "America's Prisons: A Road to Nowhere," The Huffington Post, Nov. 24, 2014. http://www.huffingtonpost.com/opedspace/americas-prisons-a-road-t_b_6204554.html

Aviva Shen, "The Problem With the DOJ's Decision to Stop Using Private Prisons: The private prison industry will still have access to its biggest cash cow: immigrants," ThinkProgress.com, Aug 18, 2016. https://thinkprogress.org/the-federal-government-is-not-actually-ending-private-prisons-40e8c8dbf976#.f0lbz8ik8

Eric E. Sterling, Esq., "Drug Laws and Snitching: A Primer," Frontline—PBS.org, http://www.pbs.org/wgbh/pages/frontline/shows/snitch/primer/

Matt Zapotosky and Chico Harlan, "Justice Department says it will end use of private prisons," The Washington Post, August 18, 2016. https://www.washingtonpost.com/news/post-nation/wp/2016/08/18/justice-department-says-it-will-end-use-of-private-prisons/?utm_term=.b22fbc039853

OPPOSING
VIEWPOINTS®
SERIES

CHAPTER 4

# How Do We Perceive Crime?

# Chapter Preface

It might seem that few could argue over the perception of crime. Criminal behavior results when an individual takes some action that leads to the commission of an unlawful act. Say for example someone breaks into a house and steals the television, that's burglary. But what if there's more to the story? What if that person is stealing the TV in order to support a drug habit? Who or what is at fault—the person for committing the act, or the addiction that led to the act? What if other factors are at play—like mental illness, or even a genetic predisposition?

As the overcrowding in our country's prisons has come to reach epidemic proportions, criminal justice experts have sought to answer these questions and examine their relationship in our determination of punishment and rehabilitation for offenders.

Some ask, what would happen if we changed our definitions of violent crime? Is there a possibility society would actually become safer? Of course, the criminal justice system exists for a purpose—to maintain law, order, and public safety. However, these experts are searching for something beyond the status quo in order to find new ways to address criminal behavior and its resulting incarceration.

Some people say that evidence shows our criminal justice system is, for all intents and purposes, the new home for people with psychological problems. Modern-day professionals are looking at the link between crime and mental illness, and what the best course of action might be in dealing with perpetrators afflicted by such illness.

Another looming question is the number of prisoners incarcerated over drug offenses. Should drug crime be dealt with as an offense, or should treatment be a consideration? Another intriguing factor in the debate over how to stem the prison population is genetics; if a person is predisposed to crime, what's the best course of action—simply locking them up?

The articles in this chapter examine our perceptions of crime and how those may contribute to the systemic problem of mass incarceration.

> "The U.S. will not be able to
> meaningfully lower its incarceration
> rate without changing how the justice
> system treats people charged with
> and convicted of violent crimes."

# America Needs to Rethink Its Approach to Violence

*Marc Schindler*

*In the following viewpoint, Marc Schindler praises the move for reform that is taking place in the United States. However, he makes the argument that in order to truly make significant change, the approach to violent crime needs to shift. He discusses the public-health approach as one alternative, as well as other inroads that can reduce prison populations while still keeping communities safe. Schindler is executive director of the Justice Policy Institute. He provides commentary for news organizations such as CNN and NPR and has also published numerous articles and book chapters.*

"Defining Violence: America Needs To Reconsider Its Approach To Violent Crime To End Mass Incarceration," by Marc Schindler, Justice Policy Institute, September 13, 2016. Reprinted by Permission.

As you read, consider the following questions:

1. What does the author say is one reason that some justice-reform bills have been rejected?
2. What made the Neighborhood Engagement Achieves Results Act of 2016 significant?
3. What are some of the "bright spots" Schindler feels optimistic about in the movement to reduce the numbers of those incarcerated?

Now more than ever, there is widespread momentum for criminal justice reform. At the federal level, this month the Department of Justice announced its plan to phase out its use of private prisons. We are also seeing shifts at the local level in how jurisdictions are responding to crime. For example, in Washington, D.C., Council Member Kenyan McDuffie (D-Ward 5) led the way for the passage of the Neighborhood Engagement Achieves Results Act of 2016, which takes a holistic approach to addressing an uptick in homicides in the nation's Capital. And during its next session, Congress will again consider a bipartisan sentencing reform bill.

While there is still lots of work to do to reform our justice systems, I am cautiously optimistic by the way the conversation has changed on these issues and some of the changes we are seeing in policy. But, I also know that with the largest prison population in the world, including a disproportionate number of people of color locked up in adult and juvenile prisons across the country, America needs significant and bold reforms to reduce the imprisonment of more than 2 million people across the country and create a system that treats people fairly, regardless of race or ethnicity.

While the nation struggles with how to address one of the greatest public policy issues in its history, a JPI report takes a new look at the issue of mass incarceration and how America responds to violent crime. The report, Defining Violence: Reducing Incarceration by Rethinking America's Approach to Violence, notes that while there is currently more support than ever for criminal justice reform, the U.S. will not be able to meaningfully lower its incarceration rate without changing how the justice system treats people charged with and convicted of violent crimes.

Debates in state legislatures and Congress around criminal justice reform are often mired down over what constitutes a violent crime and how the justice system treats violent crimes. The reality is, significant reductions in our prison and jail populations cannot happen until we rethink our approach to violent offenses. Even with all of the momentum around criminal justice reform, the latest surveys show only a one percent reduction in the national prison population, and a slight increase in jail populations.

In some places, justice reform bills have been rejected if there is a hint that someone convicted of a violent crime might benefit. The conversations on the federal and state levels, as well as recent policy reforms, have focused on reducing the incarceration of people convicted of nonviolent offenses. Yet just under half the people in prison have been convicted of a violent crime, and meaningful justice reform must include rethinking how laws, policies, and practices treat these offenses if the nation is to see sustained reductions in incarceration.

Coming at a time when there has been very little change in national prison and jail populations, Defining Violence points to bright spots that show growing public appetite for a different approach to violent crime. Many of the laws enacted that have led to high incarceration rates followed spikes in crime. But just recently when D.C. communities were responding to growing concerns around crime, D.C. Councilmember and Chair of the Council's Judiciary Committee, Kenyan McDuffie, introduced and secured passage of the Neighborhood Engagement Achieves Results Act of 2016, which adopts a public health approach to crime prevention, and does not increase justice system involvement. The bill passed the D.C. Council unanimously.

McDuffie's NEAR Act is a step in the right direction for rethinking how we approach violence in the criminal justice system. We need to be moving towards policies backed by the evidence on what works best for sentencing, corrections, and criminal justice reform. We also need to think about how the way our systems treat violence in context with larger social policy discussions. McDuffie's use of a public health approach makes the right investment in protecting our communities against violence and crime.

Along with an increasing reliance on public health approaches to violence prevention, there are other bright spots around efforts to reduce the incarceration of people convicted of violent crimes. These include, significant reductions in juvenile confinement for violent crimes; reforms spurred on by the Supreme Court around juvenile life without parole that are allowing people convicted of violent crimes long ago to finally have a chance to be released; broader reforms being offered to parole that make decisions less reliant on the offense; and law changes that are chipping away at long prison sentences for violent crimes, including mandatory minimums.

These examples give me hope that we can build on the current momentum for criminal justice reform. To achieve more significant and meaningful reform, Defining Violence makes a number of recommendations for reducing our prison populations, such as: increasing prevention and intervention approaches to violence, reducing the number of offenses that result in incarceration, and using risk assessment tools in decision-making. By rethinking America's approach to violence and the way the justice system treats violent offenses, we can significantly reduce our prison and jail populations and make our communities safer.

> *"Of course crime control and due process logics are not pristine and mutually exclusive."*

# Countries Need to Consider the Purpose of the Criminal Justice System

*Richard Garside*

*In the following viewpoint, Richard Garside examines the theories and ideas behind criminal justice, taking a special look at crime control versus effectiveness. He compares the crime control model with that of due process and delves further to point out the relationship between a system of law and order and its implications on social structures. Garside heads the Centre for Crime and Justice Studies and was previously the head of communications for Nacro, a charity dedicated to reducing crime. He has written numerous articles, speaks at conferences, and serves as a commentator on crime, criminal justice, and social harm for print and broadcast media.*

As you read, consider the following questions:

1. In a quote used by the author, why is justice compared to a "delicate plant"?
2. How do the crime control and due process models differ?
3. What do Sanders and Young say are the implications of operating criminal justice in a society with marked differences in power and wealth among its people?

"The Purpose of the Criminal Justice System," by Richard Garside, Centre for Crime and Justice Studies, March 17, 2008. Reprinted by Permission.

What is the purpose of the criminal justice system? Consult the official website—www.cjsonline.gov.uk—and you will read the following under the "aims and objectives" section:

> The purpose of the Criminal Justice System... is to deliver justice for all, by convicting and punishing the guilty and helping them to stop offending, while protecting the innocent.

Or consider the following, from Working Together to Cut Crime and Deliver Justice, the criminal justice strategic plan published in November 2007:

> The central purpose of the Criminal Justice System is to deliver an efficient, effective, accountable and fair justice process for the public.

A similar tone was set by the Policy Green Paper published in early March 2008 by the Conservative Party, entitled "Prisons with a purpose." Replete with crime control aspirations, the paper observed, in relation to prisons:

> Prisons should reduce crime in three principal ways: by incapacitating offenders, by punishing and thereby deterring others who would commit crimes, and by rehabilitating offenders.

The main challenge was that of making the prisons system and the processes associated with dealing with prisoners more effective and efficient.

With their appeal to a utilitarian efficiency and an instrumental logic—protecting the innocent and punishing the guilty—these statements offer a picture of criminal justice as being in the business of crime control. The challenge is one of effectiveness.

A rather different note was struck by Jack Straw in his first major speech as Lord Chancellor in July 2007. What was "fundamental to the welfare and happiness" of citizens, he argued, was strong public institutions, properly managed, "and above all whether all... citizens, poor or rich, low or high got justice against the powerful, and the state." He went on to draw out the implications for the justice system:

We are blessed in the United Kingdom by a judiciary whose integrity, independence, professionalism and skill are not in question. But we take such a condition for granted at our peril. Justice is a delicate plant. It has to be nurtured, protected, cared for.

The justice system on this account presents a bulwark against the potentially overweening power of the state and other vested interests. A concern for due process, checks and balances, core values and an underlying institutional strength inform this perspective, rather than the pragmatic appeal to the effective and efficient control of crime.

It was the American legal scholar Herbert Packer who first proposed that the competing logics of "crime control" and "due process" exercised varying influence on the operations of the US criminal justice process. Under the crime control model, the underlying logic of the criminal justice is to contain and repress criminal behaviour. Successful criminal detection, prosecution and conviction are hallmarks of an effective criminal justice model. The due process model, on the other hand, places at least as much emphasis on protecting the rights of the innocent as it does on convicting the guilty. The protection of individual liberty in the face of a potentially over-powerful state is a key preoccupation of the due process model.

Packer's contrast between crime control and due process was developed in the context of the US criminal justice process. Yet it is possible to consider recent debates on criminal justice in England and Wales in the categories he developed.

Of course crime control and due process logics are not pristine and mutually exclusive. The very fact that Jack Straw can both express due process concerns, while also being a senior minister responsible for the implementation of the government's criminal justice strategy suggests as much.

But disputes between crime control and due process considerations tend also to boil down to questions of degree and emphasis. Crime control advocates might argue that a misguided attachment to certain protections historically afforded to suspects hampers convictions. But the principle of appropriate protections is not, generally, denied. Due process advocates might champion enhanced protections for suspects in police custody. But one would have to search hard to find someone who would oppose any questioning of suspects in police custody.

The debate over the appropriate balance between due process protections and the crime control imperative, in other words, tends to be dominated by disagreements of a largely procedural kind. Such procedural debates are obviously vitally important. A society that shows indifference to the processes by which those deemed to have breached the laws of the land are dealt with is unlikely to be a society in which the rights of individuals are respected.

But on their own, procedural debates offer little insight into the social context and political-economic structures within which the criminal justice process operates. In order to explore this question, consider the following definition of criminal justice, taken from Andrew Sanders and Richard Young's standard textbook on the subject. Criminal Justice, they write:

> is... a complex social institution which regulates potential, alleged and actual criminal activity within procedural limits supposed to protect people from wrongful treatment and wrongful conviction.

Criminal justice practices, they go on to note, "are inherently coercive." This focus on criminal justice as a set of often coercive social regulatory institutions, and not merely a collection of "crime fighting" agencies, throws a spotlight on the broader social purpose of criminal justice, rather than merely considering its operations within the framework of a fight against crime versus the protections afforded suspects.

But then criminal justice, as a social regulatory set of institutions, operates within a society characterised by notable inequalities in wealth and power. What is the implication of this for the operations of criminal justice? For Sanders and Young they are very clear. "[I]n a society in which power, status and wealth are unequally distributed along lines such as age, gender, race, and class, much criminal justice activity will compound wider social divisions," they write. They go on to argue that the "enforcement of the criminal law... reinforces a hierarchical social order which benefits some while disadvantaging others."

Now Sanders and Young are hardly red in tooth and claw revolutionaries. Their scholarship sits squarely within the parameters of liberal critique. But while liberal scholarship has many strengths, it also has its limitations. Take, for instance, the perspective set out by the Marxist political scientist Ralph Miliband over thirty years ago, on the differences between a liberal and a Marxist view on the nature of social conflict and its resolution:

> In the liberal view of politics, conflict exists in terms of "problems" which need to be "solved". The hidden assumption is that conflict does not, or need not, run very deep; that it can be "managed" by the exercise of reason and good will, and the readiness to compromise and agree... The Marxist approach to conflict is very different. It is not a matter of "problems" to be "solved" but of a state of domination and subjection... Ultimately, stability is not a matter of reason but of force... and the notion of genuine harmony is a deception or a delusion.

The reason for quoting Miliband's analysis is that it implies a rather different take on the purpose and nature of criminal justice. From a Marxist perspective—at least if we take Miliband as the reference point—the purpose of criminal justice might be characterised as the ongoing maintenance of class domination by means of coercive force, legitimated by legal norms. Thus, of the four functions of the capitalist state identified by Miliband the first of them is the maintenance of law and order; what he dubs "the repressive function." The "state is always involved" in the processes of criminal justice, Miliband argues, if only because it defines the nature of "legal norms and sanctions."

It is not necessary to subscribe to Miliband's politics, nor Sanders and Young's liberalism, to acknowledge the critical purchase they offer to an understanding of criminal justice.

In different ways they pose the challenge to take seriously the relationship between social structures and social processes on the one hand, and normative principles in relation to criminal justice on the other.

A concern with the appropriate principles and priorities that guide the operations of the criminal justice process remains an important and necessary task. But a theory of criminal justice that does not take seriously the ways in which criminal justice might both regulate and manage underlying social antagonisms is likely ultimately to lead to bad policy and dubious outcomes.

> "*The question then arises concerning whether the hospital is the appropriate place for that individual and whether public safety is the only question at hand.*"

# The "Treatment Years" Approach Should Be Used for Mentally Ill Offenders

*Yuval Melamed*

*In the following viewpoint, Yuval Melamed takes a close look at the options in both treatment and punishment when perpetrators of crime are mentally ill. The goal, Melamed states, is to find the right balance between patient rights and maintaining public safety. After examining options around the globe, Melamed concludes the most reasonable solution to reaching that balance involves "treatment years," an approach in which a court determines the number of years for treatment based on the severity of a crime and risk to public safety. Melamed is deputy director at the Lev Hasharon Mental Health Center in Tel-Aviv, Israel.*

"Mentally Ill Persons Who Commit Crimes: Punishment or Treatment?", by Yuval Melamed, American Academy of Psychiatry and the Law, March, 2010. Reprinted by Permission.

As you read, consider the following questions:

1. In the European countries examined, what happens to an accused person if found incompetent to stand trial?
2. What U.S. case helped the idea of "guilty but mentally ill" to gain momentum?
3. What does the author claim are the benefits of the treatment years model?

## Abstract

In many countries, there continue to be conflicting opinions and mechanisms regarding the appropriateness of treatment and/or punishment for mentally ill individuals who commit crimes. The general population is concerned with public safety and often finds it difficult to accept the possibility that a mentally ill individual who commits a crime can be hospitalized and eventually discharged, sometimes after a relatively short time. In most countries the options of incarceration and hospitalization are available in concert. In some, incarceration occurs before hospitalization. In others, hospitalization is first, followed by a prison term. An additional option could be "treatment years." The court would determine the number of years of treatment required, according to the crime. This dilemma has no unequivocal solution. The goal is to reach a balance between the right of the patient to treatment and the responsibility of the courts to ensure public safety.

Should mentally ill individuals who commit crimes be referred to psychiatric treatment or should they be punished? In recent years, there has been increased awareness of patients' rights, integration of mentally ill individuals into the community, reduction of duration of hospitalization and of psychiatric hospital beds, and more ambulatory services.[1] However, rights entail corresponding civil obligations and responsibility for one's actions.[2] The public is concerned with safety and often finds it difficult to accept the possibility that a mentally ill individual who commits a crime (sometimes a serious crime) can be hospitalized and eventually discharged, sometimes after a relatively short time.

Although this outcome may be legally possible if the mental state of the patient has improved, potential danger and threats to public safety remain primary concerns. There is no easy solution to this dilemma. The question of future risk can tip the scales in the direction of not releasing the patient from responsibility because of mental illness, even in situations when it might be appropriate. There are certainly cases in which a mentally ill individual who commits a crime is sent to prison. For example, in 1999, a patient with a history of schizophrenia pushed a woman he had never met onto the New York City subway tracks in front of an oncoming train, causing her death. Previously, he had been discharged from the hospital against his will. The jurors determined that he was mentally ill but guilty, because he understood the nature and meaning of his actions and because he told the police that he knew his actions were wrong.[3]

In many countries, there is an increase in the rate of court-ordered hospitalizations of mentally ill individuals who commit crimes. There is a trend toward criminalization of compulsory hospitalization: more court-ordered admissions and fewer hospitalizations for medical reasons. This situation is apparently the outcome of overcautiousness in the civilian process of involuntary commitment in response to increased awareness of patients' rights.

In Israel, the regional psychiatrists (who are responsible for civil commitment decisions in a designated district)[4] seem to have become more lenient and do not issue commitment orders for patients whose actions may have warranted involuntary hospitalization in the past. Psychiatric committees are now also more apt to release involuntarily committed patients who appeal their confinement. Thus, some mentally ill individuals who do not receive appropriate treatment may eventually commit crimes that lead to involuntary hospitalization by court ruling.[5] For example, cases of domestic aggression that previously resulted in involuntary hospitalization, as per commitment order by the

# The Case of John Hinckley Jr.

John Hinckley Jr., 35-years after he tried to kill a president, has won his freedom.

A federal judge…has granted a request for Hinckley to leave the mental hospital…to go live full-time with his elderly mother…

…Hinckley is not allowed to contact his victims, their relatives or actress Jodie Foster, with whom he was obsessed. Hinckley also will not be permitted to "knowingly travel" to areas where the current president or members of Congress are present…Hinckley could be allowed to live on his own or in a group home after one year.

"Mr. Hinckley shall abide by all laws, shall not consume alcohol, illegal drugs… shall not possess any firearm, weapon, or ammunition and shall not be arrested for cause," Senior U.S. District Judge Paul Friedman ordered.

[…]

Hinckley already spends 17 days each month with his mother in…Williamsburg, something that bothers his neighbor Joe Mann.

"It could be a grave mistake to try to force fit him into that community with his 90-year-old mother," Mann told NPR before the ruling. "What I think of is Hinckley may be OK as long as he is on his drugs. What goes off when he misses a dose or two? Or decides, I don't need this stuff?"

[…]

Levine said the voluminous court record demonstrates Hinckley is not a threat…"This case shows that people who are ravaged by disease, mental disease, can get well and become productive members of society without imposing any threat of danger," he said.

But Justice Department prosecutors…want to be able to monitor his whereabouts and his Internet use….former prosecutor Thomas Zeno explained why.

"The question with Mr. Hinckley is because he has this basic character flaw or personality flaw as it is called, of narcissism, can he really be changed? And will he really be a different person?"…

**"John Hinckley, Who Tried To Kill A President, Wins His Freedom," by Carrie Johnson, National Public Radio, July 27, 2016.**

regional psychiatrist, may now be referred to the police and result in compulsory court-ordered hospitalization.

## The Forensic System in Europe

The responsibility for forensic services differs among countries. It may be handled by the Justice Department (e.g., Greece, Italy, and Portugal), or by the Health Department (e.g., England and Germany), or there may be joint responsibility for forensic services (e.g., Belgium). In all countries, there is a consensus that the law relates to mentally ill individuals who have schizophrenia and other psychotic disorders.

There are countries that have a dichotomous, all or none, view of criminal responsibility, such as Austria and Israel. However, most countries have a graduated view that leads to partial responsibility and/or reduced punishment or treatment.

In all countries, the suspect has the right to an attorney, even if legal representation is contrary to the will of the accused. The courts are extremely cautious with regard to the prospect of the mentally ill representing themselves. In most countries, the cost of the attorney is covered by the department of justice, and the accused is not required to participate physically in the trial, though he or she must appear in court for the verdict.

In the case of incompetence to stand trial, most countries would suspend the trial. If the accused was ill when the crime was committed and is currently ill, in all countries, the patient would be sent to the hospital for treatment. The danger to public safety and illness-related threats become considerations when the patient was ill when the crime was committed, but is not currently ill.

## Treatment or Punishment

That there are many mentally ill individuals in the prisons (including those incarcerated under circumstances like the New York case described earlier) raises the question of whether indeed it is a desirable situation.[6] Today, there is more emphasis placed on the examination of the relationship between the crime and psychotic content. There is no longer an automatic exemption from responsibility for a criminal who has a chronic psychiatric illness such as schizophrenia.

This more focused approach does not necessarily mean that more patients will find themselves behind bars.[7] In addition, the option of partial responsibility in some countries leads to some prison time. In most countries, the options of incarceration and hospitalization are available in concert. In some, incarceration occurs before hospitalization. In others, hospitalization is first, followed by a prison term. In effect, this attitude can be described as a treatment/punishment ruling that integrates both concerns and contributes to public safety.

In the United States, the concept of guilty but mentally ill began in Michigan in 1975 and gained momentum following the United States v. Hinckley trial (1982).[8] Many states added this option to the insanity defense and did not abolish it. This verdict leads to a double stigma, and more prison time, because it implies that the accused committed the crime, was aware of the wrongfulness of the crime, but had a mental disorder that interfered with compliance with the law. This course was intended to be intermediary, but it did not reduce the number of rulings of not guilty by reason of insanity. A more severe course of punishment was created—one with no limitation on punishment, including the death penalty. The emphasis is on punishment and consideration of public safety and not psychiatric treatment in prison.[9]

Guilty but mentally ill is not a defense, but rather a court ruling that the individual is guilty and a candidate for punishment. The emphasis is on punishment and consideration of public safety and not psychiatric treatment. The discussion focuses on duration of hospitalization.

The common denominator between the treatment model and the punitive model is the concern for public safety and prevention of repeated endangerment. Repeat evaluations during hospitalization are necessary. In most countries standard risk assessment is performed with the PCL-R (Psychopathy Checklist-Revised) and

HCR-20 (Historical Clinical Risk-20).[10] Re-evaluation is generally performed every six months; however, there are countries that re-evaluate only once a year or even less frequently.

In Israel, the issue is deliberated in the Supreme Court, though from a different vantage point.[11] In a case in which the patient was hospitalized by court order for many years because his mental state did not improve, but the period of hospitalization by court order was based on a nonserious crime (theft of a bicycle), The Honorable Judge Barak ruled that the duration of hospitalization should not be longer than a prison sentence would have been for the identical crime. In the event that the patient's condition would require additional treatment, he would be transferred to the civilian course of treatment.[12]

In this case, it seems that the intentions of the Court concerned allocation of responsibility, since the ruling mandates the maximum, not the minimum, duration of treatment. Throughout the years, the pendulum has swung between punishment and treatment, between complete exemption from responsibility and limiting the insanity defense. For example, the insanity defense has been partially abolished in five of the United States (Montana, Utah, Idaho, Kansas, and Nevada); however, testimony regarding mental state is still permitted and mens rea must still be proved.[13]

## Combination of the Treatment and Punitive Positions

How, then, can the matter of treatment versus punishment be settled—the right of the patient to be treated versus the right of the public to be protected? Medically, there is room for the narrow approach when there is clear evidence that the crime is directly related to the illness. Discharge should be determined by a legal committee or by the courts, as is done in many countries. In England, for example, according to the Mental Health Act of 1983, the patient under court order is discharged as per medical decision by the physician, unless there is a restriction order, which can be declared by the Crown Court for a patient who has committed a serious crime. Discharge is then handled by the Psychiatric Committee, not the treating physician.

However, this could create a situation in which a person who is no longer psychotic would have to remain in the hospital because the legal committee did not release him. The question then arises concerning whether the hospital is the appropriate place for that individual and whether public safety is the only question at hand. The dilemma is raised of how to treat a patient (who committed a crime and was found not responsible for his actions) after his recovery from the psychotic state, to prevent mental relapse with danger to the public. In many countries, there is no legal recourse for prevention, a subject that may necessitate legislation. If the individual is no longer ill, but is still dangerous, should he or she remain in the hospital or be transferred to a nonmedical incarceration facility? The opinions are divided, although many believe hospitalization is most appropriate, since the core of the problem is the illness.

Administratively, there is an option for mandatory conditional discharge and/or compulsory ambulatory care following every court-ordered hospitalization. This option would allow for closer follow-up and would enable rehospitalization in the event of deterioration of the mental state that could create a risk based on prior proven dangerousness. Discharge and transfer to the community should be gradual. After prolonged hospitalization in a closed ward, the patient needs assistance and close supervision for a designated period. The aim is to assist the patient when necessary and to protect the public. In a few countries, such as Germany and The Netherlands, discharge is always conditional, and thus appropriate community outpatient facilities are needed that are not available in all countries.

An additional option could be "treatment years." The court would determine the number of years of treatment required, according to the severity of the crime and the risk to public safety. The treatment setting would be determined by medical professionals in accord with the decision of a psychiatric committee, under court supervision when necessary, with the option to appeal. When in a psychotic state, the patient would be hospitalized but would later be a candidate for a rehabilitation program, once his condition improved. He would then be eligible to be transferred to ambulatory care, with the approval of the psychiatric committee. Ambulatory care would be mandatory after discharge, and the frequency of visits and treatment would be determined by the attending physician. Follow-up visits would be required at least monthly for severe crimes. In addition to the regular medical follow-up, legislation would be necessary to enable supervision by a parole officer who would be responsible for enforcing compulsory ambulatory treatment. If the patient's condition were to deteriorate, he would be readmitted based on the original treatment years order, until stabilized. This solution is low in cost, considering that it makes use of existing treatment facilities, with the addition of a parole officer who would have the authority to enlist the help of the police to enforce compulsory treatment when necessary. Guaranteed ongoing treatment is economical and could help avoid exacerbation of the patient's condition and thus reduce the risk of recidivism.

## Conclusions

The dilemma of whether to treat or punish has no unequivocal solution. Every option has benefits and disadvantages. These alternatives contribute to the public's peace of mind and to the patient's welfare. In the end, the patient must return to the community. The goal is to reach a balance between the rights of the patient to treatment and the responsibility to ensure public safety. The balance between patients' rights, the right to treatment, and public safety is taken into account with the "treatment years" approach.

### Endnotes

1. Christodoulou G, "Psychiatric reform revisited," World Psychiatry 8:121–2, 2009
2. Melamed Y, Ganot N, Mester R, et al, "The civil liability for damages of the criminally insane," Isr J Psychiatry Relat Sci 45:285–90, 2008

3. Waldman, A, "Woman killed in a subway station attack," The New York Times. January 4, 1999, B3

4. Kalian M, Witztum E, "The Israeli model of the 'district psychiatrist'—a fifty-year perspective," Isr J Psychiatry Relat Sci 43:181–97, 2006

5. Salize HJ, Dreissing H, "Placement and treatment of mentally ill offenders: legislation and practice in EU member states," Final report, February 15, 2005. Available at http://ec.europa.eu/health/ph_information/implement/wp/mental/docs/ev_20050530_co04_en.pdf.

6. Baillargeon J, Binswanger IA, Penn JV, et al, "Psychiatric disorders and repeat incarcerations: the revolving prison door," Am J Psychiatry 166:103–9, 2009

7. Zemishlany Z, Melamed Y, "The impossible dialogue between psychiatry and the judicial system: a language problem," Isr J Psychiatry Relat Sci 43:150–4; discussion 155–8, 2006

8. *United States v. Hinckley*, 672 F.2d 115 (D.C. Cir. 1982

9. Melville JD, Naimark D, "Punishing the insane: the verdict of guilty but mentally ill," J Am Acad Psychiatry Law 30:553–5, 2002

10. Nicholls TL, Ogloff JR, Douglas KS, "Assessing risk for violence among male and female civil psychiatric patients," the HCR-20, PCL:SV, and VSC. Behav Sci Law 22:127–58, 2004

11. Toib JA, "Civil commitment and the criminal insanity plea in Israeli law," Int J Law Psychiatry 31:308–18, 2008

12. 3854/02 Israeli Supreme Court, *Anonymous v. the Regional Psychiatric Committee*, 22 January, 2003

13. Hathaway M, "The moral significance of the insanity defence," J Crim Law 72:310–17, 2009

> *"The genetics revolution, for one, is searching for the roots of crime in our DNA."*

# Alternative Ideas Like Genomics Should Be Considered in Approaching Punishment and Rehabilitation

*Sohail Inayatullah*

*In the following viewpoint, Sohail Inayatullah explores the future of crime and prisons, mainly the debate over rehabilitation and punishment. He provides examples of social construction and offers genomics as an interesting new variable in the criminology discussion. He also identifies possibilities for the future: gene testing, gene therapy, and even genetic modification. Ultimately, the key, he maintains, is that corrections focus on differentiating among criminal types. Inayatullah is a professor at the Graduate Institute of Futures Studies at Tamkang University, Taiwan. He has written over 300 journal articles, book chapters, encyclopedia entries, and magazine pieces; is co-editor of the Journal of Futures Studies; and is associate editor of New Renaissance.*

"Crime and Prisons: Beyond the Rehabilitation and Punishment Debate," by Sohail Inayatullah, PROUT Globe, May, 2011. Reprinted by Permission.

As you read, consider the following questions:

1. What aspects are considered in the "what works" model the author discusses?
2. According to biosocial criminologist Kevin Beaver, what behavior is tied to the MAOA gene?
3. What are the differences among those who are criminals by instinct, criminals by habit, and criminals by necessity?

While the rest of the world is undergoing dynamic change—genomics, democratization in Southwest Asia, digitalization, the rise of Chindia, the development of alternative energy such as solar—prisons are often considered static. They are hidden away from the eyes of the public unless there is a prison escape or if someone released on parole re-offends. However, prisons and policing are also in the process of radical restructuring.

Generally the debate in this restructuring has been between rehabilitation, humanizing the prisons, and punishment, seeking stricter and longer punishment for offenders. But the external changes through the field of genomics, ecological design and through soft technologies such as meditation, yoga and biopsychology are changing prisons as well. Moreover, prisons themselves are being seen as organizations and thus in need of strategic planning, and indeed, some correctional facilities are attempting to become learning organizations, reflecting on their alternative futures and their desired visions. Based on literature on prisons and foresight workshops with correctional and police leaders, alternative futures of prisons are explored.

[…]

## Rehabilitation

In the USA and most developed nations, the main debate as to the futures of justice is between rehabilitation and punishment. Those on the rehabilitation side believe crimes are generally committed because of social and economic reasons. They also argue that crime and criminality is socially constructed, and thus, not a "god given" universal context but one that is created through historical practice.

The argument is: Born into a poor family, or a single parent family, a person goes to a second-rate public school that labels them under-achievers. Over time, they see themselves as not very worthwhile. Eventually (and especially if there is a nominal increase in their wealth) noticing their relative deprivation—that others are driving fancier cars, have more "perfect" wives and girlfriends, live in beautiful estates—and accompanied by a trigger event, they steal, or commit other crimes.

Imprisoning someone like that merely adds to the problem. In jail, offenders rarely learn new skills, except how to be a more successful criminal. Their peer group consists of other prisoners, with similar stories. When they are released from prison, they stay within their[5] learned behavior and thus are likely to commit crimes again. For police, it becomes the story of arresting the "usual suspects."

If you believe in this perspective—rehabilitation—the reform interventions needed are multifold:

(1) Remove class barriers. Ensure that the possibility to move from lower to middle class and even to the upper class is there for all. Society should be based on merit. Equity. Equity. Equity.

(2) Help single parent families. By ensuring that children of single-parent families do not fall into the poverty trap, the chances of future crimes is reduced. Funding can come through various programs. Ensuring a nutritious breakfast for children (for body and brain development), housing allowance, unemployment insurance, counseling; indeed, any intervention that helps those outside of the merit system get the benefits that others are getting, and that increases the possibility of them feeling they are part of society is to be encouraged. And: it is crucial that a dependency trap not be created such that there is resentment on both parties—the state providing the benefits and the recipient who now becomes a welfare victim. Social justice should not be confused for psychological entitlement.

(3) Promote finer peer groups. As children grow, and develop peer groups, intervention comes through job training, sports camps, and community clubs—again anything to ensure that children do not start on paths of crime, and that they remain integrated in the family and broader community.

(4) Create learning and healing communities. Ultimately intervention is about healing communities, reweaving the fabric of friendship, helping peers see that we are all in this together.[6]

(5) Rehabilitate through transforming the prison. The rehabilitation model in prisons as well works to ensure that when the prisoner is released he will leave behind his previous behavior and start afresh. Interventions go from the simple of changing diet (research suggests that diets rich in fruits and vegetables and low in refined sugar reduce prison violence), changing the colors of prison cells, giving prisons meaningful work, prison gardens (so inmates can connect with nature), and work training.[7]

(6) Use alternative sentencing. As much as possible, and where appropriate, keep those who have committed crimes out of prisons: whether through electronic sentencing or half-way houses, or volunteering ensure that those sentenced find ways to reconnect, to psychologically earn their way back into society.[8] European nations have especially had success with this approach.

In this model—aspects of what now are called in the social policy profession the "What works" model—the goal is to ensure the prisoner (and victim, community) is healed ... that connections between self, nature, god, and community are remade, restored. Once balance is restored, the chances of the prisoner re-offending are diminished. The scientific evidence is that this model does work.[9]

(7) Finally, if the offender or the person on the margin is from a non-dominant ethnic background there are many instances where culturally appropriate dispute resolution is important. Re-integrating back to the community may mean not using the dominant legal system but using restorative justice that is more

culturally attuned. This is not universally applicable but there are cases where culture is crucial in policing and sentencing.

## Punishment

In contrast, is the punishment model. The argument is that all the rights are given to the offender and to the marginal. And the victim—who may have been raped, or maimed—has none. In this approach, the best way to reduce present-day and future crimes is to keep serious offenders in jail. And there is evidence that backs this up—twenty-five percent of criminal activity can be reduced by lengthy prison sentences.[10] Underneath this approach is the view that if we do something wrong, we should be punished. We have sinned, whether against our community, ourselves, or our understanding of God. Merely focusing on rehabilitation sends a signal of weakness to potential criminals. It also frustrates police who tire of repeat offenders. Thus, the most extreme version of this is the death penalty. While most Western nations have eliminated it—seeing it as repugnant murder grievously committed by the State—the USA continues this ancient practice. As do most traditional feudal nations (some of which would have anadulterous woman stoned to death, a sentence generally protested by certain other nations, including the USA).

The punishment model as well supports the: (1) the war on drugs, (2) the transformation of the prison through new surveillance technologies (making it safer for guards, in particular), (3) restorative justice for victims, and (4) privatizing prisons, to make them more efficient and cost-effective.

## Genomics—A New Variable?

The debate between rehabilitation and punishment is being challenged on a multiple fronts, especially from revolutions in science and technology, hard and soft. Three are pivotal: genomics, digital technologies and soft technologies behavior modification methods such as meditation, yoga and diet.

The genetics revolution, for one, is searching for the roots of crime in our DNA. If certain individuals are more inclined toward committing crimes—as by their risk-taking proclivities—we should intervene to ensure they do not behave in this way in the future.

This means mapping our genes and our theories of the factors of crime. Intervention could take the form of gene therapy (healing the damaged gene array) or germ line intervention (ensuring the faulty gene is eliminated so that future generations do not inherit that fault).

Thus, the science of genetics joins criminology in a search for genetic solutions to crimes. These solutions can be done at various phases in the "chain" of crime, even afterwards (in rape cases, judges have sentenced individuals to take castrations drugs).

As mapping the human genome becomes cheaper, from a million dollars to 50,000 per genome to 5,000$ [11]—and very soon less than a 1000$—every child in wealthy nations at birth will most likely be given a life diagnostic map with the main risks factors identified.[12] While currently the information of genome diagnostic sites is health focused—disease identification probabilities—we can well imagine "tough-on-crime" parliaments suggesting that police use it to identify those at high-risk for offending, for example, young males who drive and are prone for alcohol abuse. [13] There is already initial evidence for the aggression or warrior gene.[14] Biosocial criminologist Kevin Beaver of Florida State University's College of Criminology and Criminal Justice argues that young males who carry the MAOA gene are more likely to join gangs and engage in violence.[15]

"While gangs typically have been regarded as a sociological phenomenon, our investigation shows that variants of a specific MAOA gene, known as a 'low-activity 3-repeat allele,' play a significant role. " Previous research has linked low-activity MAOA variants to a wide range of antisocial, even violent, behavior, but our study confirms that these variants can predict gang membership," says Beaver. "Moreover, we found that variants of this gene could distinguish gang members who were markedly more likely to behave violently and use weapons from members who were less likely to do either." [16] As the genome becomes cheaper to sequence—a map for all—and as the technology becomes more available—an application (an app) for all—not only will genomics be used after the fact—forensics—but as well as part of social policy, as central to the rehabilitation and punishment debate. If we know that an offender is more likely to have the genetic variation that enhances his likelihood for criminal behavior is more punishment warranted or does it behoove society to enhance rehabilitation … or is genetic modification the next route?

[…]

## Crime and Its Future Based on Our Views of Justice

Crime and corrections are based on our deep held, unconscious view of criminality.[20] While science and technology, hard and soft, race ahead, many penal institutions remain lost in time. The ideas that govern them remain based on traditional notions of crime and punishment (sin and hell) and traditional notions of imprisonment (the prison, the cell, the jailor, the watchful eye).

If we wish to transform these places, we need to ask what is our preferred view of justice and policing, crime and corrections? Which would be the most serious crimes? Which less serious? Would you still have prisons? If so, how would they be designed? What are the appropriate roles of other stakeholders such as police, courts, communities and others in the Department of Justice. Seen this way, the futures of crime and corrections is less about forecasting new technologies, climate change, levels of globalization, demographic shifts, or social movements, and more about asking what type of world do we really want to live in? And, what steps can we initiate today to help create that world?

## PROUT Policy and Corrections

Prout policy on prisons is focused on differentiating the type of offender.[21] Generally "criminals by instinct" require a team approach: a medical doctor, a psychologist, a counselor, a geneticist and as well, Sarkar, suggests a teacher of yoga and meditation. Quarantining them from others is crucial, as they can harm others directly and indirectly. Other types of offenders, such as "criminals by habit" require far more caution as they are well organized in their criminal activities. On the other hand, for "criminals by necessity" changing the socio-economic system so that there is social support (basic necessities) is far more important. Placing this type of offenders in prisons is nonsensical from a Proutist view. Indeed, Sarkar recommends social revolution in this case. Generally Prout policy on prisons has seven prongs.

First, Prout supports the meditation in prison program and suggests it go from a trial program to nation-wide, indeed, global.

Second, along with meditation Prout recommends the use of scientific research to alter the physical and social environment of prisons, including vegetarian food, regular exercise and yoga.

Third, Prout recommends early intervention as much as possible. This means financial support for at-risk groups: vulnerable families, single mothers with children and others who may resort to crime for opportunistic reasons.

Fourth, Prout suggests that we need to be tough on the causes of crime: poverty, injustice, alienation and lack of meaning. Social change is required.

Fifth, Prout focuses on city design. Cities need to be designed to enhance equity and prosperity, to include nature in cities, for example, thus enhancing well being. Lighting in cities is crucial, creating well lit green spaces. And, as much as impossible, decentralize industry so cities are less burdened by large populations. Decentralization is crucial to reduce crime.

Sixth, Prout recommends rethinking prison design. Intelligent use of space can reduce violence in prisons. Enhancing biodiversity through gardens can enhance the psychological well-being of inmates. Feng-shui as well can assist in making prisons places where those that wish to be healed can do so. Seventh, for repeat offenders then prisons are important. But even there, the purpose of the prison is not so much to punish, but to ensure that when released the offender can build a healthy life. Leading the world in number of offenders, as the USA currently does, is not an indicator of a successful society.

To conclude: Prout would focus on changing the social and economic conditions so that fewer enter prison. And while in prison, Prout would focus on using spiritual, biopsychological and ecological practices to increase the chance of rehabilitation. And once offenders leave prison, Prout would continue to monitor offering support and direction so there is every possibility of their reintegration in society.

# Notes

5. "New report links crime with poverty," Honolulu Advertiser (5 December 1999), A16.

6. For more on this, see S. Inayatullah, "The learning and healing organization," Executive Excellence (Vol 19, No. 12, 2003–2004), 20.

7. Randall Atlas, "Changes in Prison Facilities as a Function of Correctional Philosophy," http://cptedsecurity.com/atlas/index2.php?option=com_docman&task=doc_view&gid=19&Itemid=35. Accessed 23 February 2011.
Andrew Coyle, *The Myth of Prison Work. Kings College London International Centre for Prison Studies*, 2011.
http://www.restorativejustice.org/prison/01overview. Accessed 23 February 2011."Is it time to close the prisons ~ seeds of change", http://www.yesmagazine.org/issues/is-it-time-to-close-the-prisons. Accessed 23 February 2011.

8. See research publications at the Willem Pompe Institute for Criminal Law and Criminology, Utrecht University December 1996. Also see: http://www.esc-eurocrim.org/newsletter/July04ESCnewsletter. Accessed 23 February 2011.

9. Gene Stephens, "Preventing Crime: The Promising Road Ahead," The Futurist,(Vol 33, No. 9 Nov 1999), 29-34. Francis T. Cullen and Paul Gendreau, "From Nothing Works to What Works: Changing Professional Ideology in the 21st Century,"
The Prison Journal (Vol.81, No.3, 2001), 313-338. Jacinthe Allard, Carole Dolan and Pierre Cremer, eds, *Reflections of a Canadian Prison Warden: The Visionary Legacy of Ron Wiebe: an Unfinished Conversation*, Correctional Service of Canada, 2000. http://www.csc-scc.gc.ca/text/pblct/ronwiebe/2-eng.shtml. Accessed 23 February 2011.

10. Alfred Blumstein and Joel Wallman, eds., *The Crime Drop in America*, New York, Cambridge University Press, 2000.

11. http://bigthink.com/ideas/26394. Personal genome sequencing technology is now faster and cheaper – and fits on a table top. Accessed 21 January 2011

12. http://www.personalhealthmonitor.net/Features.html. Accessed January 10, 2010.

13. http://www.medicinenet.com/script/main/art.asp?articlekey=26119. A gene for alcoholism is discovered. Accessed 21 January 2011.

14. http://www.sciencedaily.com/releases/2009/01/090121093343.htm. Accessed 21 January 2011.

15. http://www.fsu.edu/news/2009/06/05/warrior.gene/. Accessed 21 January 2011.

16. http://www.fsu.edu/news/2009/06/05/warrior.gene/. Accessed 21 January 2011.

20. Crime and punishment is also based on the type of society. In a warrior dominated society, where issues of loyalty, honor and courage are foremost, punishment can be extreme. In warrior societies, as in Saudi Arabia or Afghanistan, hands are cut off for certain offenses. In modern societies, where bureaucratic rules are foremost, the process of law has become most important. While we can never know for sure if someone committed a crime, we do our best to ensure that the process of justice is fair. Thus, the rights of a possible criminal are read. To those who can't afford an attorney, the State provides a lawyer and a group of peer judges. The reasoning here is that it is far worse to punish an innocent than let the guilty go.

21. P.R. Sarkar, "Prout in a Nutshell." Part 2. Kolkata, India, AMPS, 1987, 1-23.

> *"In every year from 1993 to 2009, more people were admitted for drug crimes than violent crimes."*

# Drug Crimes Are the Main Driver of Imprisonment

*Jonathan Rothwell*

*In the following viewpoint, Jonathan Rothwell makes the case that drug-related crime must be viewed under two separate distinctions: 1) the number of people that have been imprisoned over a set period of time, and 2) the proportion at a specific moment in time. According to Rothwell, once the statistics are viewed this way, it's clear that drug crimes are the main force for incarceration, and that this incarceration affects blacks more than whites. Rothwell was formerly a fellow at the Brookings Institution's Metropolitan Policy Program and is now a senior economist at Gallup.*

As you read, consider the following questions:

1. In 2009, what was the median length of time for drug offenses in state prisons?
2. According to Rothwell, why would dealing with drug prosecution differently still make a positive change when it comes to mass incarceration?
3. How many more times are African Americans likely to be imprisoned in a state facility for a drug offense?

There is now widespread, bipartisan agreement that mass incarceration is a huge problem in the United States. The rates and levels of imprisonment are destroying families and communities, and widening opportunity gaps—especially in terms of race.

But there is a growing dispute over how far imprisonment for drug offenses is to blame. Michelle Alexander, a legal scholar, published a powerful and influential critique of the U.S. criminal justice system in 2012, showing how the war on drugs has disproportionately and unfairly harmed African Americans.

Recent scholarship has challenged Alexander's claim. John Pfaff, a Fordham law professor and crime statistics expert, argues that Alexander exaggerates the importance of drug crimes. Pfaff points out that the proportion of state prisoners whose primary crime was a drug offense "rises sharply from 1980 to 1990, when it peaks at 22 percent. But that's only 22 percent: nearly four-fifths of all state prisoners in 1990 were not drug offenders." By 2010 the number had dropped to 17 percent. "Reducing the admissions of drug offenders will not meaningfully reduce prison populations," he concludes.

Other scholars, including Stephanos Bibas of the University of Pennsylvania, and some researchers at the Urban Institute, have made similar points in recent months: since only a minority of prisoners have been jailed for drug offenses, only modest gains against mass incarceration can be made here.

## Stock versus flow

There is no disputing that incarceration for property and violent crimes is of huge importance to America's prison population, but the standard analysis—including Alexander's critics—fails to distinguish between the stock and flow of drug crime-related incarceration. In fact, there are two ways of looking at the prison population as it relates to drug crimes:

1. How many people experience incarceration as a result of a drug-related crime over a certain time period?
2. What proportion of the prison population at a particular moment in time was imprisoned for a drug-related crime?

The answers will differ because the length of sentences varies by the kind of crime committed. As of 2009, the median incarceration time at state facilities for drug offenses was 14 months, exactly half the time for violent crimes. Those convicted of murder served terms of roughly 10 times greater length.

## Drug crimes are the main driver of imprisonment

The picture is clear: Drug crimes have been the predominant reason for new admissions into state and federal prisons in recent decades. In every year from 1993 to 2009, more people were admitted for drug crimes than violent crimes. In the 2000s, the flow of incarceration for drug crimes exceeded admissions for property crimes each year. Nearly one-third of total prison admissions over this period were for drug crimes.

Violent crimes account for nearly half the prison population at any given time; and drug crimes only one fifth. But drug crimes account for more of the total number of admissions in recent years—almost one third (31 percent), while violent crimes account for one quarter.

## Being imprisoned and being in prison: The wider picture

So, as Michelle Alexander argued, drug prosecution is a big part of the mass incarceration story. To be clear, rolling back the war on drugs would not, as Pfaff and Urban Institute scholars maintain, totally solve the problem of mass incarceration, but it could help a great deal, by reducing exposure to prison. In other work, Pfaff provides grounds for believing that the aggressive behavior of local prosecutors in confronting all types of crime is an overlooked factor in the rise of mass incarceration.

More broadly, it is clear that the effect of the failed war on drugs has been devastating, especially for black Americans. As I've shown in a previous piece, blacks are 3 to 4 times more likely to be arrested for drug crimes, even though they are no more likely than whites to use or sell drugs. Worse still, blacks are roughly nine times more likely to be admitted into state prison for a drug offense.

During the period from 1993 to 2011, there were three million admissions into federal and state prisons for drug offenses. Over the same period, there were 30 million arrests for drug crimes, 24 million of which were for possession. Some of these were repeat offenders, of course. But these figures show how largely this problem looms over the lives of many Americans, and especially black Americans. A dangerous combination of approaches to policing, prosecution, sentencing, criminal justice, and incarceration is resulting in higher costs for taxpayers, less opportunity for affected individuals, and deep damage to hopes for racial equality.

> *"One third of state inmates and one quarter of federal inmates committed their offenses under the influence of illicit drugs."*

# Drug Laws Can't Be Blamed for Mass Incarceration

*David W. Murray, Brian Blake, and John P. Walters*

*In the following viewpoint, David W. Murray, Brian Blake, and John P. Walters argue that data has been distorted in order to show that drug-related crime has led to an increase in incarceration rates. The authors look at prison sentences, recidivism rates, and the relationship of drug use in the commission of crime in an attempt to show that dismissing drug crime is not only misleading but also dangerous. Murray co-directs the Center for Substance Abuse Policy Research at the Hudson Institute. He formerly served as associate deputy director (Supply Reduction) for the Office of National Drug Control Policy. Blake is a senior fellow at the Hudson Institute and Walters is chief operating officer.*

"The Real Connection of Drugs to Crime," by David W. Murray, Brian Blake & John P. Walters, Hudson Institute, October 20, 2015. Reprinted by Permission.

As you read, consider the following questions:

1. Why do federal prisons hold a larger proportion of drug offenders than state prisons?
2. What nondrug offenses are now driving the federal inmate population, according to the authors?
3. According to Bureau of Justice Statistics data used by the authors, how many of the drug-offense prisoners released in 2005 committed another offense within the next five years?

Few topics have been more distorted by politicians and media than claims about the criminal justice system in its various forms. When the offense involves illicit drugs (use, possession, or trafficking), the distortion becomes pronounced.

In large measure, a complicated set of data have been made even more difficult to grasp because of tendentious (and often false) assertions forwarded by drug legalization advocates, who seek to advance their own "reforms" by first misrepresenting the criminal justice facts. Moreover, though drug use overall is subject to confusion, distortion is even greater when marijuana is the drug in question.

An example of agendas distorting understanding is the effort to blame drug laws for the growth in incarceration. That effort seeks to convince a public otherwise disinclined to accept more drugs that current drug laws have created the supposed injustice of "mass incarceration." This is demonstrably untrue.

To answer with the facts, we will address several distinct dimensions of legal institutions concerning illicit drugs: prison sentences, recidivism of released prisoners, and the relationship of drug use to the commission of criminal acts. (We addressed the parallel issue of drug arrests in a previous study, showing that they are far fewer in proportion to drug use than drug reform advocates claim.)

We start with prison inmates, found in both state and federal prisons, and contrast the cumulative numbers of those imprisoned with those entering in a single year. In all cases, we will find that the proportion of drug offenses to the overall number of prisoners has been much overstated. Cumulatively, all drug offenders in both systems constitute 20 percent of inmates (303,800 out of 1,508,636 sentenced inmates).

## The Federal Prison System

The federal system holds 13 percent of all prisoners, but contains the larger proportion of drug offenders. This happens because many trafficking offenses, be they interstate or international, are specifically federal in nature. But even as the total number of prisoners has grown, the drug-offender percentage has declined steadily.

There were 52,568 federal prisoners in 1989 (those "under jurisdiction"), and by 2014, there were 191,374 (those "sentenced"— the categories shifted slightly over time, yielding slight variation in respective calculations). Yet the percentage of drug offenders in the total peaked in 1996, when it stood at 59.6 percent.

A 2014 publication from the White House showing the cumulative total of federal prisoners broken down to show drug offenses as the most serious charge, reveals that the proportion of drug offenders had dropped to 44 percent of all offenders in 2011. By 2014, the most recent data on sentenced drug offenders in the federal prison system shifted back to 50 percent of all federal inmates, an increase from the previous ratio due largely to recent inmate releases.

When we turn to inmates entering federal prison in a single year, data are more current, but show the same trajectory. In 1998, the proportion of drug offenders incarcerated for that year was 41 percent (vs. 57.8 percent of the 1998 cumulative "jurisdiction" figure).

By 2014, according to the United States Sentencing Commission (USSC), drug offenders (of all types) had fallen to only 32 percent (of 75,836 entering federal inmates, 22,193 were drug offenders). Importantly, 96.6 percent of entering inmates who were drug offenders were convicted of trafficking offenses, while only 0.9 percent were convicted of simple possession.

We can further break these data down by drug type, and by nature of the drug offense. Methamphetamine resulted in the largest subset of drug types with more than 6,304 incarcerations, while heroin produced 2,431.

Though recent legislative reforms have altered the mandatory sentencing guidelines regarding powder cocaine offenses (based on weight) compared to crack offenses (a former ratio of 100 to 1 has been amended to 18 to 1), there were only 4,959 powder cocaine convictions in 2014, compared to 2,439 crack convictions. Moreover, the number of crack cocaine inmates sentenced for simple possession was 0.3 percent, or no more than 7 people.

Finally, marijuana federal incarcerations totaled only 3,971. Marijuana offenses are overwhelmingly (97.6 percent) for trafficking, with a "simple possession offense" representing only 75 individuals (or 1.9 percent), with that conviction often resulting from downward plea-bargaining from more serious offenses.

To show the emphasis on traffickers, when asked in Congressional testimony how many drug possession offenders the Drug Enforcement Administration (DEA) refers for federal prosecution, Acting Deputy Administrator Jack Riley stated, "virtually none."

What, then, is currently driving the changing distribution of the federal inmate population? To a large extent it is a rising number of immigration offenses, according to a study by the Congressional Research Service. This fact is echoed for single-year entry for prisoners as well: in 2014 the USSC shows 29 percent were immigration offenders, while 32 percent were drug offenders.

## The State Prison System

The state prison system is larger, holding 1,317,262 sentenced prisoners cumulatively in 2014. The state prison inmate population has also grown over time, and the absolute number of drug offenders within that total has nearly doubled since 1989 from 120,100 to 208,000 (sentenced) in 2014.

Yet just as with the federal system, the percentage of drug offenders has declined since the peak year 1990 when it stood at at 22 percent. For 2014, those whose most serious offense involved drugs were only 16 percent of sentenced state prison inmates (drug possession offenses are only 3.6 percent of all state inmates).

While there has been a marked increase in the state prison population over the past few decades as America has gotten more serious about combatting crime, the data do not support the idea that drug offenses are the primary driver of those increases. Further, with regard to the current push to decriminalize or legalize drug use, there is no support for the assertion that convictions for drug use/possession are responsible for the sharp increases in either state or federal prison inmates.

## Sentencing Reform and Recidivism

And what of sentencing reforms leading to the release of large numbers of federal drug offenders? A substantial problem is recidivism, or re-offending within a relatively short period of time, as we have elsewhere recently argued.

Yet the press persists in misrepresentation. According to the Economist, advocating for prisoner release, "Given how high America's incarceration rate is, it is fair to say reducing it won't precipitate a crime wave. Many convicts serving long sentences were never generally dangerous, or have mellowed with age, and no longer pose a threat to the public."

But the data show otherwise. According to a Bureau of Justice Statistics study of prisoners released in 2005 and tracked for five years, 32 percent were drug offenders. Of these, fully 77 percent of those released re-offended within that five- year-period (57 percent of all offenders re-offended at only one year).

It is worth noting two features of a further breakdown of the 404,638 released prisoners in the study. First, the outcome is the same regardless of the type of drug offense (trafficking or possession); that is, either type of offense has comparable re-offense rates. Drug possession offenders had 78 percent recidivism, drug trafficking offenders, 75 percent.

Second, the percent of re-offenses where the subsequent crime specifically involved drugs reached 51 percent. More compelling, violent crimes were fully 25 percent of drug inmates' recidivating offenses.

These data clearly show if drug offenders are released through sentencing reform, both drug and violent crime will follow; to the extent that they are released early, the effect is to compress their criminal impact into a shorter period.

Further, inmates' prior arrest history matters. In this study, for all offenders, the mean number of prior arrests per released prisoner was nearly 11.

For those who had ten or more prior arrests, 86 percent re-offended within 5 years. (Even for those aged 40 and over, the recidivism for drug offenders was 71 percent.)

## Drug Use and the Commission of Crimes

Finally, there is the role of drugs in the commission of crime. According to another Bureau of Justice Statistics study, one third of state inmates and one quarter of federal inmates committed their offenses under the influence of illicit drugs. That holds for all crimes, not just drug offenses.

For state prisoners, 69 percent used drugs "regularly," and for 59 percent, that drug was marijuana (with 30 percent using cocaine/crack).

For federal prisoners, 64 percent used drugs "regularly," with 53 percent using marijuana (and 28 percent using cocaine/crack).

Even for federal trafficking offenders, 34 percent were using drugs at the time of the offense.

The same pattern holds for violent offenders. Of them, 49 percent of both federal and state offenders used drugs in the month prior to the offense. The number using drugs at the time of the violent offense reached 28 percent of state and 24 percent of federal prisoners. Homicide-specific rates of drug use in the month prior to the offense were 49 percent and 45 percent, respectively for state and federal prison inmates, with a respective 27 percent and 17 percent using at the time of the homicide.

## Policy Conclusions

By these data, we may conclude the following:

1. Sentencing reforms that result in the early release of prison inmates will increase the number of future crimes, and crime victims, through recidivism, while the effect will be concentrated in time, thereby stressing law enforcement and rehabilitation services.

2. Drug intoxication (including the most prevalent drug, marijuana), is deeply implicated in crime commission, including violent crime. It follows that enabling greater drug use will magnify the criminal impact, with the corollary that efforts to reduce drug use prevalence should help lower the incidence of crime.

3. In particular, decriminalizing or legalizing marijuana will have virtually no impact on prison overcrowding, but the attendant increase in drug-use prevalence nationwide will likely lead to increased commission of crimes, including non-drug offenses and violent offenses.

# Periodical and Internet Sources Bibliography

*The following articles have been selected to supplement the diverse views presented in this chapter.*

Lindsay Hodges Anderson, "Experts talk about reducing crime through a holistic approach," Harvard Gazette, April 23, 2009. http://news.harvard.edu/gazette/story/2009/04/experts-talk-about-reducing-crime-through-a-holistic-approach/

Brian Boutwell and J.C. Barnes, "Is Crime Genetic? Scientists don't know because they're afraid to ask," The Boston Globe, March 6, 2016. https://www.bostonglobe.com/ideas/2016/03/06/crime-genetic-scientists-don-know-because-they-afraid-ask/3lhGUVuNsfdJXjvhtaxPHN/story.html

Mitchell Chamberlain, "Are Genetics Responsible for Criminal Behavior? Many Prisoners Share a Gene Linked to Personality Disorder," Medical Daily, Sept. 13, 2016. http://www.medicaldaily.com/are-genetics-responsible-criminal-behavior-many-prisoners-share-gene-linked-397741

Samantha Cowan, "Defining Violence: It's Not as Simple as You Think," TakePart.com, Sept. 19, 2016. http://www.takepart.com/article/2016/09/19/defining-violence

Inga Fryklund, "The Link Between Drugs and Violence," The Huffington Post, July 26, 2016. http://www.huffingtonpost.com/inge-fryklund/the-link-between-drugs-an_b_11095430.html

Kathleen Miles, "Just How Much the War on Drugs Impacts Our Overcrowded Prisons, In One Chart," The Huffington Post, March 10, 2014. http://www.huffingtonpost.com/2014/03/10/war-on-drugs-prisons-infographic_n_4914884.html

Richard Prince, "How Media Have Shaped Our Perception of Race and Crime," The Root, Sept. 4, 2014. http://www.theroot.com/blog/journal-isms/how_media_have_shaped_our_perception_of_race_and_crime/

Regis University, "What Causes Someone to Exhibit Criminal Behavior?" 2016. http://criminology.regis.edu/criminology-programs/resources/crim-articles/what-causes-someone-to-exhibit-criminal-behavior

Filip Spagnoli, "Crime and Human Rights: Why Do We Impose Criminal Punishment?" The Daily Journalist, May 4, 2013. http://thedailyjournalist.com/thethinker/crime-and-human-rights-why-do-we-impose-criminal-punishment/

Ana Swanson, "A shocking number of mentally ill Americans end up in prison instead of treatment," The Washington Post, April 30, 2015. https://www.washingtonpost.com/news/wonk/wp/2015/04/30/a-shocking-number-of-mentally-ill-americans-end-up-in-prisons-instead-of-psychiatric-hospitals/?utm_term=.f675889f6255

Treatment Advocacy Center, "How Many Individuals with Serious Mental Illness are in Jails and Prisons?" November 2014 (update). http://www.treatmentadvocacycenter.org/storage/documents/backgrounders/how%20many%20individuals%20with%20serious%20mental%20illness%20are%20in%20jails%20and%20prisons%20final.pdf

OPPOSING VIEWPOINTS® SERIES

# CHAPTER 5

# How Do We Handle Crime?

# Chapter Preface

Most people would agree that there should be consequences for criminal conduct and that people who break the law should be punished in some fashion for doing so. Prisons are intended to restrain violent offenders and punish those who have committed crimes against society. In an ideal world, while under incarceration, rehabilitation would take place to help change behavior and return ex-offenders to the community as contributing members. The key, it would seem, is finding the proper balance between punishment and rehabilitation.

Because the United States has the world's largest prison population, it becomes increasingly important that we deal with offenders effectively—and fairly. But how do we solve these problems—what is the best tack to take? Prisons are now homes for many individuals with mental illness and addiction issues. In instances where mental illness or addiction are factors in criminality, it would seem that treatment should take precedence over rehabilitation, and individuals such as these may not receive adequate services in a prison environment.

Similarly, some argue that the mandatory minimums related to drug offenses have led to a surge of nonviolent drug offenders being locked away in federal prisons with no hope of negotiating sentences. The solution they see? Smarter sentencing.

As overcrowding has become increasingly problematic in the United States, criminal justice experts have begun to seek punishment and rehabilitation options that do not involve incarceration. They argue that prison may not be the answer at all for some offenders and offer up alternatives such as work and education programs; counseling and psychotherapy; and drug-treatment programs.

Other ideas for reform include helping to address injustice and rights inequalities from the outset through police training and improving police interactions with the communities they serve.

The following chapter examines ideas on incarceration alternatives. The authors discuss their potential effectiveness, their effect on society as a whole, and offer opinions on whether these strategies could have a significant and positive impact on America's prison problem.

> "*When properly implemented, work programs, education and psychotherapy can ease prisoners' transitions to the free world.*"

# Rehabilitation, Not Punishment, Should Be the Focus in Criminal Justice

*Etienne Benson*

*In the following viewpoint, Etienne Benson looks at the models of punishment and rehabilitation and aims to show that the latter must be the focus in criminal justice. He argues that work programs, education, and psychotherapy can make a positive difference and that a strictly punitive approach, in the end, can do more harm than good. Benson worked as a science writer for the American Psychological Association's publication Monitor on Psychology.*

As you read, consider the following questions:

1. When compared to the national average, how much higher is the mental illness rate among the prison population?
2. According to Benson, what services do psychologists provide in the prison system?
3. What are some of the risk factors for criminal behavior mentioned by the author?

I t's not a very good time to be a prisoner in the United States. Incarceration is not meant to be fun, of course. But a combination of strict sentencing guidelines, budget shortfalls and a punitive philosophy of corrections has made today's prisons much more unpleasant—and much less likely to rehabilitate their inhabitants— than in the past, many researchers say.

What is the role for psychologists? First and foremost, they are providing mental health services to the prison population, which has rates of mental illness at least three times the national average.

More broadly, they are contributing a growing body of scientific evidence to political and philosophical discussions about the purpose of imprisonment, says Craig Haney, PhD, a psychologist at the University of California, Santa Cruz.

"Psychology as a discipline now has a tremendous amount of information about the origins of criminal behavior," says Haney. "I think that it is important for psychologists to bring that information to bear in the debate on what kind of crime control policies we, as a society, should follow."

## The punitive turn

Until the mid-1970s, rehabilitation was a key part of U.S. prison policy. Prisoners were encouraged to develop occupational skills and to resolve psychological problems—such as substance abuse or aggression—that might interfere with their reintegration into society. Indeed, many inmates received court sentences that mandated treatment for such problems.

Since then, however, rehabilitation has taken a back seat to a "get tough on crime" approach that sees punishment as prison's main function, says Haney. The approach has created explosive growth in the prison population, while having at most a modest effect on crime rates.

As a result, the United States now has more than 2 million people in prisons or jails—the equivalent of one in every 142 U.S. residents—and another four to five million people on probation or parole. A higher percentage of the population is involved in the criminal justice system in the United States than in any other developed country.

Many inmates have serious mental illnesses. Starting in the late 1950s and 1960s, new psychotropic drugs and the community health movement dramatically reduced the number of people in state mental hospitals. But in the 1980s, many of the mentally ill who had left mental institutions in the previous two decades began entering the criminal justice system.

Today, somewhere between 15 and 20 percent of people in prison are mentally ill, according to U.S. Department of Justice estimates.

"Prisons have really become, in many ways, the de facto mental health hospitals," says former prison psychologist Thomas Fagan, PhD. "But prisons weren't built to deal with mentally ill people; they were built to deal with criminals doing time."

## The mentally ill

The plight of the mentally ill in prisons was virtually ignored for many years, but in the past decade many prison systems have realized—sometimes with prodding from the courts—that providing mental health care is a necessity, not a luxury, says Fagan.

In many prison systems, psychologists are the primary mental health care providers, with psychiatrists contracted on a part-time basis. Psychologists provide services ranging from screening new inmates for mental illness to providing group therapy and crisis counseling.

They also provide rehabilitative services that are useful even for prisoners without serious mental illnesses, says Fagan. For example, a psychologist might develop special programs for substance abusers or help prisoners prepare for the transition back to the community.

But they often struggle to implement such programs while keeping up with their regular prison caseloads. "We're focused so much on the basic mental health services that there's not enough time or emphasis to devote to rehabilitative services," says Robert

Morgan, PhD, a psychologist at Texas Tech University who has worked in federal and state prisons and studies treatment methods for inmates.

Part of the problem is limited resources, says Morgan: There simply aren't enough mental health professionals in most prisons. Haney agrees: "Many psychologists in the criminal justice system have enormous caseloads; they're struggling not to be overwhelmed by the tide."

Another constraint is the basic philosophical difference between psychology, which is rehabilitative at heart, and corrections, which is currently punishment-oriented.

"Right now there's such a focus on punishment—most criminal justice or correctional systems are punitive in nature—that it's hard to develop effective rehabilitative programs," says Morgan.

## Relevant research

To help shift the focus from punishment to rehabilitation, psychologists are doing research on the causes of crime and the psychological effects of incarceration.

In the 1970s, when major changes were being made to the U.S. prison system, psychologists had little hard data to contribute.

But in the past 25 years, says Haney, they have generated a massive literature documenting the importance of child abuse, poverty, early exposure to substance abuse and other risk factors for criminal behavior. The findings suggest that individual-centered approaches to crime prevention need to be complemented by community-based approaches.

Researchers have also found that the pessimistic "nothing works" attitude toward rehabilitation that helped justify punitive prison policies in the 1970s was overstated. When properly implemented, work programs, education and psychotherapy can ease prisoners' transitions to the free world, says Haney.

Finally, researchers have demonstrated the power of the prison environment to shape behavior, often to the detriment of both prisoners and prison workers.

The Stanford Prison Experiment, which Haney co-authored in 1973 with Stanford University psychologist and APA Past-president Philip G. Zimbardo, PhD, is one example. It showed that psychologically healthy individuals could become sadistic or depressed when placed in a prison-like environment.

More recently, Haney has been studying so-called "supermax" prisons—high-security units in which prisoners spend as many as 23 hours per day in solitary confinement for years at a time.

Haney's research has shown that many prisoners in supermax units experience extremely high levels of anxiety and other negative emotions. When released—often without any "decompression" period in lower-security facilities—they have few of the social or occupational skills necessary to succeed in the outside world.

Nonetheless, supermax facilities have become increasingly common over the past five to ten years.

"This is what prison systems do under emergency circumstances—they move to punitive social control mechanisms," explains Haney. "[But] it's a very short-term solution, and one that may do more long-term damage both to the system and to the individuals than it solves."

> "*Mandatory minimum sentences also address two widely acknowledged problems with the criminal justice system: sentencing disparity and unduly lenient sentences.*"

# Punishment Is Necessary, But Mandatory Minimum Sentences May Not Be

*Evan Bernick and Paul J. Larkin, Jr.*

*In the following viewpoint, Evan Bernick and Paul J. Larkin, Jr., examine two proposed pieces of legislation and their potential effect on mandatory minimum sentences and criminal justice reform. They conclude that the Smarter Sentencing Act could resolve the harsh sentences related to small-scale drug offenses without dismantling decades of progress toward public safety improvement. Bernick is assistant director of the Center for Judicial Engagement at the Institute for Justice and was a visiting legal fellow at the Heritage Foundation. His work has appeared in Time, USA Today, Fox News.com, The Washington Times, The Chicago-Sun Times, and the National Review Online. Larkin is senior legal research fellow at the Heritage Foundation's Center for Legal and Judicial Studies.*

As you read, consider the following questions:

1. What led to the Anti-Drug Abuse Act of 1986?
2. Why do advocates against mandatory minimums claim that sentencing disparities still exist?
3. What reasons do the authors give in stating that the Safety Valve Act could cause overcorrection of the system?

I s justice best served by having legislatures assign fixed penalties to each crime? Or should legislatures leave judges more or less free to tailor sentences to the aggravating and mitigating facts of each criminal case within a defined range?

The proliferation in recent decades of mandatory minimum penalties for federal crimes, along with the tremendous increase in the prison population, has forced those concerned with criminal justice in America to reconsider this age-old question. The Supreme Court of the United States has upheld lengthy mandatory terms of imprisonment over the challenge that they violate the Eighth Amendment's prohibition against cruel and unusual punishments.[1] The question remains, however, whether mandatory minimums are sound criminal justice policy.

Today, public officials on both sides of the aisle support amending the federal mandatory minimum sentencing laws. Two bills with bipartisan support are currently under consideration. Senators Patrick Leahy (D–VT) and Rand Paul (R–KY) have introduced the Justice Safety Valve Act of 2013,[2] which would apply to all federal mandatory minimums. Senators Dick Durbin (D–IL) and Mike Lee (R–UT) have introduced the Smarter Sentencing Act, which would apply to federal mandatory minimums for only drug offenses.[3]

In what follows, this paper will explain how mandatory minimums emerged in the modern era, summarize the policy arguments for and against mandatory minimums, and evaluate both the Justice Safety Valve Act and the Smarter Sentencing Act. The bottom line is this: Each proposal might be a valuable step forward in criminal justice policy, but it is difficult to predict the precise impact that each one would have. This much, however, appears likely: The Smarter Sentencing Act is narrowly tailored to address one of the most pressing problems with mandatory minimums: severe sentences for relatively minor drug possession crimes.[4]

## The Modern History of Mandatory Minimum Sentences

For most of the 19th and 20th centuries, federal trial judges had virtually unlimited sentencing discretion.[5] In the 1960s and 1970s, influential members of the legal establishment criticized that practice,[6] concluding that that unrestrained discretion gave rise to well-documented sentencing disparities in factually similar cases.[7] Over time, that scholarship paved the way for Congress to modify the federal sentencing process through the Sentencing Reform Act of 1984.[8] That law did not withdraw all sentencing discretion from district courts; it did, however, establish the United States Sentencing Commission and directed it to promulgate Sentencing Guidelines that would regulate and channel the discretion that remained.[9]

Congress also decided to eliminate the courts' discretion to exercise leniency in some instances by requiring courts to impose a mandatory minimum sentence for certain types of crimes. For example, Congress enacted the Armed Career Criminal Act[10] in 1984 as part of the same law that included the Sentencing Reform Act of 1984.[11] The Armed Career Criminal Act demands that a district court sentence to a minimum 15-year term of imprisonment anyone who is convicted of being a felon in possession of a firearm if he has three prior convictions for "a violent felony or a serious drug offense."[12] Two years later, concerned by the emergence of a new form of cocaine colloquially known as "crack," Congress passed the Anti-Drug Abuse Act of 1986,[13] which imposes mandatory minimum terms of imprisonment for violations of the federal controlled substances laws.[14]

Congress could have allowed the U.S. Sentencing Commission to devise appropriate punishment for those offenses, at least as an initial matter. Instead, Congress forged ahead and preempted the commission by decreeing that offenders should serve defined mandatory minimum terms of imprisonment when convicted of those crimes.[15]

District courts may depart downward from those mandatory minimum sentences only in limited circumstances. For example, the Anti-Drug Abuse Act of 1986 has two exceptions to the mandatory minimum sentencing requirement. The first occurs if a defendant cooperates with the government and the government files a motion for a downward departure from the statutory minimum.[16] Absent such a motion, the district court cannot reduce a defendant's sentence based on that exception. [17] The second exception involves the so-called safety valve that allows judges to avoid applying mandatory minimums, even absent substantial assistance.[18] The safety valve, however, has a limited scope: It applies only to sentences imposed for nonviolent drug offenses[19] where the offender meets specific criteria relating to criminal history, violence, lack of injury to others, and leadership.[20] Otherwise, a district court must impose the sentence fixed by the Anti-Drug Abuse Act of 1986. With regard to the Armed Career Criminal Act, no federal law authorizes a district court to impose a term of imprisonment less than the one required by that statute.

The Armed Career Criminal Act and the Anti-Drug Abuse Act of 1986 are the two principal modern federal statutes requiring mandatory minimum terms of imprisonment—but they are by no means the only ones. Mandatory minimums have proliferated and have increased in severity. Since 1991, the number of mandatory minimums has more than doubled.[21] Entirely new types of offenses have become subject to mandatory minimums, from child pornography to identity theft.[22] During that period, the percentage of offenders convicted of violating a statute carrying a mandatory minimum of 10 years increased from 34.4 percent to 40.7 percent.[23]

## The Arguments For and Against Mandatory Minimum Sentences

There are powerful arguments on each side of this debate. The next two sections summarize the arguments pro and con on mandatory minimum sentences as each side of that debate would make its case.[24]

### The Assault on Mandatory Minimum Sentences

Mandatory minimum sentences have not eliminated sentencing disparities because they have not eliminated sentencing discretion; they have merely shifted that discretion from judges to prosecutors. [25] Judges may have to impose whatever punishment the law requires, but prosecutors are under no comparable obligation to charge a defendant with violating a law carrying a mandatory minimum penalty.[26] As a practical matter, prosecutors have unreviewable discretion over what charges to bring, including whether to charge a violation of a law with a mandatory minimum sentence, and over whether to engage in plea bargaining, including whether to trade away a count that includes such a law. Moreover, even if a prosecutor brings such charges against a defendant, the prosecutor has unreviewable discretion whether to ask the district court to reduce a defendant's sentence due to his "substantial assistance" to the government.[27]

What is more, critics say, unbridled prosecutorial discretion is a greater evil than unlimited judicial discretion. Prosecutors are not trained at sentencing and do not exercise discretion in a transparent way.[28] Critics also claim that prosecutors, who stand to gain professionally from successful convictions under mandatory minimums, do not have sufficient incentive to exercise their discretion responsibly.[29]

Indeed, nowhere else in the criminal justice system does the law vest authority in one party to a dispute to decide what should be the appropriate remedy. That decision always rests in the hands of a jury, which must make whatever findings are necessary for a punishment to be imposed, or the judge, who must enter the judgment of conviction that authorizes the correctional system to punish the now-convicted defendant.[30]

Furthermore, they contend, mandatory minimum sentences do not reduce crime. As University of Minnesota Law Professor Michael Tonry has concluded, "the weight of the evidence clearly shows that enactment of mandatory penalties has either no demonstrable marginal deterrent effects or short-term effects that rapidly waste away."[31] Nor is it clear that mandatory minimum sentences reduce crime through incapacitation. In many drug operations, if a low-level offender is incapacitated, another may quickly take his place through what is known as the "replacement effect."[32] In drug cases, mandatory minimum sentences are also often insensitive to factors that could make incapacitation more effective, such as prior criminal history.[33]

In theory, mandatory minimum sentences enable the government to "move up the chain" of large drug operations by using the assistance of convicted lower-level offenders against senior offenders. The government can reward an offender's cooperation by moving in district court for a reduction of the offender's term of imprisonment below whatever term is required by law.[34] In reality, however, critics argue that the value of that leverage is overstated. The rate of cooperation in cases involving mandatory minimums is comparable to the average rate in all federal cases.[35]

Further, only certain defendants in cases involving organized crime—those who are closest to the top of the pyramid—will be able to render substantial assistance.[36] The result is that sentencing reductions go to serious offenders rather than to small-scale underlings. The practice of affording sentence concessions to defendants who assist the government is entrenched in American law, but the quantity-driven drug mandatory minimums are uniquely problematic because they can render each low-level co-conspirator responsible for the same quantity of drugs as the kingpin.[37]

Statutes imposing mandatory minimum sentences result in arbitrary and severe punishments that undermine the public's faith in America's criminal justice system. Consider the effect of those provisions in the Anti-Drug Abuse Act of 1986. Drug offenses, which make up a significant proportion of mandatory minimums, can give rise to arbitrary, severe punishments.[38] The difference between a drug quantity that triggers a mandatory minimum and one that does not will often produce a "cliff effect."[39] While someone with 0.9 gram of LSD might not spend much time incarcerated, another fraction of a gram will result in five years behind bars.

In fact, it is easy to find examples of unduly harsh mandatory minimums for drug offenses. A financially desperate single mother of four with no criminal history was paid $100 by a complete stranger to mail a package that, unbeknownst to her, contained 232 grams of crack cocaine. For that act alone, she received a sentence of 10 years in prison even though the sentencing judge felt that this punishment was completely unjust and irrational.[40]

In some cases, mandatory minimums have been perceived as being so disproportionate to a person's culpability that the offender has altogether escaped punishment. Florida Judge Richard Tombrink "nullified" the 25-year mandatory sentence of a man who possessed (without an intent to distribute) hydrocodone pills.[41] Juries also have the power to nullify by acquitting someone they would otherwise have convicted if not for the disproportionately harsh sentence. Although defendants cannot demand that the trial judge explicitly instruct the jury that it has the power to nullify, in mandatory contexts, a judge troubled by the length of the sentence a defendant must receive for a conviction can allow the jury to learn what those penalties are in the hope that the jury exercises this power sua sponte.[42]

Finally, critics maintain that mandatory minimum sentences are not cost-effective. The certainty of arrest, prosecution, conviction, and punishment has a greater deterrent effect than the severity of punishment. If a one-year sentence for a crime has the same deterrent effect as a five-year sentence, the additional four years of imprisonment inflict unnecessary pain on the offender being

# Reforming Mandatory Minimums

## The Problem

Mandatory minimum, three strikes you're out, and truth in sentencing laws are typically overly punitive. They often impose excessively long sentences for crimes. Their consequences are felt throughout the country: The average prison stay has increased 36 percent since 1990. The federal inmate population grew more than 400 percent since the late 1980s; now, their prisons are 39 percent beyond capacity.

Research has shown that increasing time served does not help keep the public safe. Studies show that longer sentences have minimal or no benefit on future crime. Even worse, research shows a strong correlation between increased prison time and repeat offenses, meaning prison may create more serious and violent offenses when overused. For example, a 2002 study indicates that sentencing low-level drug offenders to prison may increase the likelihood they will commit crimes upon release.

[...]

## Successes

Several states have done this while continuing to see crime fall to historic lows:

*New York.* New York State passed the "Rockefeller drug laws," imposing harsh mandatory sentences for drug possession in 1973. As a direct result, the state's prison population increased six-fold with striking racial disparities. In 2009, to slow the growth of its prison system, New York removed the law's mandatory minimums for low-level drug offenses, choosing instead to allow judges to use their discretion to determine appropriate sentence lengths or decide to send someone to treatment instead. Since 2009, the number of people sent to prison and the length of sentences has declined statewide. Sentencing disparities between minority and white defendants also narrowed by one-third. Now, those sent into treatment have only a 36 percent chance of committing a repeat offense, versus 54 percent for those incarcerated before the new law went into effect.[...]

"Reforming Mandatory Minimums," © Law Enforcement Leaders.

incarcerated and, to borrow from economics, impose a "dead weight" loss on society. Mandatory minimum sentences, therefore, waste scarce criminal justice resources.

## The Defense of Mandatory Minimums

On the other hand, a number of parties defend the use of mandatory minimum terms of imprisonment. They argue that mandatory minimum sentences reflect a societal judgment that certain offenses demand a specified minimum sanction and thereby ensure that anyone who commits such a crime cannot avoid a just punishment.

A nation of more than 300 million people will necessarily have a tremendous diversity of views as to the heinousness of the conduct proscribed by today's penal codes, and a bench with hundreds of federal district court judges will reflect that diversity. The decision as to what penalty should be imposed on a category of offenders requires consideration of the range of penological justifications for punishment, such as retribution, deterrence, incapacitation, education, and rehabilitation. Legislatures are better positioned than judges to make those types of judgments,[43] and Americans trust legislatures with the authority to make the moral and empirical decisions about how severely forbidden conduct should be sanctioned. Accordingly, having Congress specify the minimum penalty for a specific crime or category of offenses is entirely consistent with the proper functioning of the legislature in the criminal justice processes.

Mandatory minimum sentences eliminate the dishonesty that characterized sentencing for the majority of the 20th century. For most of that period, Congress vested district courts with complete discretion to select the appropriate period of confinement for an offender while also granting parole officials the authority to decide precisely whether and when to release an inmate before the completion of his sentence.

That division of authority created the inaccurate impression that the public action of the judge at sentencing fixed the offender's punishment while actually leaving that decision to the judgment of parole officials who act outside of the view of the public. At the same time, Congress could escape responsibility for making the moral judgments necessary to decide exactly how much punishment should be inflicted upon an individual by passing that responsibility off to parties who are not politically accountable for their actions. The entire process reflected dishonesty and generated cynicism, which corrodes the professional and public respect necessary for the criminal justice system to be deemed a morally defensible exercise of governmental power.

Mandatory minimum sentences also address two widely acknowledged problems with the criminal justice system: sentencing disparity and unduly lenient sentences. Mandatory minimums guarantee that sentences are uniform throughout the federal system and ensure that individuals are punished commensurate with their moral culpability by hitching the sentence to the crime, not the person.[44]

In fact, the need to use mandatory minimums as a means of addressing sentencing variances has become more pressing in the wake of the Supreme Court's 2005 decision in *United States v. Booker*.[45] Booker excised provisions of the Sentencing Reform Act of 1984 that had made the Sentencing Guidelines binding upon federal judges.[46] The result, unfortunately, has been a return to the type of inconsistency that existed before that statute became law. According to the Department of Justice, Booker has precipitated a return to unbridled judicial discretion: "[For] offenses for which there are no mandatory minimums, sentencing decisions have become largely unconstrained."[47] Booker therefore threatens to resurrect the sentencing disparities that, 30 years ago, prompted Congress to enact the Sentencing Reform Act. Mandatory minimum sentences may be the only way to eliminate that disparity today.

Mandatory minimum sentences also prevent crime because certain and severe punishment inevitably will have a deterrent effect.[48] Locking up offenders also incapacitates them for the term of their imprisonment and thereby protects the public.[49] In fact, where the chance of detection is low, as it is in the case of most drug offenses, reliance on fixed, lengthy prison sentences is preferable to a discretionary sentencing structure because mandatory sentences enable communities to conserve scarce enforcement resources without losing any deterrent benefit.[50]

Finally, the available evidence supports those conclusions. The 1990s witnessed a significant drop in crime across all categories of offenses,[51] and the mandatory minimum sentences adopted in the 1980s contributed to that decline.[52]

Moreover, mandatory minimums are an important law enforcement tool. They supply the police and prosecutors with the leverage necessary to secure the cooperation and testimony of low-level offenders against their more senior confederates.[53] The evidence shows that mandatory minimums, together with the Sentencing Guidelines promulgated by the U.S. Sentencing Commission, have produced more cooperation and accomplice testimony in organized crime cases.[54]

It is a mistake to condemn mandatory minimum sentences because of the cost of imprisoning offenders. Opponents of mandatory minimums decry the high cost of housing a large number of inmates for a lengthy period of time and point to other criminal justice programs—e.g., the FBI, Federal Public Defenders, and victim advocates—that can better use those funds. That argument, however, does not consider both sides of the ledger. Imprisonment reduces the number of future victims of crime and thereby reduces the costs that they and the rest of society would otherwise suffer. Society is entitled to decide how to spend its funds, and underwriting the cost of incapacitating proven criminals is certainly a legitimate use of resources. Moreover, this efficiency-based criticism mistakenly assumes that Congress will not increase the budget for the Justice Department to use a valuable criminal justice tool: imprisonment.

In any event, there is no guarantee that any funds saved by reducing the length of offenders' sentences will go to other components of the criminal justice system. Indeed, there is no criminal justice "lockbox" into which all saved or unspent funds are dumped, and it is dishonest to pretend that funds not given to the Federal Bureau of Prisons will necessarily be used elsewhere in the criminal justice system rather than for non–criminal justice government programs.

Finally, the arguments against mandatory minimum sentences are, at their core, just a sleight of hand. The principal objection to mandatory minimum sentences is not that they are mandatory, but that they are severe or that they are required for drug offenses. No one would object to a mandatory 30-day sentence for possession of heroin or a mandatory one-year sentence for rape (in fact, the objection likely would be that those mandatory sentences are too short). Critics are concerned less about the mandatory nature of federal sentences than they are about their length and their use in drug cases.

## Potential Reforms: The Justice Safety Valve Act and the Smarter Sentencing Act

The U.S. Senate is considering two bills that would revise the federal sentencing laws in the case of mandatory minimum sentences. These bills differ significantly in their details, but they have the common goal of ameliorating some of the harsh results that those laws can produce.

### The Justice Safety Valve Act of 2013

As noted above, Section 3553(f) of Title 18 contains a "safety valve" that allows judges to exempt certain drug and other offenders from mandatory minimum sentences. The Justice Safety Valve Act would add a new subsection (g) to Section 3553.[55] That provision would expand the existing safety valve by allowing a judge to depart downward from any mandatory minimum "if the court finds that it is necessary to do so in order to avoid imposing" an unjust sentence. [56] Judges would need to state on the record their reason(s) for not imposing a mandatory minimum sentence, but they could reduce every sentence required by law to the punishment that the court deemed appropriate in each case.[57]

### The Smarter Sentencing Act of 2013

The other law, called the Smarter Sentencing Act, operates in a different and far more limited manner.[58] To start with, it would not apply to every mandatory minimum sentence. Instead, it would amend Section 3553(f), which applies only to nonviolent drug crimes. The Smarter Sentencing Act would permit a district judge to impose sentences without regard to any mandatory minimum if the court finds that the defendant has no more than two criminal history points, as defined by the U.S. Sentencing Guidelines, and the defendant was not convicted of a disqualifying offense, such as a violent crime.[59]

Finally, the act would make retroactive the Fairness in Sentencing Act of 2010,[60] which reduced the disparity between the amount of crack cocaine and powder cocaine needed to trigger mandatories and eliminated the five-year mandatory minimum sentence for simple possession of crack cocaine.[61] It is sensible as a matter of policy to apply that statute retroactively. The Fairness in Sentencing Act of 2010 reduces the crack-to-powder ratio used in calculating a mandatory minimum sentence from 100:1 to 18:1. If the higher ratio is unnecessary to serve the legitimate purposes of punishment, there is no obvious reason why it should not be applied retroactively. After all, if Congress decides that a particular method of calculating a sentence of imprisonment is unduly severe on a going-forward basis, it makes little sense to continue to apply that penalty to offenders already suffering under it.

## Comparing the Two Proposals

Each bill would grant district courts greater discretion to depart downward from a mandatory minimum sentence than current law allows. The Safety Valve Act would allow such departures in every case in which there is a mandatory minimum sentence, while the Smarter Sentencing Act permits that result only in connection with violations of the controlled substances laws and only if the defendant satisfies certain requirements.

Neither the Justice Department nor the Government Accountability Office has analyzed the potential effect of either proposal, so Americans are left with uncertainty about those proposals' likely effects. In theory, the Safety Valve Act could result in a greater number of downward departures than the Smarter Sentencing Act because the former would apply to every mandatory minimum statute. It is uncertain, however, just how often district courts would depart downwards in non-drug cases and how many years of imprisonment courts would shave off the amount now required by law for those offenses.

Moreover, the Safety Valve Act could pose a risk of overcorrection. That bill, for example, would authorize a district court to disregard a mandatory minimum sentence "if the court finds that it is necessary to do so in order to avoid" imposing a sentence that would "violat[e]" the purposes of federal criminal punishment, which are to impose a sentence that is "sufficient, but not greater than necessary" to, among other "things, reflect the seriousness of the offense," "provide just punishment," "afford adequate deterrence," and "protect the public from further crimes of the defendant."[62] Even though the act would require district courts to provide a written statement of the reasons for any downward departure,[63] that provision would, on its face, appear to grant district courts virtually unfettered discretion to issue a sentence below the statutory minimum. Furthermore, the Safety Valve Act supplies district courts with no objective standards, thereby denying an appellate court the criteria needed to determine whether the district court had abused its discretion.

Given that the Sentencing Guidelines are no longer mandatory, the Safety Valve Act might effectively return to district courts the broad discretion that they enjoyed before the Sentencing Reform Act of 1984. The result would be to make every current mandatory minimum sentence into a mere recommendation, thereby accelerating the transformation of federal sentencing law back to the "bad old days" of unjustified sentencing disparities—a risk that must be considered.

The Smarter Sentencing Act is a far narrower remedy than the Safety Valve Act because it addresses perhaps the most troubling aspect of mandatory minimums: their capacity to impose arbitrary and unduly severe sentences on relatively low-level offenders in controlled substances cases. That problem is particularly acute in drug cases, because an additional gram of a controlled substance quantity can have an enormous impact on sentencing even though that additional gram has little marginal bearing on the offender's moral culpability.[64] By removing the mandate in cases where offenders, despite having a slightly more substantial criminal history, otherwise qualify for the safety valve and by substantially decreasing mandatory sentences for nonviolent drug offenses, the Sentencing Act would mitigate the evils of the "cliff effect" that some critics have identified.

Perhaps, in the long term, the Safety Valve Act might be preferable policy. For now, however, such sweeping reform might be a bridge too far. The immediate and most urgent problem facing America's criminal justice system is that district courts must impose unduly severe mandatory minimum sentences on certain small-scale drug offenders. The Smarter Sentencing Act focuses on remedying that problem while leaving for another day the issue of whether there should be mandatory minimum sentences imposed on, for example, violent criminals. The Smarter Sentencing Act takes a smaller step than the Safety Valve Act toward the revision of the federal mandatory minimum sentencing laws, but a smaller step might enhance federal sentencing policy while avoiding the risks noted above.

## Conclusion

Mandatory minimum sentences are the product of good intentions, but good intentions alone do not make good policy; good results are also necessary. Congress was right to be concerned about reducing sentencing disparity and ensuring that sentences are neither unduly lenient nor unduly harsh.

Nonetheless, just as law should be tempered with equity, so should rigid sentencing rules leave room for adjustment in certain cases where a legislatively fixed sentence would be manifestly unjust. No statute can account for every variable in every case, and the attempt to do so with mandatory minimums has given rise to punishments in some small-scale drug possession cases that are completely out of whack with the purpose of the federal sentencing laws.

The problem, however, is remediable. Granting district courts some additional limited sentencing discretion would improve the status quo by eliminating some unjust sentences without obviously undercutting the incapacitative, deterrent, and educative benefits of the criminal law. The Smarter Sentencing Act seeks to mitigate the "cliff effect" in the context of nonviolent drug offenses. Doing so could ameliorate some of the extremely harsh sentences that district courts have imposed without taking a bite out of the efforts that the government has made over the past four decades to improve public safety.

## Endnotes

1. See *Ewing v. California*, 538 U.S. 11 (2003) (upholding application of the California "three strikes" law); *Harmelin v. Michigan*, 501 U.S. 957 (1991) (upholding mandatory sentence of life imprisonment for a drug offense).
2. The Justice Safety Valve Act of 2013, S. 619, 113th Congress (2013). See infra Appendix A.
3. The Smarter Sentencing Act of 2013, S. 1410, 113th Congress (2013). See infra Appendix B.
4. Both the Justice Safety Valve Act and the Smarter Sentencing Act would revise the front end of the correctional process by amending federal mandatory minimum sentencing laws in order to permit district court judges to depart downwards in a larger number of cases than the law currently allows. An alternative would be to revise the back end of the correctional process by amending the federal good-time (or earned-time) laws in order to allow the Federal Bureau of Prisons to grant prisoners additional credit toward an early release, perhaps even in cases in which the prisoner was sentenced under a mandatory minimum sentencing law. For a discussion of potential reform of the federal good-time laws, see, e.g., Paul J. Larkin, Jr., Clemency, Parole, Good-Time Credits, and Crowded Prisons: Reconsidering Early Release, 11 Geo. J.L. & Pub. Pol'y 1 (2013). Of course, it also is possible to reform both ends of the process. For a list and discussion of the various possible front and back-end reforms, see, e.g., Urban Institute, Stemming the Tide: Strategies to Reduce the Growth and Cut the Cost of the Federal Prison System (Nov. 2013), available at http://www.urban.org/UploadedPDF/412932-stemming-the-tide.pdf.
5. See, e.g., *Mistretta v. United States*, 488 U.S. 361, 363 (1989); Larkin, supra note 4, at 7–8.

6. Judge Marvin E. Frankel criticized the sentencing disparities resulting from leaving district courts complete freedom to impose a sentence within the range authorized by Congress. See Marvin E. Frankel, "Criminal Sentences: Law Without Order" (1973); Marvin E. Frankel, Lawlessness in Sentencing, 41 U. Cin. L. Rev. 1 (1972). His work was particularly important in drawing attention to the "lawlessness" of the status quo. See Kevin R. Reitz, Sentencing Reform in the States, 64 U. Colo. L. Rev. 645, 650 n.21 (1993) (finding that Frankel's work "charted the general outline of sentencing reform through the 1980s and into the 1990s").

7. See, e.g., S. Rep. No. 97–307, at 956 (1981) ("glaring disparities…can be traced directly to the unfettered discretion the law confers on those judges and parole authorities [that implement] the sentence."); Ilene Nagel, "Structuring Sentencing Discretion: The New Federal Sentencing Guidelines, "80 J. Crim. L. & Criminology 883, 895–97 (1990) (detailing studies demonstrating widespread sentencing disparities in the pre–Sentencing Guidelines era); William Austin & Thomas A. Williams III, A Survey of Judges' Responses to Simulated Legal Cases: Research Note on Sentencing Disparity, 68 J. Crim. L. & Criminology 306 (1977) (finding that judges sentencing in the pre–Sentencing Guidelines era imposed different sentences despite having the identical case information); Kate Stith & Steve Y. Koh, The Politics of Sentencing Reform: The Legislative History of the Federal Sentencing Guidelines, 28 Wake Forest L. Rev. 223 (1993) (recounting the legislative history of the Sentencing Reform Act of 1984 and describing how Frankel's work inspired the legislators instrumental in pushing sentencing reform).

8. Sentencing Reform Act of 1984, Pub. L. No. 98-473, Ch. II, 98 Stat. 1987 (codified as amended at 18 U.S.C. §§ 3551-3586 (2006)).

9. See 28 U.S.C. § 991 (2006) (establishing the Commission and describing its duties); Mistretta, 488 U.S. at 363–70.

10. 18 U.S.C. § 924 (2006).

11. Both the Sentencing Reform Act of 1984 and the Armed Career Criminal Act were enacted as part of the Comprehensive Crime Control Act of 1984, Pub. L. No. 98-473, 98 Stat. 1976 (1984).

12. 18 U.S.C. § 924(e).

13. Anti-Drug Abuse Act of 1986, Pub. L. No. 99–570, 100 Stat. 3207 (1986).

14. See, e.g., Chapman v. United States, 500 U.S. 453 (1991); Paul J. Larkin, Jr., "Crack Cocaine, Congressional Inaction, and Equal Protection," 37 Harv. J.L. & Pub. Pol'y 241, 241–42 (2013). While drug quantities are for the most part pegged to five- and 10-year sentences, some drug offenses can result in life imprisonment. See 21 U.S.C. § 841(b)(1)(B), 960(b)(2)(A)–(C), (G) & (H).

15. See Stith & Koh, supra note 7, at 259 (describing a "growing public concern about crime and a new President, Ronald Reagan, keenly interested in toughening and expanding federal anticrime measures"); U.S. Sentencing Comm'n, Mandatory Minimum Penalties in the Federal Criminal Justice System 23 (2011) (describing the new drug mandatory minimums as a "response to a number of circumstances, including the increased incidence of drug use and trafficking and well-publicized tragic incidents such as the June 1986 death of Boston Celtics' first-round draft pick, Len Bias.")

16. Section 3553(e) of Title 18 provides that, "[u]pon motion of the Government, the court shall have the authority to impose a sentence below a level established by statute as a minimum sentence so as to reflect a defendant's substantial assistance in the investigation or prosecution of another person who has committed an offense."

17. See, e.g., Melendez v. United States, 518 U.S. 120 (1996); Wade v. United States, 504 U.S. 181 (1992).

18. See, e.g., 139 Cong. Rec. 27, 842 (daily ed. Nov. 8, 1993) (statement of Sen. Hatch urging that a safety valve could restore "a small degree of discretion to the courts for a small percentage of nonviolent drug cases.").

19. See 18 U.S.C. § 3553(f) (applies only to offenders convicted under "401, 404, or 406 of the Controlled Substances Act…or section 1010 or 1013 of the Controlled Substances Import and Export Act.").

20. See 18 U.S.C. § 3553(f): "(1) the defendant does not have more than 1 criminal history point, as determined under the sentencing guidelines; (2) the defendant did not use violence or credible threats of violence or possess a firearm or other dangerous weapon (or induce another participant to do so) in connection with the offense; (3) the offense did not result in death or serious bodily injury to any person; (4) the defendant was not an organizer, leader, manager, or supervisor of others in the offense, as determined under the sentencing guidelines and was not engaged in a continuing criminal enterprise, as defined in section 408 of the Controlled Substances Act; and (5) not later than the time of the sentencing hearing, the defendant has truthfully provided to the Government all information and evidence the defendant has concerning the offense or offenses that were part of the same course of conduct or of a common scheme or plan, but the fact that the defendant has no relevant or useful other information to provide or that the Government is already aware of the information shall not preclude a determination by the court that the defendant has complied with this requirement."

21. See U.S. Sentencing Comm'n, Mandatory Minimum Penalties in the Federal Criminal Justice System 71 (2011) (hereafter Mandatory Minimum Penalties).

22. See, e.g., Protection of Children from Sexual Predators Act of 1998, Pub. L. No. 105–314, 112 Stat. 2974 (codified at 18 U.S.C. § 2241 (2006)); Identity Theft and Assumption Deterrence Act of 1998, Pub. L. No. 105–318, 112 Stat. 3007 (codified at 18 U.S.C. § 1028 (2006)).

23. See U.S. Sentencing Comm'n, supra note 21, at 75. Ironically, in 1990, slightly more than half of offenders convicted of a mandatory minimum sentence offense violated a statute mandating five years of imprisonment, whereas in 2010, that number declined to 39.9 percent. Id.

24. For an excellent discussion of the arguments pro and con, see Eric Luna & Paul G. Cassell, "Mandatory Minimalism," 32 Cardozo L. Rev. 1 (2010).

25. See, e.g., Jeffrey T. Ulmer, Megan C. Kurlychek, & John H. Kramer, "Prosecutorial Discretion and the Imposition of Mandatory Minimum Sentences," 44 J. Res. Crim. & Delinq. 427, 451 (2007) ("Our findings support the long-suspected notion that mandatory minimums are not mandatory at all but simply substitute prosecutorial discretion for judicial discretion.")

26. Internal Justice Department policies regulate a federal prosecutor's exercise of charging discretion. Those policies seek to prevent a nationwide occurrence of disparate charging decisions by limiting a prosecutor's decision not to charge the most serious provable offense. See, e.g., Memorandum from U.S. Attorney General Eric Holder on Department Policy on Charging and Sentencing to All Federal Prosecutors (May 19, 2010), available at http://www.talkleft.com/holder-charging-memo.pdf; and Memorandum from U.S. Attorney General Eric Holder on Department Policy on Charging Mandatory Minimum Sentences and Recidivist Enhancements in Certain Drug Cases to the United States Attorney and Assistant Attorney General for the Criminal Division (Aug. 12, 2013), available at http://www.popehat.com/wp-content/uploads/2013/08/holder-mandatory-drug-minimums-memo.pdf. Those policies, however, are not judicially enforceable. See *United States v. Caceres*, 440 U.S. 741 (1979) (ruling that federal courts may not exercise

their supervisory power to exclude evidence obtained in violation of an agency's internal rules).

27. See, e.g., David Bjerk, "Making the Crime Fit the Penalty: The Role of Prosecutorial Discretion Under Mandatory Minimum Sentencing," 48 J. Law & Econ. 591, 622 (2005) ("[P]rosecutors generally have the discretion to prosecute a defendant for a lesser charge than the initial arrest charge, and the use of such discretion can have dramatic effects on sentencing with respect to mandatory sentencing laws."); Michael A. Simons, "Departing Ways: Uniformity, Disparity, and Cooperation in Federal Drug Sentences," 47 Vill. L. Rev. 921, 934 (2002) ("Whether a defendant is eligible for a substantial assistance departure is almost completely discretionary—and that discretion rests entirely with the prosecution.").

28. See, e.g., Albert W. Alschuler, "Sentencing Reform and Prosecutorial Power: A Critique of Recent Proposals for "Fixed" and "Presumptive" Sentencing," 126 U. Pa. L. Rev. 550, 551 (1978) (arguing that prosecutorial discretion is "usually exercised by people of less experience and less objectivity than judges"); Hon. Anthony M. Kennedy, "Speech at the American Bar Association Annual Meeting," Aug. 9, 2003, available at http://www.supremecourt.gov/publicinfo/speeches/viewspeeches.aspx?Filename=sp_08-09-03.htm ("The trial judge is the one actor in the system most experienced with exercising discretion in a transparent, open, and reasoned way.").

29. See Reevaluating the Effectiveness of Mandatory Minimum Sentences: Hearing Before the S. Comm. on the Judiciary, 113th Cong. 4 (2013) (statement of Hon. Brett Tolman arguing that "institutional pressures to prosecute with an eye toward identifying and using mandatory minimum statutes to achieve the longest potential sentence in a given case are severe").

30. See, e.g., *United States v. Booker*, 543 U.S. 220 (2005) (ruling that the Sixth Amendment Jury Trial Clause limits the sentence that a trial judge may impose to one that rests on the jury's findings or the defendant's admissions).

31. See Barbara S. Vincent & Paul J. Hofer, "The Consequences of Mandatory Minimum Prison Terms: A Summary of Recent Findings," Federal Judicial Center (1994), available at http://www.fjc.gov/public/pdf.nsf/lookup/conmanmin.pdf/$file/conmanmin.pdf.

32. See, e.g., Alfred Blumstein & Allen J. Beck, "Population Growth in U.S. Prisons, 1980—1996," 26 Crime & Just. 17, 57 (1999) ("Incarceration of even three hundred thousand drug offenders does little to reduce drug sales through deterrence or incapacitation as long as the drug market can simply recruit replacements."); Larkin, supra note 14, at 247–48 & n.35.

33. See U.S. Sentencing Comm'n, Measuring Recidivism: The Criminal History Computation of the Federal Sentencing Guidelines (2004), available at http:// www.ussc.gov/publicat/Recidivism_General.pdf ("In general, as the number of criminal history points increases, the risk of recidivating within two years increases"); Jane L. Fryod, Safety Valve Failure: Low-Level Offenders and the Federal Sentencing Guidelines, 94 Nw. U. L. Rev. 1471, 1491 (2000) ("[T]he [Sentencing] Guidelines provide graduated, proportional increases in sentence severity for additional misconduct or prior convictions, whereas mandatory minimums sentences do not.").

34. See 18 U.S.C. § 3553(3) (2006).

35. See Luna & Cassell, supra note 24, at 19.

36. See Stephen J. Schulhofer, "Rethinking Mandatory Minimums," 28 Wake Forest L. Rev. 199, 212 (1993) ("Defendants who are most in the know, and thus have the most 'substantial assistance' to offer, are often those who are most centrally involved in conspiratorial crimes.").

37. Id. at 213.

38. In fiscal year 2010, 77.2 percent of defendants convicted of violating a statute carrying a mandatory minimum were convicted of a drug trafficking offense. U.S. Sentencing Comm'n 2011, supra note 21, at 72.

39. Schulhofer, supra note 36, at 209.

40. See Steven Nauman, *Brown v. Plata*; "Renewing the Call to End Mandatory Sentencing," 65 Fla. L. Rev. 855, 866–67 (2013). In another case, a man who attempted suicide by overdosing on Vicodin received 15 years in prison because he possessed 31 pills. His sentencing judge lamented, "I do believe this is an inappropriate sentence for you … but there are restraints placed on my ability to stray from the statutory framework that would result in [your] early release." See Erin Fuchs, "10 People Who Received Outrageous Sentences for Drug Convictions," Business Insider, Apr. 23, 2013, available at http://www.businessinsider.com/10-most-outrageous-mandatory-minimum-2013-4?op=1.

41. See id. Upon failing to find an alternative to the sentence, Judge Tombrink declared the statute unconstitutional because his conscience would not permit him to execute the sentence, and he did not want to waste the taxpayers' money. See id.

42. See Kristen K. Sauer, "Informed Conviction: Instructing the Jury About Mandatory Sentencing Consequences," 96 Colum. L. Rev. 1232, 1232 (1995).

43. See, e.g., *Gregg v. Georgia*, 428 U.S. 153, 186 (1976) (lead opinion) ("The value of capital punishment as a deterrent of crime is a complex factual issue the resolution of which properly rests with the legislatures, which can evaluate the results of statistical studies in terms of their own local conditions and with a flexibility of approach that is not available to the courts.").

44. See, e.g., Mandatory Minimum Penalties, supra note 21 (describing how critics of indeterminate sentencing during the pre-Guidelines era urged that a system of determinate sentencing would increase sentencing effectiveness by requiring sentences that are "more certain, less disparate, and more appropriately punitive"); Prepared Statement of David B. Muhlhausen, Senior Policy Analyst, Heritage Foundation, to the U.S. Sentencing Comm'n 9 (May 27, 2010) ("[M]andatory minimum sentences that establish long incarceration or death sentences for very serious and violent crimes can be justified based solely on the doctrine of just deserts.").

45. 543 U.S. 220 (2005).

46. See, e.g., Paul J. Larkin, Jr., "Parole: Corpse or Phoenix?," 50 Am. Crim. L. Rev. 303, 321–26 (2013).

47. Prepared Statement of Sally Quillian Yates, U.S. Attorney, Northern District of Georgia, to the U.S. Sentencing Comm'n 7 (May 27, 2010).

48. See, e.g., Steven N. Durlauf & Daniel S. Nagin, "Imprisonment and Crime: Can Both Be Reduced?," 10 Criminology & Pub. Pol'y 13, 37–38 (2011) (finding that certainty of punishment may have a large deterrent effect); Charles R. Tittle & Alan R. Rowe, "Certainty of Arrest and Crime Rates: A Further Test of the Deterrence Hypothesis," 52 Soc. Forces 455 (June 1974) (finding that certainty of imprisonment deters the commission of offenses).

49. See, e.g., Shlomo Shinnar & Reuel Shinnar, "The Effects of the Criminal Justice System on the Control of Crime: A Quantitative Approach," 9 Law & Soc'y Rev. 581 (1975) (suggesting violent crime can be significantly reduced by mandatory incarceration due to the incapacitation of offenders); Robert S. Mueller III, Mandatory Minimum Sentencing, 4 Fed. Sent'g Rep. 230 (1992) ("[T]he imposition of prescribed minimum prison terms enhances public safety by incapacitating dangerous offenders for substantial periods, thus preventing numerous instances of death, injury, and loss of property.").

50. See, e.g., Gary S. Becker, "Crime and Punishment: An Economic Approach," 76 J. Pol. Econ. 169, 178–85 (1968); Richard A. Posner, An Economic Theory of the Criminal Law, 85 Colum. L. Rev. 1193, 1212–13 (1985).

51. See Steven D. Levitt, "Understanding Why Crime Fell in the 1990s," 18 J. of Econ. Persp. 163, 163 (2004) (describing the phenomenon).

52. See Stanley Sporkin & Asa Hutchinson, "Debate, Mandatory Minimums in Drug Sentencing: A Valuable Weapon in the War on Drugs or a Handcuff on Judicial Discretion?," 36 Am. Crim. L. Rev. 1279, 1283 (1999) (statement of Rep. Hutchinson) ("[M]andatory minimum penalties appear to be effective. Violent crime has declined seven years in a row.").

53. See Reevaluating the Effectiveness of Federal Mandatory Minimum Sentences: Hearing Before the S. Comm. on the Judiciary, 113th Cong. 3 (2013) (statement of Scott Burns, Executive Director, National District Att'ys' Ass'n) ("Mandatory sentences have been extremely helpful to state and local prosecutors as leverage to secure cooperation from defendants and witnesses and solve other crimes or, in a drug distribution case, 'move up the chain' and prosecute those at higher levels of sophisticated trafficking organizations."); Prepared Statement of Raymond W. Kelly, Commissioner, New York Police Department, to the U.S. Sentencing Comm'n 4 (July 10, 2009) (testifying that the potential application of more severe penalties in federal court "has convinced a number of suspects to give up information.").

54. See, e.g., John C. Jeffries, Jr., & John Gleeson, "The Federalization of Organized Crime: Advantages of Federal Prosecution," 46 Hastings L.J. 1095, 1119–21 (1995) (finding that mandatory minimums have "produced far more cooperation and accomplice testimony in organized crime cases than occurred in the pre-Guidelines era.").

55. The Justice Safety Valve Act is reprinted in Appendix A.

56. Subsection 3553(a) of Title 18 sets forth various factors that federal judges may consider in imposing sentence, which include, among other things, criminal history, offense gravity, deterrence, and the need to protect the public.

57. See Justice Safety Valve Act, § 2.

58. On January 30, 2014, the Senate Judiciary Committee voted to send to the floor a revised version of the original bill. Appendix B contains the version approved by the committee. An additional salutary feature of the bill reported out of the Senate Judiciary Committee can be seen in Section 7. Section 7 would impose four new requirements on the federal government: (1) It directs the Attorney General, within one year, to prepare a report that lists all federal criminal offenses, the punishment authorized for a violation of each offense, the mens rea elements required by each offense, and the number of federal prosecutions brought within the last 15 years; ( 2) Section 7 directs each specified federal regulatory agency within one year to prepare a similar report listing all federal criminal offenses enforced by the agency, the punishment authorized for a violation of each offense, the mens rea elements required by each offense, and the number of cases that the agency referred to the Justice Department for prosecution within the past 15 years; (3) Section 7 directs the Attorney General, within two years, to have publicly available without cost an index of each criminal offense listed in the report that is accessible without cost on the website of the Department of Justice; and (4) within two years, each federal agency must have a similar list of regulatory offenses that is publicly accessible without charge on its agency website. The Heritage Foundation has previously supported the concept of having federal authorities "count the crimes" and has highlighted the problems posed by enacting criminal laws and regulations that lack adequate mens rea requirements. See, e.g., Paul Rosenzweig, Ignorance of the Law Is No Excuse, But It Is Reality, The Heritage Foundation Backgrounder No. 2812 (June 17, 2013), http://www.heritage.org/research/

reports/2013/06/ignorance-of-the-law-is-no-excuse-but-it-is-reality; Paul Rosenzweig, Congress Doesn't Know Its Own Mind—And That Makes You a Criminal, The Heritage Foundation Legal Memorandum No. 98 (July 18, 2013), http://www.heritage.org/research/reports/2013/07/congress-doesnt-know-its-own-mind-and-that-makes-you-a-criminal; Defining the Problem and Scope of Over-criminalization and Over-federalization: Hearing Before the H. Comm. on the Judiciary, 112th Congress (2013) (testimony of John G. Malcolm, Rule of Law Programs Policy Director and the Ed Gilbertson and Sherry Lindberg Gilbertson Senior Legal Fellow, The Heritage Foundation).

59. See Appendix B, § 2.

60. See Fair Sentencing Act of 2010, Pub. L. No. 111-220, § 2, 3, 124 Stat. 2372 (codified at 21 U.S.C. §§ 841, 960 (2012)).

61. See Appendix B, §§ 3–4.

62. See Justice Safety Valve Act, § 2, and 18 U.S.C. § 3553(a).

63. See Justice Safety Valve Act, § 3.

64. The same cannot be said for, say, the use of a firearm to commit a crime.

> "*The current lack of political representation for communities of color undermines trust in government, disadvantages depressed communities, and creates the context for racial tension.*"

# The Entire Criminal Justice System Needs a Smarter Approach

## Michele L. Jawando and Chelsea Parsons

*In the following viewpoint, Michele L. Jawando and Chelsea Parsons go beyond the mass incarceration aspect of the criminal justice system and delve into improving police-community relations. They argue that four steps: increasing the use of special prosecutors, enhancing data collection in police-involved fatalities, implementing implicit bias training, and increasing federal oversight of police conduct could help reform the system, helping to address injustices and right inequalities. Jawando serves as vice president for legal progress at the Center for American Progress. She has appeared and been cited in The Washington Post, Politico, CNN, NBC, MSNBC, PBS, FOX, and Huffington Post Live. Parsons, vice president of guns and crime policy at the Center for American Progress, has appeared on CNN, MSNBC, and NPR. She has been cited in USA Today, The Washington Post, The Wall Street Journal, the Los Angeles Times, and The Economist.*

"4 Ideas That Could Begin to Reform the Criminal Justice System and Improve Police-Community Relations", by Michele L. Jawando and Chelsea Parsons, Center for American Progress, December 18, 2014. Reprinted by Permission.

As you read, consider the following questions:

1. How many reports of misconduct were there in 2010 according to The Cato Institute?
2. According to the authors, how can improved data collection help in the development of new laws and policies?
3. What is implicit bias?

From the shooting death of unarmed teenager Michael Brown, to the heavily militarized police response, to the protests in the wake of Brown's death, to the failure of the grand jury to indict Officer Darren Wilson for his role in the shooting, the events in Ferguson, Missouri, have turned up the heat on a long simmering debate over the persistent inequalities in our criminal justice system. Other recent events have made the urgent need to act even more clear: In Staten Island, New York, a grand jury decided not to indict New York Police Officer Daniel Pantaleo for causing the death of another unarmed black man, Eric Garner, even though the officer's actions were caught on tape. Days earlier, a police officer shot and killed Tamir Rice, a 12-year-old in Cleveland, Ohio, while he played with a toy gun.

At the center of this debate has been a conversation about inequities in the basic functioning of the criminal justice system—including police practices, the use of force and aggressive policing, arrest and prosecution policies, the severity of criminal sentences, and the disparate impact many of these policies have on communities of color. Little wonder there is a deep-seated sentiment within communities of color that the criminal justice system is inherently rigged against them and that the institutions supposedly designed to protect them are failing them, or even worse, targeting them. Moreover, the gap between black and white views on law enforcement, the criminal justice system, and race relations in this country only seems to be growing. This ever-widening gulf further complicates our attempts to understand exactly what is at issue in cases such as the deaths of Brown and Garner, the failure of the grand juries in those cases to indict the officers responsible, and the opportunity to think through ideas and options for concrete solutions to address the underlying problems.

While reflection is important after moments such as this, we are now tasked with the obligation of figuring out how to move forward, learn from these incidents, and turn a moment of anger and frustration into an opportunity to make positive change in our criminal justice system. Much of this work is already underway. Following the unrest in Ferguson, President Barack Obama announced a three-year, $263 million package to increase police officers' use of body-worn cameras and expand local law-enforcement training. The president is preparing to issue an executive order calling for additional oversight of various federal programs that provide military surplus equipment to local law-enforcement agencies and for the establishment of a presidential taskforce examining crime reduction and efforts to build public trust. Additionally, U.S. Attorney General Eric Holder announced the release of updated Department of Justice, or DOJ, guidance, for federal law-enforcement agencies that will create rigorous new standards and robust safeguards that seek to end racial profiling by federal law enforcement. Another promising development from the Obama administration includes the DOJ announcement that it "has enlisted a team of criminal justice researchers to study racial bias in law enforcement in five American cities and recommend strategies to address the problem." These data will not only help inform smart and more effective policing models, but they will also help to close some of the looming racial divides by identifying prejudiced behavior and developing processes to address bias in all aspects of policing.

These are excellent steps, but they are not a panacea. More must be done to implement new innovations in policing and other aspects of the justice system that will improve police accountability and reduce the degree to which the harshest aspects of criminal justice fall disproportionately on communities of color. The United

States needs to embrace a smarter approach to criminal justice that recognizes that the propensity to focus on race is not the answer to create safe communities. The failure to ensure that our judicial and legal systems treat all Americans equally has divided too many of our communities. We must give voice to the legitimate and widespread concerns about trust in the criminal justice process. As Americans, we have a responsibility to build inclusive communities where families thrive and where compassion, not fear, is the core value.

This issue brief offers four ideas to reform the criminal justice system, including improved police training; data collection and accountability; repairing the fractured relationship between police and community; and, in instances where lives are taken, the promise of a diligent, independent, and thorough investigation and prosecution, when appropriate. This is certainly not intended as a final assessment of what needs to be done to reform policing and the criminal justice system in the United States, but rather as an opening salvo in an ongoing conversation about crime and justice in this country.

## 1. Increase the use of special prosecutors in police misconduct investigations

In recent weeks, the role of the prosecutor and the grand jury system has come under intense scrutiny. The failure of grand juries to indict either Officer Darren Wilson for his role in Brown's death or Staten Island Officer Daniel Pantaleo for his role in Garner's death have raised significant questions about the ability of local prosecutors to remain impartial in cases involving local law enforcement in the same jurisdiction. Prosecutors rely on local police officers to make arrests, investigate cases, interrogate suspects, and testify at trial. Police officers, in turn, rely on prosecutors to convert their arrests into convictions and assist with investigations. The prosecutor's office is charged with responsibility for prosecutions in its jurisdiction. However, in most instances of fatalities involving officers, "prosecutors generally use special grand juries ... to investigate and gather evidence before determining if an arrest and indictment are warranted." In cases involving alleged police misconduct, questions about prosecutors' sympathies for the defendant—sympathies that may prevent the prosecutor from being an effective advocate for the state—provide an opportunity to consider alternatives to address perceived conflicts of interests.

The Cato Institute's "National Police Misconduct Reporting Project" shows 4,861 unique reports of misconduct in 2010, including 127 fatalities associated with excessive force. Additionally, according to the Bureau of Justice Statistics, 70 percent of black people who have experienced the use of police force against them feel that the force was excessive. Black people are three to five times more likely than whites to believe that police misconduct frequently occurs in their city, and black Americans are three times more likely to say that it occurs very often in their neighborhood. As discussed below, no precise figures exist for the number of people killed by the police in the United States, but police departments each year voluntarily report about 420 "justifiable police homicides" to the Federal Bureau of Investigation. Rarely do deaths involving police lead to murder or manslaughter charges. Philip Stinson, a criminologist at Bowling Green State University, has found that between 2005 and 2011, 41 officers were charged with murder or manslaughter for on-duty shootings, but police departments reported 2,600 justifiable homicides to the FBI.

The perception, real or perceived, is that local prosecutors have far too great of an interest to protect and justify the actions of local law enforcement. The perceived bias in the system has led to the erosion of trust that is needed to build public safety between law enforcement and local communities, suggesting that viable alternatives should be considered.

Some states have established permanent special prosecutors' offices. Maryland handles a variety of cases, from violations of election law to police misconduct, through an independent special prosecutor. In 1972, the state of New York created a special prosecutor's office to explore police corruption in New York City.

According to the New York Law Journal, the special prosecutor's office in New York "established a remarkable track record in fairly, objectively and successfully investigating and prosecuting police officers and others in the criminal justice system suspected of criminality." In 1990, the office was disbanded, but recently, there have been calls to reinstate the office to investigate and potentially prosecute alleged police brutality cases that result in the death of an unarmed subject.

There are several approaches employed in states across the country that could serve as a model for reform. States could provide state attorney generals additional prosecutorial authority over fatalities involving police and create permanent "special prosecutors" that are housed within the state office of the attorney general to provide a level of insulation from local law enforcement. As suggested by Joshua Deahl, an appellate attorney with the District of Columbia' Public Defender Service, the special prosecutor's responsibilities could "be limited to the oversight, investigation and prosecution of police or public official misconduct, keeping them independent from other policing functions." Alternatively, states such as Wisconsin have "officer-involved-death" statutes. In Wisconsin, this requires that at least two independent investigators examine cases.

Finally, automatic referral outside the jurisdiction in fatal cases involving police is a possibility. In that instance, a prosecutor from outside the jurisdiction in question would lead the investigation. The requirement of an independent, outside party could address perceived conflict of interest issues with local officials. Whether by state statute requiring an out-of-jurisdiction investigator or state executive action automatically assigning fatalities cases involving police to attorney generals or special prosecutors, all states should adopt practices to ensure that all investigations of homicides involving police are conducted by a neutral prosecutor other than the office that typically works with the police department that is the subject of the investigation.

## 2. Enhance the collection of data on fatalities involving police

In the immediate aftermath of the deaths of Brown and Garner, many commentators, community members, and policymakers around the country asked what should be relatively easy questions to answer: How often do police officers kill unarmed individuals? Are the deaths of Brown and Garner isolated incidents or examples of a larger trend of inappropriate use of force by police officers in communities around the country, and are communities of color disproportionately affected?

Unfortunately, these are not easy questions to answer. As a number of reporters discovered over the past few months, there are significant gaps in the collection and analysis of data related to fatalities involving officers; these gaps make it very difficult to assess the scope of the problem either nationwide or in individual states and localities. The primary source for data about homicides in the United States is the FBI's Uniform Crime Reporting, or UCR, program, through which federal, state, and local police agencies voluntarily report information about certain designated crimes, including homicides. Police agencies are asked to submit more detailed information about homicides, including demographic information about the victim and offender, the type of weapon used, the relationship between the perpetrator and offender, and some limited information about the circumstances of the killing, such as whether the homicide occurred during the commission or attempted commission of a felony. As part of this Supplementary Homicide Report, the FBI also collects information about deaths of individuals deemed "justified," which includes two categories of homicides: felons killed by law-enforcement officers in the line of duty and felons killed by private individuals during the commission of a felony.

There are a number of problems with these data. First, police departments' reporting of homicide data to the UCR program is voluntary. And because police departments are not required to submit these data, many choose not to. For example, Florida does not provide any data to the UCR program, and other states submit these data in a piecemeal and incomplete fashion. So while FBI data tell us that between 2009 and 2013, law-enforcement officers killed 2,102 felons nationwide in the line of duty and used firearms in 99 percent of these cases, this is likely a very incomplete total count of fatalities involving police. Indeed, a comparison with another source of homicide data—the Centers for Disease Control, which compiles information on deaths based on death certificates—demonstrates the limitations of the FBI data. For 2012, the FBI reports 426 justifiable homicides nationwide; the CDC reports 550 such fatalities. Although these two sources use slightly different definitions, the disparity between the two numbers helps demonstrate the scope of the data gap. Additionally, the FBI only counts homicides by police officers that are deemed justified, so deaths by officers that do not fall into that category— such as shootings in which an officer is determined to have acted criminally—will not be included in the FBI count. Second, the data that local police agencies voluntarily provided to the FBI about officer-involved fatalities include limited information about the context and circumstances of those incidents and what immediately precipitated the fatal event, including whether the victim was armed.

But even with this incomplete data set, there is evidence of a racial disparity in instances of police shootings of civilians. An analysis of FBI Supplementary Homicide data conducted by the independent, nonprofit news service ProPublica found that from 2010 to 2012, police killed young black men at much higher rates than their white peers: 31.17 per million for black males between the ages of 15 and 19 versus 1.47 per million for white males in the same age group. This analysis found that young black men in this age group were 21 times more likely to be shot by police than young white men. Reporters from Vox, a news website, obtained more detailed information from the FBI about each of the justifiable homicides reported in 2012 and found that a disproportionate number of reported felons who were killed by police were black.

In order to develop smart laws and policies to address law enforcement's inappropriate and illegal use of force, we need to understand the scope and nature of the problem. The federal government must improve data collection and require state and local law enforcement to provide detailed information about deaths caused by police officers. On December 11, 2014, Congress passed the Death in Custody Reporting Act of 2013, a bill that would mandate such reporting by states and would give the U.S. attorney general the discretion to reduce federal law-enforcement funding to states that fail to comply by as much as 10 percent. This legislation would require states to submit demographic information about the victim, details about the time and location of the death, the law-enforcement agency involved, and "a brief description of the circumstances surrounding the death." The attorney general would then be required to conduct a study of this information in order to "determine means by which such information can be used to reduce the number of such deaths."

This legislation would be a significant step forward in addressing the current data gap on fatalities involving police, and President Obama should sign it into law as soon as possible. However, in order for this legislation to have the maximum beneficial impact, the administration must implement detailed regulations outlining exactly what kind of information about each of these incidents are required to be reported under the catch-all language in the legislation to ensure that states are reporting crucial information— including whether the victim was armed, whether the officer or officers involved had any relevant disciplinary history related to the use of force, and other key details regarding events precipitating the fatal event. Additionally, the regulations should provide that, absent "extraordinary circumstances," the attorney general will exercise the discretion to impose the 10 percent funding penalty on states that fail to comply by the second year that the law is in effect.

The next Congress should also act to expand the reporting mandate on states to include full participation in the FBI Supplementary Homicide Report to provide details on all homicides in a jurisdiction, not just those involving police. This information would provide a crucial baseline for understanding homicides in the states and help inform law-enforcement practices going forward. In particular, states should be required to provide information about homicides in which individuals invoke "stand-your-ground" defenses, another area in which there is an extreme paucity of reliable data.

## 3. Implement implicit bias training for all federal law-enforcement officers and state and local police involved in federal task forces

"Black Lives Matter" is one of the most evocative statements being chanted from protesters participating in demonstrations in the wake of the recent killings of Michael Brown, Eric Garner, and Tamir Rice. The statement itself has become a point of contention, but the statement speaks to perhaps the most important and most difficult issue that has arisen out of the recent protests: the subtle and stark differences that make up white and black experiences in America. While these divisions are often felt writ large by communities of color, the disparities seem to be particularly acute between white and black individuals, and the data seem to support these perceptions. The discrepancies in outcomes with similar circumstances between races can be interpreted through the lens of implicit bias. Researchers who seek to measure implicit biases often point to psychological and neurological factors inherent in unconscious racial associations. This has shown, as one researcher recently noted, "that hidden biases operating largely under the scope of human consciousness influence the way that we see and treat others, even when we are determined to be fair and objective." Findings show that implicit bias can be contradictory to an individual's stated beliefs. The presence of implicit bias has been used to explain disparities among races in both access to and quality of health care, treatment in the criminal justice system, and housing.

For instance, despite reporting very little explicit bias, approximately two-thirds of the nation's health clinicians were found to harbor a statistically significant implicit bias against blacks and Latinos. Additionally, unconscious views about race help explain the disproportionate arrest and incarceration of African Americans for drug offenses. Research shows that although whites engage in drug offenses at rates higher than blacks do, blacks are almost four times more likely to be arrested for these offenses compared to whites. The data also reveal that black men were sent to prison on drug charges at 11.8 times the rate of white men, and black women are sent to prison on drug charges at 4.8 times the rate of white women.

Likewise, the realm of housing shows a striking racially based implicit bias when African Americans look to rent or buy housing. When renting, blacks were told about the availability of 11.4 percent fewer units as compared to whites and shown 4.2 percent fewer units. When it came to home buying, blacks were also told about 17 percent fewer homes than whites and shown 17.7 percent fewer homes.

According to David R. Williams, a Harvard sociologist, the "frightening point" is that because implicit bias is "an automatic and unconscious process, people who engage in this unthinking discrimination are not aware of the fact that they do it." A 2012 study found that officers were quicker to shoot an armed black person and slower to refrain from shooting an unarmed black person than they were with members of any other racial group. Similar results were found in a study of the Denver, Colorado, police department. When asked to press a button labeled "shoot" or "don't shoot," Denver police officers were "uniformly faster to shoot an armed black target, relative to an armed white target, and uniformly faster to press the 'Don't shoot' button for an unarmed white target, relative to an unarmed black target."

If these are indeed unconscious reactions, what can actually be done about implicit bias, especially in policing? There are promising policies available that may mitigate the effects of bias. A key element is training. Training recommendations do not reduce bias; rather, they raise consciousness about them. Research has suggested that by making one aware of unconscious biases, these malleable biases may be reduced. The federal government should require training on implicit bias in police academies and ongoing state and local departmental training as a condition of federal grants. Law-enforcement recruits should be challenged to identify key police decisions and scenarios that are at greatest risk of manifesting bias—such as traffic stops, consent searches, reasonable suspicion to frisk, and other procedures—and then reflect on the potential impact of implicit bias on their perceptions and behaviors in those scenarios. Furthermore, seasoned officers should be similarly challenged at in-service and other training venues.

In addition, police departments should be encouraged to take steps to increase diversity among law-enforcement professionals. The federal government should condition receipt of certain grant funding by state and local law-enforcement agencies—perhaps funding for surplus military equipment—on the implementation of hiring and retention policies designed to increase diversity in police departments. Ideally, the composition of personnel should reflect the diversity of the community that is serves. Finally, law-enforcement agencies need to eschew colorblindness and acknowledge real group and individual differences, such as through ongoing diversity and multiculturalism training. Research suggests that a colorblind ideology generates greater amounts of implicit bias than a multicultural perspective does.

## 4. Increase the federal government's oversight of police conduct

The day-to-day operations of police departments across the country are largely handled at the state and local level. The federal government does have a role in local policing, primarily through the provision of federal funding for law enforcement for a variety of programs such as crime deterrence initiatives, hiring of officers, purchasing equipment, training, and creation of cross-jurisdiction task forces. A Brennan Center for Justice analysis found that at least $3.8 billion is given to state and local governments each year in federal criminal justice grants. The federal government also becomes involved when a complaint is made to the Department of Justice Office of Civil Rights about issues relating to police officer conduct. The complaints regard either an individual incident in which an officer allegedly violated the civil rights of a community member or an incident in which an entire police department has engaged in a "pattern or practice" of violating the civil rights of the community. In those cases, the DOJ conducts extensive investigations and, upon finding violations of civil rights, commences or threatens litigation against the offending jurisdictions, which often results in consent decrees that reform police practices in the jurisdiction.

However, the DOJ engages in relatively little proactive activity to shape police practices on the ground in communities across the country. While the DOJ may enter into a detailed consent decree with a particular jurisdiction that outlines specific policies and practices that officers must implemented on the ground, it does not offer this guidance on a broader basis to law-enforcement agencies across the country. The DOJ should take a more proactive role in providing guidance to local police agencies about best practices— for issues such as use of force, racially discriminatory practices, or officer accountability—before police department practices deteriorate to the point of systematically violating the civil rights of members of the community. While the DOJ has issued some general guidance for police departments over the years, there are certainly lessons learned from pattern and practice investigations of individual police departments—along with innovative new policies and practices that have arisen from those investigations—that could and should be shared with law enforcement across the country. In recent months, the DOJ has done more of this by issuing guidance to law enforcement on maintaining order during protests and the appropriate circumstances under which federal officers may consider a person's race or ethnicity.

The DOJ should take a more active approach in setting expectations for police conduct nationwide and ensure compliance with those standards by conditioning participation in federal task forces on the adoption of certain standards, policies, and training and through penalties in federal funding. The Brennan Center recently released a report offering an innovative new approach for rethinking federal funding for law enforcement called "Success-Oriented Funding" that would better connect provision of federal funding with achievement of clearly-established goals. The federal government has an obligation to ensure that police officers in communities around the country are not violating the civil rights of the people they are charged to serve and protect and should be more proactive in ensuring that police agencies are properly training and supervising their officers before individual misconduct rises to the level of systemic violations of civil rights.

## Conclusion

These four recommendations, along with President Obama's recent actions, are among a set of reforms that are needed to address injustice and inequalities in the criminal justice system, particularly with respect to police misconduct. The challenges that the criminal justice system face, however, do not operate in a vacuum; but rather, they reflect broader challenges in our culture and in our democracy. Ferguson, Missouri—where even though "two in three Ferguson residents are black, the city government is almost entirely white"—underscores the lack of representation of people of color and raises significant concerns over a lack of reflective representation in our democracy.

One new challenge in ensuring full civic participation of people of color is an increasing trend in laws and practices that restrict voter access. In 2013, the U.S. Supreme Court's *Shelby County v. Holder* ruling weakened the landmark Voting Rights Act of 1965.

November 4, 2014, marked the first Election Day in 50 years in which voters went to the polls without many important protections. As a result, many states imposed suppressive new voting laws that make it harder for eligible voters to cast their ballots. Unsurprisingly, the 2014 election had the worst voter turnout in 72 years. Suppressive voter laws also affect the composition of local grand juries. In many states, the list generated for juror selection uses the names of registered voters. State laws that make it harder to register to vote—by limiting same-day registration, imposing stringent voter ID laws, and eliminating the so-called "golden week" when voters can register and immediately cast ballots—deleteriously prevent potential jurors from appearing on juror lists. This dilutes the pool of potential grand jurors and inaccurately reflects the make up of local communities. The lack of diversity on the grand juries in Ferguson and Staten Island underscores this lack of reflectiveness.

The current lack of political representation for communities of color undermines trust in government, disadvantages depressed communities, and creates the context for racial tension. This threatens our democracy. Racial and ethnic diversity in elected office can result in positive policy changes for all Americans. Instead of crafting more barriers to representation and excluding communities from the juror's box, we should actively seek to promote opportunities for participation in civic life. Instead of denying the right to vote, we should strive to engage all citizens in our democracy. Addressing efforts to curtail the right to vote and to limit participation in the democratic process are crucial to promoting the kinds of robust democratic institutions and rebuilding the public's confidence in those institutions to both reform and build confidence in policing and prosecution. Poverty, lack of representation, and perceived bias of local law enforcement combine to create a combustible situation that presents significant challenges to communities across the country. We should make every effort to address these challenges and strive to make a more inclusive, fair, and just America.

> *"During the early part of the national prison boom, all of the states walked lockstep together to increase their use of the prison."*

# Ending Mass Incarceration Requires a Focus on State Policy

*Peter Wagner*

*In the following viewpoint, Peter Wagner argues that states, not the federal government, are responsible for increasing prison growth. In the original article, he uses graphs to illustrate the differences in rates and numbers across the country. He says we now have the benefit of this data to show how individual states' policy choices have affected criminal justice and prisons in those areas. Wagner is an attorney and the executive director of the Prison Policy Initiative, which he co-founded in 2001. In 2013, he was given the Champion of State Criminal Justice Reform Award by the National Association of Criminal Defense Lawyers.*

"Tracking State Prison Growth in 50 States," by Peter Wagner, Prison Policy Initiative, May 28, 2014. Reprinted by Permission.

As you read, consider the following questions:

1. What percentage of incarcerated individuals are behind bars as a result of federal-level policy?
2. What effect have the prison populations in New York and California had on the national incarceration rate?
3. What does Wagner say accounts for the year-to-year variations in the graphs he discusses?

Over the last three decades of the 20th century, the United States engaged in an unprecedented prison-building boom that has given our nation the highest incarceration rate in the world. Among people with experience in criminal justice policy matters, the "hockey stick curve" of the national incarceration rate is well known; but until now more detailed data on the incarceration rates for individual states has been harder to come by. This briefing fills the gap with a series of more than 100 graphs [see online] showing prison growth (and sometimes decline) for every state in the nation to encourage states to confront how their criminal policy choices undermine our national welfare.

Ending the U.S. experiment with mass incarceration requires us to focus on state policy because individual states are the most active incarcerating bodies in the nation.

Most (57%) people incarcerated in the United States have been convicted of violating state law and are imprisoned in a state prison. Another 30% are confined in local jails — which are outside the scope of this briefing — generally either for minor violations of state law or because they are waiting to be tried for charges of violating state law. Federal-level policy directly accounts for only the 10% of people behind bars in the U.S.; they have either been convicted of violating a federal law or are being detained by the immigration authorities and are awaiting potential deportation to another country.

## FOUR GUIDING PRINCIPLES FOR FUTURE POLICY DECISIONS

[D]eciding whether incarceration is justified requires an analysis of social costs versus benefits. This equation should weigh the importance of recognizing the harm experienced by crime victims, appropriately addressing those harms, and reinforcing society's disapproval of criminal behavior. However, the committee stressed that future policy decisions should not only be based on empirical evidence but also should follow these four guiding principles, which have been notably absent from recent policy debates on the proper use of prisons:

- *Proportionality*: Criminal offenses should be sentenced in proportion to their seriousness.

- *Parsimony*: The period of confinement should be sufficient but not greater than necessary to achieve the goals of sentencing policy.

- *Citizenship*: The conditions and consequences of imprisonment should not be so severe or lasting as to violate one's fundamental status as a member of society.

- *Social justice*: Prisons should be instruments of justice, and as such their collective effect should be to promote society's aspirations for a fair distribution of rights, resources, and opportunities.

**"U.S. Should Significantly Reduce Rate of Incarceration; Unprecedented Rise in Prison Population 'Not Serving the Country Well,' Says New Report," by Dana Korsen and Chelsea Dickson, The National Academies of Sciences, Engineering, and Medicine. April 30, 2014.**

In the aggregate, these state-level policy choices have been the largest driver of our unprecedented national experiment with mass incarceration, but not every state has contributed equally or consistently to this phenomenon. In the U.S., each state is responsible for making its own policy choices about which people to lock up and how for long. We can't end our nation's experiment with mass incarceration without grappling with the wide variety of state-level criminal justice policies, practices and trends.

Take, for example, the comparison of the incarceration rate for the United States with data from individual states. Minnesota has long been less likely to incarcerate than other states, but also, like the country as a whole, markedly increased its use of imprisonment in the late 20th century. On the other extreme, Alabama and Louisiana have consistently maintained above-average rates of incarceration, and their use of the prison continues to grow.

But another, contrary, trend is visible: the recent rapid decline of imprisonment in the populous states of New York (starting in 1999) and California (beginning in 2006 and accelerating in 2009). The number of people incarcerated in those two states is so large that prison population changes within those states are, in large part, responsible for the recent drop in the national incarceration rate. So, while the United States incarceration rate has dropped for four years in a row, over that same time period 15 states have made policy choices that increased their individual incarceration rates.

Although individual state comparisons are probably the most informative, regional data reveal significant patterns as well. For example, the South has consistently had a higher rate of incarceration than the other regions of the United States.

All of the yearly variations indicate one of two things: either a change in criminal justice policy or, less often, a change in data collection practices. As always, a comprehensive understanding of the larger political and social climate in any given state is key to successfully interpreting incarceration data. For example, the large drop in California's prison population is the result of both an order from the U.S. Supreme Court to reduce unconstitutional overcrowding in state prisons and a legislative change that sends people who would previously have gone to state prison to local jails, which are both exempt from the Supreme Court's order. To be sure, the California prison population drop is still notable because the state's prison population is dropping faster than the jail population is increasing, but the actual decline in the number of people incarcerated in California is not as large or as quick as the Supreme Court ordered.

During the early part of the national prison boom, all of the states walked lockstep together to increase their use of the prison. In the last decade, some individual states gradually started to reverse direction. As more states realized that mass criminalization is counterproductive, the aggregate national figures also reversed. Two decades ago, the idea of reducing any given state's use of incarceration would have required a great deal of imagination. Today, we have the benefit of being able to compare states that have made dramatically different criminal justice policy choices.

With this briefing we give state-level policymakers and advocates another opportunity to get involved, and to look at the larger context of incarceration in their state and to develop strategies that will make their communities stronger and safer. This briefing is just a starting point. It's time to get going.

> *"It's inconceivable that we routinely dump nonviolent offenders in prison cells with violent ones, even in local jails and holding tanks."*

# We Need to Embrace Alternative Strategies for Dealing with Offenders

*Bo Lozoff and Human Kindness Foundation*

*In the following viewpoint, Bo Lozoff makes the case that the current methods we use to handle crime have not made our society safer; he says they've only made the problem worse. Lozoff provides solutions for reform that he believes can make a positive difference. He covers such aspects as how we deal with drugs, violent and nonviolent offenders, thinking beyond rehabilitation, and each individual's own role in seeking change. Lozoff is a director at the Human Kindness Foundation—as part of this work he has corresponded with prisoners for over 20 years. He authored the book* We're All Doing Time: A Guide to Getting Free.

"Seven Ways to Fix the Criminal Justice System", by Bo Lozoff, Renaissance Universal. Reprinted with Permission of Bo Lozoff and Human Kindness Foundation.

As you read, consider the following questions:

1. What does Lozoff say is the most pervasive myth when it comes to the criminal justice system?
2. How does the author define what he calls "socially sanctioned hatred"?
3. According to Lozoff, what does restorative justice do for an offender?

How can we reduce the frightening levels of crime and violence that plague our society today? The usual answer from politicians and the media is that we have to be tougher on crime. If we had the guts to crack down like, say, those Singaporeans, then we'd straighten this country out.

But that's just a myth, and a dangerous one, because it is actually preventing us from solving the crime problem. Here's the reality: America now locks up prisoners at a rate five times greater than most industrialized nations, a rate of incarceration second only to Russia. The number of inmates in state and federal prisons has more than quadrupled, from fewer than 200,000 in 1970 to 948,000 in 1993. Prisoners currently sleep on floors, in tents, in converted broom closets and gymnasiums, or in double or triple bunks in cells that were designed for one inmate. I have visited about 500 prisons and, I can tell you, they are not country clubs (though they certainly are a luxury item: The average new prison cell costs $53,100 to construct). For the most part, they are terrifying and miserable places that will seem as shameful to us in a hundred years as the infamous nineteenth-century "snake-pit" insane asylums seem to us today.

Approximately 240,000 brutal rapes occur in our prison system each year, and most of the victims are young, nonviolent male inmates, many of them teen-age first offenders. After being raped, or "punked out," many of these young men are forced to shave their body hair and dress effeminately so they can be sold among "roosters" as sexual slaves for packs of cigarettes. This sometimes continues for the entire length of their incarceration. They are traumatized beyond imagination. Michael Fay's caning in Singapore was child's play compared to the reception he would have had in nearly any state prison in America. We are not soft on criminals.

The above, however, should not lead you to believe that our prisons are teeming with violent, dangerous people. Just the opposite: More than half of all US prisoners are serving time for non-violent offenses. Please let that sink in, because it's probably not the image you've received from the media. Instead, we've been led to imagine a legion of dangerous criminals cleverly plotting to get out and hurt us again. The truth is that most prison inmates are confused, disorganized, and often pathetic individuals who would love to turn their lives around if given a realistic chance. Unfortunately many of those nonviolent offenders will no longer he nonviolent by the time they leave prison.

But perhaps the most pervasive myth distorting our view of criminal justice is that increasing arrests and imprisonment is an effective strategy for reducing crime. Again, here's the shocking reality: The rate of violent crime hasn't significantly increased or decreased in the past fifteen years. And yet, the prison population in the US more than doubled during the 1980s. What's more, the threat of prison does not seem to deter criminal behavior. Around 62 percent of all prison inmates nationwide are arrested again within three years. Prisons are not scaring criminals away from crime; they are incapacitating them so they are hardly fit for anything else.

In other words, the criminal justice system that we're paying for so dearly simply isn't working. And yet we keep on throwing more money into it. So how do we start fixing what's broken? Here are seven places to begin:

## Learn to recognize the influence of socially sanctioned hatred.

What I mean by socially sanctioned hatred is simple: We human beings seem to have a built-in temptation to objectify other groups of people in order to feel superior to them or to find a scapegoat for all our problems. It's reflected in language, in words like "nigger," "Faggot," "slant-eyes," "gook," and so on. Certainly, among most of us, that kind of prejudicial speech is not acceptable. And yet, among decent people, from liberal to conservative, it is still socially acceptable to call criminals "scum," "sleaze bags," or "animals." We hear that one demented soul kidnapped and killed a little girl, and a few weeks later, when a teenager steals our car radio, we are ready to strap the two of them together in the gas chamber. "I'm sick of these animals," we say. "They're all alike. Let them fry."

People who break the law are not all alike. They are an enormously diverse group of human beings.

## Make drugs a public health problem instead of a criminal justice problem.

Drug cases are clogging our nation's prisons. Some 61 percent of federal prison inmates are there for drug offenses, up from 18 percent in 1980. And all this incarceration is doing nothing to solve the drug problem. Many wardens, judges, and other officials know this, but it has become political suicide to discuss decriminalization.

We need to insist upon a more mature dialogue about the drug problem. Keep in mind that the high-level drug dealers aren't cluttering up our prisons; they're too rich and smart to get caught. They hire addicts or kids, sometimes as young as eleven or twelve, to take most of the risks that result in confinement.

But it's not the dealers who create the drug problem anyway. Among the poor, drugs are a problem of alienation and isolation, of feeling unknown, unimportant, powerless, and hopeless. Among the affluent, they are an attempt to keep up with or escape from an insanely frenzied lifestyle that has almost nothing to do with simple human joys such as friendship or hearing the birds sing.

We need to address these issues in ourselves, our families, and our communities. At the same time, we must press for changes in drug laws. I'm not advocating that we "legalize" all drugs, because it's not that simple. But we do have to "decriminalize" their use, treating the problem as the public-health issue it is. Doing so would have tremendous benefits. Without drug offenders, our prisons would have more than enough room to hold all the dangerous criminals. As a result, we wouldn't need to build a single new prison, saving us some $5 billion a year. And if we spent a fraction of that money on rehabilitation centers and community revitalization programs, we'd begin to put drug dealers out of business in the only way that will last -by drying up their market.

## Separate violent and nonviolent offenders right from the start.

It's inconceivable that we routinely dump nonviolent offenders in prison cells with violent ones, even in local jails and holding tanks. What are we thinking? I know one fellow who was arrested for participating in a Quaker peace vigil and was jailed in lieu of paying a ten-dollar fine. In a forty-eight- hour period, he was savagely raped and traded back and forth among more than fifty violent prisoners. That was twenty years ago, and since then he has had years of therapy, and yet he has never recovered emotionally. His entire life still centers around the decision of one prison superintendent to place him in a violent cellblock in order to "teach him a lesson."

Most nonviolent offenders do in fact learn a lesson: how to be violent. Ironically; we spend an average of $20,000 per year, per inmate, teaching them this. For less than that we could be sending every nonviolent offender to college.

None of us, including prison staff, should accept violence as a fact of prison life, and it would be easy not to. We could designate certain facilities as zero-violence areas and allow inmates to live there as long as they don't commit-or even threaten to commit-a single violent act. The great majority of prisoners would sign up for such a place, I can assure you. Only about 10 percent of the prison population sets the terrorist tone for most institutions, and they are able to do that because the administration gives no support to the 90 percent of inmates who just want to do their time, improve themselves in some way, and get out alive.

To make matters worse, in most prisons when an inmate is threatened he or she is the one who gets locked up in a little cell for twenty-four hours a day, while those doing the threatening remain in the open population. We must revise this practice and begin to expect prisoners to be nonviolent. And we need to support them in this by offering conflict-resolution trainings such as the 'Alternatives to Violence" programs currently being conducted by and for convicts around the country. Such trainings should be required for all prisoners and staff.

## Regain compassion and respect for those who wrong us.

Over the past twenty years, we have increasingly legitimized cruelty and callousness in response to the cruelty and callousness of criminals. And with the recent elections and new crime bills, we are rushing even further down this low road. In a number of prisons across the country we have reduced or eliminated the opportunity for inmates to earn college degrees, clamped down on family visits, and restricted access to books and magazines. And now there is even a growing public sentiment to strip prisons of televisions and exercise facilities. It's as if we want to make sure inmates are miserable every second of the day. We no longer want them to get their lives together. We just want them to suffer In the long run, however, this approach will not make us happy, nor will it keep our children safe from crime. In fact, as I see it, this vengeful attitude may actually be leading our young people toward violence. The peak age for violent crime in America is now eighteen, and it's edging downward every year. Our children sense that it's all right to be mean and violent toward people they don't like. They are not learning compassion or reconciliation. Don't expect a youngster to be able to master the difference between an enemy you define and an enemy he or she defines.

Taking the "high road" does not mean being lenient toward criminals. I'm certainly not advocating that we open the prison doors and let everybody out. In fact, I feel that there are many types of behavior that can cause a person to yield his or her right to stay in free society. But we need to work intensively with people who break the law; we have to structure our responses in ways that show them that they have value, that we believe in them, and that we need them. We must relegate prison to the status of last resort after all other measures have failed.

## Allow for transformation, not merely rehabilitation.

Our ideas of rehabilitation usually revolve around education, job skills, and counseling. But many ex-cons have told me they left prison merely better-educated and -skilled criminals. Until they felt their connection and value to others, nothing ever reached into their hearts. Take this letter from a former inmate, for example:

> Dear Bo, Man, I went through a time of hating you and Sita before I came to my senses. Let me explain: When you met me in prison and looked into my eyes, you didn't buy the evil son of a bitch that I portrayed to the world. I believed it myself. But you two looked at me with respect. Man, I hated your guts for that. I'm serious, I have never felt a worse punishment than your respect. Cops and cons could beat on me all day long, I was used to that from the time I was a kid But for somebody to see the good in me—man, that was unbearable. It took a long time, but it finally wore me down and I had to admit that I'm basically a good person. I've been out for three years now. Not even close to a life of crime anymore. Thanks seems puny but thanks.

If we forget that in every criminal there is a potential saint, we are dishonoring all of the great spiritual traditions. Saul of Tarsus persecuted and killed Christians before becoming Saint Paul, author of much of the New Testament. Valmiki, the revealer of the Ramayana, was a highwayman, a robber, and a murderer. Milarepa, one of the greatest Tibetan Buddhist gurus, killed thirty- seven people before he became a saint. Moses, who led the Jews out of bondage in Egypt, began his spiritual career by killing an Egyptian. If we forget that Charles Manson is capable of transformation, that doesn't reveal our lack of confidence in Manson, it shows our lack of confidence in our own scriptures. We must remember that even the worst of us can change.

Over the past twenty years I've had the privilege of knowing thousands of people who did horrible things and yet were able to transform their lives. They may not have become saints, but I have seen murderous rage gradually humbled into compassion, lifelong racial bigotry replaced by true brotherhood, and chronic selfishness transformed into committed altruism. The promises of every great spiritual tradition are indeed true: Our deepest nature is good, not evil.

## Join and support the restorative justice movement.

For decades our justice system has been run according to the tenets of "retributive justice," a model based on exile and hatred. "Restorative justice" is a far more promising approach. This model holds that when a crime occurs, there's an injury to the community; and that injury needs to be healed. Restorative justice tries to bring the offender back into the community; if at all possible, rather than closing him out.

Whereas retributive justice immediately says "Get the hell out of here!" when someone commits a crime, restorative justice says "Hey, get back in here! What are you doing that for? Don't you know we need you as one of the good people in this community? What would your mama think?" It's an entirely opposite approach, one that, I think, would result in stronger and safer communities.

I'm not saying that every offender is ready to be transformed into a good neighbor. Advocates of restorative justice are not naive. Sadly, prisons may be a necessary part of a restorative justice system. But even so, prisons can be environments that maximize opportunities for the inmates to become decent and caring human beings.

One of the more powerful initiatives within the restorative justice movement is the creation of victim-offender reconciliation programs (VORPs), which bring offenders and victims face to face. When offenders come out of those meetings you hear them say things like: "I feel so ashamed now of what I did, because I never realized how much I affected someone else's life," or "I never meant to do that. I was just being selfish." Meanwhile, some of the classic responses from victims are: "I really wanted to go in there hating those guys but I discovered they're just people. They really weren't as bad as I thought they'd be," or "I was expecting to see someone evil, and instead I saw somebody stupid." Such victim-offender interaction humanizes both the injury and the healing process.

What can you do? If you become the victim of a crime, insist upon meeting your assailant. Insist upon being involved with the process of his or her restoration. Join or create a VORP in your community. Tour your local jail or prison to see first-hand what your taxes pay for. Go in with a church group or civic group to meet inmates. Become a pen pal to a prisoner who is seeking to change his or her life. Talk to your friends and colleagues about employing ex-cons (in nationwide surveys, most employers admit they won't hire a person with a criminal record, so where are they supposed to work?). Please reclaim your power and your responsibility, because the retributive system you have deferred to is not serving your best interests.

## Take the issue of crime and punishment personally.

I first became an activist in the '60s during the civil rights movement in the South and, I can tell you, standing up against the Klan was not the hardest stuff. Nearly everybody was against the Klan. The activism that took the most courage was raising the consciousness of our own friends and families. The same goes for our attitudes toward prisoners today. If somebody at your workplace says "I'm glad they fried that animal," you have to have the guts to say "Come on, Bob, that's beneath you to talk like that." And you have to be willing to be mocked as a bleeding-heart liberal for doing so.

Just as with civil rights, and women's rights, we have to recognize that the national shame over our prison system is affecting us all, and it's getting worse every day. This doesn't mean that we all have to become crusaders for prison reform, but we do have to be more mindful of what we say and who and what we vote for.

We have to realize that we are all a part of this problem. If you vote, if you pay taxes, if you are afraid to walk alone at night, you are already involved. And so we all must make real changes-not just political ones, but also in our personal attitudes and lifestyles.

## Periodical and Internet Sources Bibliography

*The following articles have been selected to supplement the diverse views presented in this chapter.*

Greg Berman, "Alternatives to incarceration are cutting prison numbers, costs and crime," The Guardian, July 4, 2013. https://www.theguardian.com/commentisfree/2013/jul/04/alternatives-incarceration-prison-numbers

Robbie Couch, "Some States Are Closing Prisons and Turning Them Into Homeless Shelters, Reentry Centers," The Huffington Post, Feb. 5, 2015. http://www.huffingtonpost.com/2015/02/05/closing-state-prisons_n_6614220.html

Ruth David, "Ten Alternatives To Prison," Forbes, April 19, 2006. http://www.forbes.com/2006/04/15/prison-justice-alternatives_cx_rd_06slate_0418alter.html

James Gilligan, "Punishment Fails. Rehabilitation Works," The New York Times, Dec. 19, 2012. http://www.nytimes.com/roomfordebate/2012/12/18/prison-could-be-productive/punishment-fails-rehabilitation-works

Christopher Ingraham, "Here's how much Americans hate mandatory minimum sentences," The Washington Post, Oct. 1, 2015. https://www.washingtonpost.com/news/wonk/wp/2015/10/01/heres-how-much-americans-hate-mandatory-minimum-sentences/?utm_term=.191deefa72ff

Leon Neyfakh, "Why Are So Many Americans in Prison?: A provocative new theory," Slate.com, Feb. 6, 2015. http://www.slate.com/articles/news_and_politics/crime/2015/02/mass_incarceration_a_provocative_new_theory_for_why_so_many_americans_are.html

Brad Parks, "How to fix America's mass incarceration problem," New York Post, Nov. 1, 2015. http://nypost.com/2015/11/01/how-to-fix-americas-mass-incarceration-problem/

Jason Pye, "9 facts about mandatory minimums and the Smarter Sentencing Act," FreedomWorks, March 18, 2015. http://www.freedomworks.org/content/9-facts-about-mandatory-minimums-and-smarter-sentencing-act

Howard Samuels, "Prison vs. Rehab: What Really Works," The Huffington Post, May 25, 2011. http://www.huffingtonpost.com/ dr-howard-samuels/prison-vs-rehab-what-real_b_571055.html

David M. Shapiro, "President Obama should curb mass incarceration with clemency," The Hill, Dec. 9, 2016. http://thehill.com/blogs/ pundits-blog/civil-rights/309757-president-obama-should-curb-mass-incarceration-with-clemency

Maya Schenwar, "The Quiet Horrors of House Arrest, Electronic Monitoring, and Other Alternative Forms of Incarceration," Mother Jones, Jan. 22, 2015. http://www.motherjones.com/ politics/2015/01/house-arrest-surveillance-state-prisons

Sarah Stillman, "Get Out of Jail, Inc. Does the alternatives-to-incarceration industry profit from injustice?" The New Yorker, June 23, 2014. http://www.newyorker.com/magazine/2014/06/23/ get-out-of-jail-inc

# For Further Discussion

## Chapter 1

1. Inimai M. Chettiar makes the assertion that mass incarceration threatens American democracy because of its harmful effects, not just in monetary cost, but in its injustices related to race and poverty. Do you think Chettiar overstates the problem or do you agree with his assertion? What are your reasons?

2. Allison Schrager argues that part of the solution to today's prison overcrowding starts with more police on the street. Do you think this is true? Why or why not?

3. Marc Mauer and Nazgol Ghandnoosh attempt to demonstrate that the incarceration rate and crime have a limited relationship through statistics from three states. Looking at the statistics, did you come to the same conclusion? Do you agree that prison populations can be reduced without risking public safety?

## Chapter 2

1. In its argument, the Friends Committee on National Legislation says sociologist Bruce Western calls prison "the new poverty trap." Do you think there are things a person could do to escape this trap? Do you think the government needs to intervene to stop this cycle? Or do you think a combination of both is needed? What are your reasons?

2. Stephanos Bibas discusses numerous considerations when it comes to mass incarceration. Among them, he mentions strengthening families, paying more attention

to the victims of crime, a focus on work, and the power of religion. Of these, which do you think would provide a more positive outcome more quickly, and why do you think that would be the case?

3. Shafaq Hasan makes an argument for paying prisoners a living wage, one beyond the extremely low rate most are currently paid. But he raises questions within his argument, such as how much should an inmate be paid for work, how should the wage be determined, should it be determined by the type of job performed? How much do you think a prison worker should earn per hour? Do you think some jobs should pay more than others? If so, which ones?

# Chapter 3

1. In his argument that drugs are not the only issue when it comes to mass imprisonment, Jonathan Simon states that "the modern law of murder and manslaughter can be considered, in some respects, a triumph of progress." What does Simon mean by this statement, and do you agree or disagree with him?

2. Nathan Benfield makes a case that private prisons are a beneficial way to address the growing need for prison facilities. He states that private prisons offer higher quality care than facilities run by the government. Would you investigate this further or were you satisfied with evidence he provided to back this statement? Give your reasons.

3. In his argument against private prisons, Alex Friedmann discusses some of the differences between private-prison employees and employees working in civil service. If you worked in the prison system, would you rather work for a private prison or one run by the government, or would that matter? Why do you feel this way?

## Chapter 4

1. Marc Schindler makes the conclusion that rethinking our country's approach to violence and the way violent offenses are treated could greatly reduce our prison populations as well as make communities safer. Do you agree with his conclusion or do you believe there are other considerations he hasn't taken into account?

2. Yuval Melamed asserts that a "treatment years" approach could help in reaching a balance between patient rights and public safety when it comes to mentally ill offenders. Do you think treatment should outweigh punishment? Why or why not? Do you think it's possible that people could take advantage of a treatment model?

3. Sohail Inayatullah discusses the new work in genomics and its relationship to criminal behavior. If scientists are finding that certain genes can affect criminal behavior, how do you think that will affect how we handle crime in the future?

## Chapter 5

1. Evan Bernick and Paul J. Larkin, Jr. examine mandatory minimum sentences. Do you think without mandatory minimum sentences judges could be fair in how they decide the fate of the offenders in their courtrooms? Do you think certain people might get away with crimes while others get sent to prison? Do you think it's easy for a judge to be impartial?

2. Michele L. Jawando and Chelsea Parsons argue that a key part to reform in our criminal justice system is improving police-community relations. Why do you think it is so crucial that these relationships improve? Do you think there are things communities could do to help improve relationships with their local police forces?

3. As part of his argument for fixing the criminal justice system, Bo Lozoff says we need to regain compassion and respect for those who wrong us. Why do you think he includes that in his argument? Do you think our society has the vengeful attitude Lozoff mentions? Do you see this attitude in other aspects of our culture, such as television shows, video games, websites, or blogs?

# Organizations to Contact

*The editors have compiled the following list of organizations concerned with the issues debated in this book. The descriptions are derived from materials provided by the organizations. All have publications or information available for interested readers. The list was compiled on the date of publication of the present volume; the information provided here may change. Be aware that many organizations take several weeks or longer to respond to inquiries, so allow as much time as possible.*

**American Correctional Association (ACA)**
206 N. Washington Street, Suite 200, Alexandria, VA 22314,
(703) 224-0000
website: www.aca.org

As one of the largest and oldest criminal justice organizations, the American Correctional Association (ACA) states in the preamble to its declaration of principles that the treatment of criminals by society is for the protection of society. Part of the association's mission is to improve correctional standards and develop adequate facilities. The organization conducts studies and makes recommendations for laws, regulations, and policies that might improve operations. It also publishes *Corrections Today* magazine, with articles such as "Good Eats Culinary Arts Training Adds Flavor to Reentry Program"; the journal *Corrections Compendium*; and an electronic newsletter, *ACAConnect*.

**American Civil Liberties Union (ACLU)**
125 Broad Street, 18th Floor, New York, NY 10004
(212) 549-2500
website: www.aclu.org

The American Civil Liberties Union (ACLU) has worked to defend the civil liberties of American citizens since 1920. As part of its work, the organization regularly publishes materials on the Bill of

Rights, as well as prisoners' rights. This includes reports such as "Banking on Bondage: Private Prisons and Mass Incarceration." The ACLU also publishes the newsletter Civil Liberties and handbooks on individual rights.

### Brennan Center for Justice
120 Broadway, Suite 1750, New York, NY 10271
(646) 292-8310
email: brennancenter@nyu.edu
website: www.brennancenter.org

Part of the NYU School of Law, The Brennan Center for Justice is a nonpartisan law and policy institute seeking to improve the systems of democracy and justice in the United States. Its aim is to hold the country's political institutions and laws accountable to the ideals of democracy and equal justice for all. The Center's work includes fighting to end mass incarceration. Examples of titles it has published include "A National Agenda to Reduce Mass Incarceration" and "Paying for Your Time: How Charging Inmates Fees Behind Bars May Violate the Excessive Fines Clause."

### Brookings Institution
1775 Massachusetts Avenue NW, Washington, DC 20036
(202) 797-6000
email: communications@brookings.edu
website: www.brookings.edu

Since 1927, the Brookings Institution has served as a sociopolitical think tank conducting specialized research in government, economics, foreign policy, and other areas. The institution has published papers such as "More Prisoners Versus More Crime Is the Wrong Question" and articles such as "How Digital Technology Can Reduce Prison Incarceration Rates." It also publishes the Policy Brief Series and the Brookings Review.

**Center for American Progress**
1333 H Street NW, 10th Floor, Washington, DC 20005
(202) 682-1611
website: www.americanprogress.org

An independent nonpartisan policy institute, the Center for American Progress is dedicated to improving the lives of all Americans, through strong and progressive ideas, leadership, and action. Among the issues it covers are courts, criminal justice, poverty, and race and ethnicity. It publishes columns, reports, issue briefs, infographics, and more. It has published "8 Facts You Should Know About the Criminal Justice System and People of Color."

**Friends Committee on National Legislation (FCNL)**
245 Second St, NE, Washington, DC 20002
(800) 630-1330
website: www.fcnl.org

Founded in 1943 by members of the Religious Society of Friends (Quakers), The Friends Committee on National Legislation (FCNL) lobbies Congress and the administration to help advance peace, justice, opportunity, and environmental stewardship. It is concerned with issues such as criminal and economic justice, including mass incarceration, policing, poverty, and income inequality. Among its resources are newsletters, statements, press releases, and updates. One of its statements is titled FCNL Applauds Justice Department Phasing Out Private Prisons

**The Heritage Foundation**
214 Massachusetts Ave NE, Washington DC 20002-4999
(202) 546-4400
email: info@heritage.org
website: www.heritage.org

The Heritage Foundation was founded in 1973 as a conservative think tank focused on strengthening the American economy, society, and the nation as a whole. It publishes commentary, legal memorandums, and issue briefs, as well as a weekly newsletter, The

Agenda. Among its publications are titles including "Theories of Punishment and Mandatory Minimum Sentences" and "A Guide to Prison Privatization."

## National Prison Project
915 Fifteenth Street NW, 7th Floor, Washington, DC 20005
(202) 393-4930
website: www.aclu.org/prison

The National Prison Project was formed by the American Civil Liberties Union in 1972. It offers resources and litigates cases with the goal of protecting and preserving the Eighth Amendment rights of criminal offenders. The project opposes practices such as electronic monitoring and prison privatization. Publications from the project include booklets such as the Prisoners' Assistance Directory and reports such as "A Death Before Dying" and "End the Abuse."

## Prison Policy Initiative
PO Box 127, Northampton, MA 01061
website: www.prisonpolicy.org

The Prison Policy Initiative is a nonprofit, nonpartisan organization founded to put the issue of mass incarceration on the national agenda. It conducts research, performs media work, and organizes to help shape national reform campaigns. Among its published reports includes titles such as "Punishing Poverty: The High Cost of Probation Fees in Massachusetts" and "Detaining the Poor: How Money Bail Perpetuates an Endless Cycle of Poverty and Jail Time."

## The Sentencing Project
1705 DeSales Street NW, 8th Floor, Washington, DC 20036
(202) 628-0871
email: staff@sentencingproject.org
website: www.sentencingproject.org

Founded in 1986, the Sentencing Project aims to be a leader in changing the way people in the United States think about crime and punishment. It provides public defenders with sentence advocacy training so offenders might be able to receive alternative sentences with more positive and constructive outcomes than incarceration. Through its work, the organization has increased public awareness and understanding of the sentencing process and alternative sentencing programs. Among its publications are reports such as "Fewer Prisons, Less Crime" and "Ending Mass Incarceration: Social Interventions That Work."

### US Department of Justice, Federal Bureau of Prisons (BOP)

320 First Street NW, Washington, DC20534
(202) 307-3198
website: www.bop.gov

The Federal Bureau of Prisons (BOP) is a subdivision of the US Department of Justice. It oversees the nation's prison facilities and helps to ensure public safety through the incarceration of dangerous criminals. BOP seeks to provide work and other opportunities for self-improvement within its prisons in order to help offenders make an easier transition and productive return to society once released. BOP keeps an online archive of news articles related to its operations and corrections. This archive contains titles such as "Institutions Prepare Inmates for Reentry" and "Paving the Way to a Successful Reentry."

# Bibliography of Books

Michelle Alexander. *The New Jim Crow: Mass Incarceration in the Age of Colorblindness*. New York: The New Press, 2012.

Ernest Drucker. *A Plague of Prisons: The Epidemiology of Mass Incarceration in America*. New York: The New Press, 2013.

Ava DuVernay. *13*. (Film documentary). Netflix. Oct. 7, 2016.

Natalie Faulk. *The Downfall of American Corrections: How Privatization, Mandatory Minimum Sentencing, and the Abandonment of Rehabilitation Have Perverted the System beyond Repair*. Seattle, WA: CreateSpace Independent Publishing Platform, 2016.

Flores Forbes. *Invisible Men: A Contemporary Slave Narrative in the Era of Mass Incarceration*. New York: Skyhorse Publishing, Inc., 2016.

Marie Gottschalk. *Caught: The Prison State and the Lockdown of American Politics*. Princeton, NJ: Princeton University Press, 2014.

Gwendolyn Hemphill. *The High Price I Had To Pay 3: From the White House to Federal Prison, Sentenced to 11 Years as a Non-Violent Offender*. New York: Voices International Publications Inc, 2015.

Tara Herivel and Paul Wright. *Prison Profiteers: Who Makes Money from Mass Incarceration*. New York: The New Press, 2009.

Elizabeth Hinton. *From the War on Poverty to the War on Crime: The Making of Mass Incarceration in America*. Cambridge, MA: Harvard University Press, 2016.

Daniel Karpowitz. *College in Prison: Reading in an Age of Mass Incarceration*. New Brunswick, NJ: Rutgers University Press, 2017.

James Kilgore. *Understanding Mass Incarceration: A People's Guide to the Key Civil Rights Struggle of Our Time*. New York: The New Press, 2015.

Mary D. Looman and John D. Carl. *A Country Called Prison: Mass Incarceration and the Making of a New Nation*. New York: Oxford University Press, 2015.

Susan L. Miller. *After the Crime: The Power of Restorative Justice: Dialogues between Victims and Violent Offenders*. New York: NYU Press, 2011.

Naomi Murakawa. *The First Civil Right: How Liberals Built Prison America*. New York: Oxford University Press, 2014.

Robert Perkinson. *Texas Tough: The Rise of America's Prison Empire*. New York: Metropolitan Books, 2010.

Maya Schenwar. *Locked Down, Locked Out: Why Prison Doesn't Work and How We Can Do Better*. Oakland, CA: Berrett-Koehler Publishers, 2014.

Jonathan Simon. *Mass Incarceration on Trial: A Remarkable Court Decision and the Future of Prisons in America*. New York: The New Press, 2016.

Steven Teles and David Dagan. *Prison Break: Why Conservatives Turned Against Mass Incarceration*. New York: Oxford University Press, 2016.

Scott Thomas Anderson. *The Cutting Four-piece: Crime and Tragedy in an Era of Prison Overcrowding*. Folsom, CA: The Coalition for Investigative Journalism, 2015.

The Washington Post. *Justice For None: How the Drug War Broke the Legal System*. New York: Diversion Books, 2015.

Thomas Wills. T*he Rise of America's Prisons: The War on the Poor*. Seattle, WA: CreateSpace, 2014.

Ruth Wilson Gilmore. *Golden Gulag: Prisons, Surplus, Crisis, and Opposition in Globalizing California*. Oakland, CA: University of California Press, 2007.

# Index

## W

## Y